THE WAR IN THE SHADOWS

The Battle of the Spymasters in WWII

Charles Whiting

SAPERE
BOOKS

THE WAR IN THE SHADOWS

Published by Sapere Books.

24 Trafalgar Road, Ilkley, LS29 8HH

United Kingdom

saperebooks.com

ISBN: 978-1-80055-825-0.

TABLE OF CONTENTS

For anyone who is tired of life, the thrilling life of a spy should be the very finest recuperator.

Lord Baden-Powell

INTRODUCTION

I suppose I met my first spy when I was seventeen. I met him in the most unlikely of places — a crowded barrack room in an echoing ancient Belgian *caserne* which housed three-hundred-odd British soldiers waiting to go up the line. Most of us were pretty young and nervous and made friends easily, as if we needed the reassurance of company around ourselves all the time.

But he was different. He kept to himself. He was much older too — perhaps thirty. But in spite of his age and obvious fitness, his ill-fitting uniform was brand new, as if he had only recently joined the Army like the rest of us. Yet on his breast he wore the pale blue, upturned wings of a man who had made three combat jumps behind enemy lines. I knew the badge, although it was a very rare insignia indeed. This was the first time I had ever seen anyone wearing it. But it was not only the badge which caught my attention. It was his eyes that were immediately noticeable; they were hard, a little cruel, and very wary. Here, I thought, was a man whom you could neither like nor dislike at the outset: a man you could not pin down easily and say that he was this or that with confidence.

He was pleasant enough when he was sober, indulging in the usual chitchat about the war and, when asked, giving his opinion of how long it would be before we were sent to the front. But when he was drunk, which was often, he was truculent and tough, and not a man one would dare to cross. The washed-out light blue eyes would blaze, and the young soldiers took care to get out of his way quickly as he came staggering down between the rows of three-tiered wooden bunks — still stamped with the eagle of the Wehrmacht, whose soldiers had slept in them some two months ago.

On one of those drunken evenings he told me a little of his story. Even when he had his fill of the weak, gassy wartime Belgian beer and black-market cognac, he still wasn't too communicative. He had acted for a year as a courier for the SOE. Just before the Battle of Arnhem he had been dropped with a large sum of money for the Dutch underground; but instead of delivering it to the patriots, he had headed for the fleshpots of Amsterdam, spending the money on whores and drink — till the SOE caught up with him. Whatever his rank had once been — perhaps that of a captain — it had been stripped off him, and he had been hastily directed to this Belgian reinforcement unit, from whence he would be sent to the front.

Soon after his little confession, he vanished as abruptly as he had appeared in our midst. Whether he had "gone on the trot," as many did during that icy winter, or had been sent to the line to take his chance with the infantry — eight weeks' life expectancy at that time — I don't know. I never saw him again, and today, so long afterwards, I can't even remember his name.

Since then I have probably known three or four other spies, and all of them seem to have possessed something of the characteristics of that lonely, broken ex-agent: a superficial wariness, which is immediately noticeable because it is so unnecessary or unwarranted, with a streak of recklessness and brutality underneath, mixed with a certain psychological incompleteness. They seem somehow never to have grown up. Some, like my ex-SOE man, felt that, if they could fool the Germans so completely for so long, they could also escape the much more cold-blooded and pragmatic London spymasters.

They all seem to be suckers in the end. Believing themselves to be the chessmasters at the outset, they find out when it is too late that they are merely expendable pawns of fate. Belatedly, they realize that their infantile desire to know what went on behind the keyhole and to use that knowledge for power or payment has sacrificed them to a dawn firing squad or a thug with a rubber truncheon.[1]

In *The War in the Shadows* there are, therefore, no heroes, just victims. Sometimes the victims deserve their fate like Snow, the Twenty Committee's creation, a triple agent, taking both German and British money and dealing out death to all and sundry in the interests of self-preservation. Sometimes one would have wished a better fate for them, as for the three young men of Otto Skorzeny's *Operation Grab*, pleading for mercy to the American captors with: "We have been captured by the Americans without having fired a single shot, because we did not wish to become murderers. We were sentenced to death and are now dying for criminals who have not only us, but also — and that is worse — our families on their conscience." Their plea did not help. They were shot one snowy morning in Belgium on December 23, 1944. Spying is, after all, a dangerous operation.

In the end, although the war was won by the Allies, the men and women who felt they had contributed so much by their activities in the darkened, dangerous back alleys of the great conflict, lost. All of them lost, whether they were British, American, Czech, French, Dutch, Russian or German.

---

[1] In this context it is interesting to note that the chief German spymaster in World War II, Admiral Canaris, was known by his family in Low German dialect as a boy as the *der Kieker* — the "*peeper.*"

There had been victories, of course. The first rounds had gone to the Germans without doubt. Then the British had rallied. The Russians and the Americans took a hand. By 1944 it was clear that the Allies were winning; and by winter of that year the back of the German resistance was broken. But the casualties among the victors were appalling. The whole of the Russian espionage ring had been executed or imprisoned, or had "turned," betraying their former friends and co-workers by the score. The SOE had lost nearly two-thirds of its key agents, with virtually every one of its female agents dead or permanently crippled, mentally or physically, by the concentration camps. And if the "Jedburgh" teams parachuted by the OSS into Europe had become the most decorated group of Americans in the war, they had paid for the honor in mind and body.

As for the Germans, Reinhard Heydrich, the "man with the iron heart," died in agony following an eight-day battle for his life after he had been attacked by Czech SOE agents; his former captain in the Navy and greatest rival, Admiral Canaris, the gentle, white-haired head of the Abwehr, ended his life not at the hands of the enemy but at those of his own countrymen. Naked, his body covered with weals and sores from the beatings he had received from men who had once indirectly been his colleagues, he swung back and forth in agony as the thin piano wire, attached to the meat-hook, cut deeper and ever deeper into his emaciated neck.

Admittedly the man he called his "dear young friend," SS General Schellenberg, escaped to live a few years more. But did he really escape? Did any of the survivors escape? Like so many of them who survived and wrote about their experiences, he felt the deprivation of the spurious glamor and heady excitement of the strange spy battle as acutely as any addict cut off from his favorite drug.

In short *The War in the Shadows* is the story of a bitter defeat for both victor and vanquished. It is not a nice book either, but then there are no more "nice" books, are there?...

BOOK ONE: THE SPIES GO TO WAR

The trade of a spy is a very fine one, when the spy is working on his own account. Is it not in fact enjoying the excitements of a thief, while still retaining the character of an honest citizen ... ? The only excitement which can compare with it is that of the life of a gambler.

Honoré de Balzac

1939: THE FIRST ROUND TO THE GERMANS

"Ye have scarce the soul of a louse," he said, *"but the roots of sin are there."*

Rudyard Kipling

1 — INCIDENT ON A FAR FRONTIER

The man who was going to start World War II mopped his high forehead. It was warm — damnably warm that August 2, 1939. The evening sky was a molten grey, the sun a great burning copper ball on the horizon. Although it would soon be dark, the tar was still melting in the streets, and sweating Berliners, usually so energetic and active, sought the shadows as they went limply about the damp pleasures of the summer evening.

But it was not only the sticky heat that caused the big tough SS man to sweat as he raced his open tourer up the Nollendorfplatz, through the Potsdamerstrasse, towards the Reich Security Headquarters in the Prinz-Albrecht Palais. He wondered why he had been summoned to see "the old man" at this time of the evening and in such haste.

A few minutes earlier he had been just about to leave his apartment when he had heard the ringing of the special phone linking him directly with headquarters. The big man had hesitated. Reluctantly he had picked up the curved phone with its ivory-tipped base, then, as he remembered many years later: "Firstly, there was seldom anything good that came to me over that phone," and "secondly, I had a date with a new girl friend." But there would be no time for new girl friends that evening. A harsh voice at the other end had snapped: "Here the adjutant's office. Please come to the boss's office as quickly as possible. When can you be here?" And without waiting for an answer, the harsh unknown voice had rapped: "Good, then be here in twenty minutes. *Heil Hitler!*"

With a somewhat sinking feeling, he had realized that he was off on a new mission: one that could only mean violent death for someone or other. Thirty years later, when the details of his true record would first come to light, the German papers would call him "Hitler's James Bond."

Alfred Naujocks had first encountered political violence while a student of engineering at the University of Kiel. There, after a series of roughhouses with Communist students, he had managed to get his nose smashed and mangled. In 1931 the heavy-jawed, thin-lipped northerner with pronounced right-wing views had joined the black guards — Hitler's SS, which at that time were trying to recruit a better class of people than those to be found in the storm troops, the long-established Nazi paramilitary organization. Naujocks felt he fitted the bill perfectly. Although he was studying engineering, his real interests lay in history and philosophy.

Four years later Naujocks transferred to the SD, the SS's security organization. He found that his new bosses, in particular cold-eyed Reinhard Heydrich, were not particularly interested in his intellectual capacities but rather in the size of his muscles, the quickness of his physical reaction, and his ability to use a silenced pistol. Swiftly over the next few years he became what William L. Shirer has called in his monumental *Rise and Fall of the Third Reich* "a sort of intellectual gangster" who could be relied upon to carry out any kind of secret unsavory mission.

He stage-managed a revolt in Slovakia so that Hitler could use the spontaneous expression of the people's will to put pressure on Czechoslovakia before his final takeover of the defenseless little country. He disposed of an exiled German who was running a propaganda radio station directed against Germany from nearby Prague. In that particular action he received his first wound, being shot through the hand in a firefight with the exiled German. He helped to "fix" Russian Army Marshal Tukhachevsky, making it appear to Stalin that the former was a traitor, working in Germany's interests. As a result, the marshal and 35,000 other senior Russian officers were "liquidated;" when Germany invaded Russia in 1941, the cream of her experienced officers were no longer available to defend their "Little Russia."

In the late thirties Alfred Naujocks, whose main interests were easy women, airy philosophizing about his country's role in history, and violent action, was involved in a dozen such clandestine operations of which he was inordinately proud. But "the master agent of the Führer," as he called himself then, had not yet carried out a mission for his boss, Reinhard Heydrich, which could be compared with the one to be given him this hot August day. The successful execution of this mission would involve Germany in a war that would change the face of Europe and leave the Continent stricken and ruined, with over 30 million of its citizens dead.

With a screech of protesting brakes, Naujocks pulled up in front of the Prinz-Albrecht Palais, ran up the steps, and passed the motionless SS guards, whose white sword belts were the only lightness against their somber black uniforms. Breathlessly he dashed up the great staircase and entered the lobby to Heydrich's office. Two other high officers were already waiting. Heinrich "Heini" Mueller, head of the Gestapo; and his chief rival in the field of criminal investigation, another former plainclothes policeman like himself, Arthur Nebe, head of the Criminal Investigation Police. Naujocks liked neither of the two men, but he clicked his heels together and shouted *"Heil Hitler."*

Mueller, the Bavarian ex-cop, looked up, his penetrating brown eyes hooded by nervously twitching eyelids, then raised a wide, massive hand with fingers as square as a matchbox. "*Heil Hitler*," he said laconically, without much conviction.

Nebe, to be hunted one day for his life by the very man who now sat opposite him, did not utter the expected formula. Instead, he said: "What, you here too, Naujocks?" Naujocks laughed to himself. As he related later, "It did me good to see the two of them nervous, especially the mighty "Gestapo" Mueller, who usually knew everything that was going on. Today he was completely in the dark. And he could hardly hide his nervousness. "But then," he told himself, "it was always the same, those who were closest to Heydrich were the most afraid of him."

Suddenly the little green light above the door to Heydrich's room began to flash. Naujocks forgot the other two. Automatically he squared his shoulders and rose to his feet, tugging at his jacket. An adjutant appeared and clicked his heels. "*Der Gruppenführer lasst bitten*" (the Group leader requests your presence) he announced formally. The three of them passed through the door.

Slowly Heydrich rose from his big desk and said casually: "Take a seat, gentlemen."

Naujocks did as commanded, thinking that Heydrich made, as always, an impressive figure. He was tall, blond, and immaculately dressed, his highly intelligent face marred only by small restless foxlike eyes, which darted cunningly back and forth from one face to the others. The head of the Reich's security services rose and walked over to the corner with the lithe grace of the champion fencer he was. Yet again, just as his face was marred by those eyes, his splendid powerful figure was marred by fat hips, a disturbingly feminine aspect which made him appear more sinister than ever.

While the three other men sat silently in the soft chairs in the corner, the 35-year-old SS General walked up and down without saying a word. In spite of the heat outside, Naujocks felt (as he wrote later) "an ice-cold shudder run down [his] spine."

Suddenly Heydrich stopped his pacing. Turning to face them, he said coldly, "Gentlemen, I have asked you to come here to discuss with you the execution of an order which has come from the Führer himself." He paused momentarily, then added in that high-pitched, feminine voice of his, "Today we are concerned with a matter which goes far beyond anything else we have ever done before."

Quickly he explained in that nervous, staccato manner of his: "We are concerned with a mission which will attract worldwide attention. For it we will need two hundred men. That means two hundred people who will be in the know." He paused and turned the full force of his cunning little eyes on Naujocks.

The tough "intellectual gangster" shuddered in spite of himself; he knew that this man, whom Hitler himself had named "the man with the heart of iron," would not hesitate one moment to "get rid" of anyone who crossed him or stood in the path of his boundless ambition.

Reinhard (Pure Heart) Heydrich had had a chip on his shoulder ever since his earliest youth. As a boy he was not interested in athletics. In addition, he was burdened by a high-pitched falsetto voice and fat girlish hips. It was not surprising, therefore, that his schoolmates, cruel as children always are, made fun of the pale-faced, girlish schoolboy whose main pleasure was to play the violin. If that had not been bad enough, young Heydrich thought he was Jewish, as did his schoolmates. The result was that in his early days at Halle High School, the other boys teased him unmercifully with their cries of "Yid," "sissy," and worse.

Almost instinctively the blond-haired, blue-eyed son of a musician realized that if he did not want to remain a worm for the rest of his life, a person completely at the mercy of his fellows, he would have to be tougher, crueller, bolder, more ambitious, and more powerful than the rest of the "mob," as he called them contemptuously to himself. Deliberately he set out to toughen himself up and to stand out as a superior individual in the eyes of his schoolmates.

He took to walking back and forth from school along the curb, never deflecting from his course even when adults got in his way. Generally they, as well as the other boys, moved away when they saw him coming. But if anyone challenged his right to continue his undeflected course, then it always came to a minor battle, the tall, pale-faced Heydrich throwing himself into it with a reckless courage that bordered almost on mania. If that were not enough, Heydrich took to showing off in front of the boys who had once mocked him so mercilessly. Once he climbed on the school roof during lessons and in full view of the horrified staff and students, he balanced his way precariously along the edge of the gutter with a hundred-foot drop to the cobbles below.[2]

---

[2] He was to perform a similar feat many years later. Arriving in Switzerland for a conference, he found to his anger that the Swiss were not flying the German swastika flag. Immediately he drove through the night to the nearest German consulate; obtaining a flag there, he shinned up the roof and then in complete darkness climbed the flag pole to hoist the swastika. Next morning the amazed Swiss were surprised to see it flying above the hotel.

Later as a young cadet in the German Navy he transferred his aggressiveness to fencing, becoming a German champion, and to his unrelenting pursuit of women. And he was not particular in his choice — they were all the same to him. He took them, conquering them with either brute force or money, and then left them as soon as he had his way. But eventually his womanizing caught up with him. In 1931 the young naval lieutenant with the cruel features and long-fingered musician's hands was kicked out of the Navy because of an unsavory affair with a young woman.

In the depressed Germany of 1931 there was little that an ex-officer could do. He was offered a job as a glider instructor, but he turned it down on his new wife's advice and applied to join the SS. In Munich for an interview, ex-chicken farmer Heinrich Himmler gave him exactly twenty minutes to draw up a plan for a future SS counterespionage organization. Heydrich, who had always been an avid reader of novels about the British Secret Service, racked his brains to remember what he could of those novels and within the prescribed time managed to draw a plan which impressed the pedantic head of the SS. He was accepted.

Heydrich made an amazing career. With the fervor and energy of the newly converted, he organized the Security Service, a combination of the National Socialist secret service and secret police, stamping out a rigidly efficient organization that was soon to be the terror of the regime's enemies. But not only of its enemies; its members, too. Himmler himself, who called Heydrich a "born intelligence officer," was a little scared of him, as were his closest associates such as Mueller, Nebe and Naujocks. The man who was called "the living card index, a brain which held all the threads and wove them all together," was in 1939 an SS general and head of the Reich's entire security.

But in spite of his great power and overwhelming ambition, there was something almost pathological in the way that he tried to keep to himself. He disdained the company of his associates and even when the Reichsführer — Himmler himself — offered to speak with him in the familiar "thou" form, Heydrich politely requested his boss "not to force this great honor" on him.[3] Although he was an accomplished violinist and loved to perform, he shunned the people who would have liked to have listened to his playing. When the other National Socialist bigwigs such as his own chief took to giving great parties, Heydrich ordered his wife to live modestly and keep company away. Lina Heydrich did not need to be ordered. She had only contempt for Frau Himmler. Privately she ridiculed the "Madame Reischsführer and her size fifty knickers!"

But sometimes the burning rage broke through the icy surface. Once after a long-drawn-out drinking session with his blonde Nordic wife, he staggered to the mirror and shouted at his Lina: "Just look at his nose, his face — typically Jewish! A real Jewish lout!" And on another occasion he stormed into his brilliantly lit bathroom and, before anyone could stop him, snatched out his revolver, crying: "At last I've got you, scum!" Crazy with anger, he pumped two shots at the great mirror and watched it crumble his image before him. Then all energy draining out of him, he let the revolver fall.

One writer has commented on this episode: "The man with the split personality had shot at his reflection because at last he had met his other half — but he had met him only in the

---

[3] Told to the author by Frau Heydrich in 1971.

23

mirror and could never get rid of him; that other half was to accompany him to the end."

Today it is generally accepted that Heydrich was not Jewish, in spite of having a grandmother with — for Germany — the typical Jewish given name of Sarah. Yet all the same, Heydrich himself felt he had Jewish blood in his veins — and that in a country dedicated to getting rid of the "Jewish pollution." And this pathologically exaggerated feeling of Heydrich that he belonged and yet did not belong made him a fearsome technocrat of death. He was not taken in by the Hitler myth, just as he was not taken in by Himmler's racial myth. Indeed, he actually helped Jews to escape from Nazi Germany. He was motivated solely by expediency and his own burning ambition, which one day might well take him to the very top of the German state. Soon, indeed, he would tell two intimates that he would be the first to do away with Hitler if the "old man makes a mess of things."

Such was the iron-hearted man who now faced the other three in the quiet Berlin office and planned the start of World War II. After letting them absorb the instruction about the "two hundred men in the know," Heydrich turned to Mueller, whom he had brought personally to Berlin from Munich in spite of the objections of the Party. "You will provide at least fifty people from the concentration camps. As only dead people can keep their mouths shut.. As was often the case with Heydrich, he did not finish his sentence. Instead, he commented: "You understand?"

Mueller nodded and snapped "*Jawohl*," actually clicking his heels together under the table. "They'll be liquidated. No problem."

"Fine," Heydrich said.

"What about the others?" Naujocks interjected.

"I'll pick them out myself. The best men available. Real SS men, who are scared of nothing."

"And how are we to keep the operation secret?" Naujocks asked, realizing that something really big was being planned but not knowing quite what.

Heydrich narrowed the slanting eyes which gave him a Mongolian appearance. He answered his subordinate's question with one of his own: "What would you do, Naujocks?"

His heart beating a little faster than normal, the big agent said: "Subject them to a special oath." As he uttered them, he knew his words were foolish. Only dead men didn't talk. But dare Heydrich kill his own agents in cold blood? What about himself? Now he was one of those in the know.

Heydrich shook his head. "We can't take that risk. I'll tell you what is going to happen to those concerned with this operation. Nobody is going to harm them." He paused, a mocking smile on his thin lips, while the other three stared at him expectantly. "However afterwards they will be given plentiful opportunities to sacrifice themselves for their fatherland. They will be allowed to die a soldier's death at the front!"

Cynically he stared down at their shocked faces.

Naujocks was the first to break the silence. "At the front!" he breathed unbelievingly.

"Yes, at the front," Heydrich echoed his words. "There is going to be a war... and we are going to be the ones who will start it." His words were harsh and cold, devoid of emotion. "Together with the men that we will select tomorrow morning..."

On Tuesday, August 22, 1939, Adolph Hitler called the military leaders of the Third Reich to his mountain home at Berghof to tell them of the momentous decision: Germany was going to war with Poland. He spoke for four hours in a long involved monologue, his pugnacity increasing as the hours passed until, with eyes bulging and face red with fury, he screamed at the assembled generals: "Close your hearts to pity! Act brutally! Eighty million people must obtain what is their right!"

And then suddenly he was calm, his rage gone in a matter of moments. Tomorrow, he announced, he would give them the date of his attack on Poland. There was no question of backing down now. All he needed was a justification for the war, which would look good to both the German people and the neutrals. As he told the generals with cynical frankness: "I shall give a propaganda reason for starting the war — never mind whether it is plausible or not. The victor will not be asked afterwards whether he told the truth. In starting and waging a war, it is not right that matters but victory..."

None of the generals knew that day as they filed wearily out of the great conference room that Reinhard Heydrich had been working on that "propaganda reason" ever since that meeting nearly three weeks before with Naujocks. Then he had told Naujocks and the other two that "a chosen group of men in Polish uniforms will attack from the direction of Poland a selected town in Germany on the border area. There must be firing. Houses will have to be set on fire. Every detail must be genuine."

Turning to Naujocks, he had then said: "You, Naujocks, as my special agent will have an especially dangerous mission. You will lead the attack on the German radio station at Gleiwitz near the Polish border with a handful of men dressed in rough Polish civilian clothes. You will force your way into the station and capture it. One of your men will violently harangue Germany over the air in Polish so that it will appear that the Poles have captured the place ... As Gleiwitz is linked to the major German network, most of Germany will hear the speech. Most of Germany will also hear the cries of the wounded and the German employees crying for help."

That had been in the first week of August. Now *Operation Himmler* (which had been seized upon eagerly by Hitler) was almost ready, worked out to the last detail. Heydrich's agents had been posted around the areas so that the Wehrmacht, which had not been let in on the plot, would not interfere by mistake when the shooting started. Admiral Canaris, head of the Army's Secret Service, the Abwehr, and one of Heydrich's greatest rivals, although he had once been the latter's commanding officer in the Navy, had been co-opted to find the 250 Polish uniforms needed. And Heinrich Mueller had found his "canned goods," the concentration camp inmate, who was going to be found dead at the scene of the "incident." Because Heydrich wanted the journalists who would be flown to the spot afterwards to see blood, the unfortunate victim would be first killed by a lethal injection and then gunshot wounds faked.

Meanwhile, in the middle of August, Naujocks had taken up his post at the Hotel Oberschlesischen Hof in the little border town of Gleiwitz, while his select group of agents took up residence in the remaining hotels and pensions. They avoided each other and looked the other way, if they happened to bump into one another in the street. They, too, had been equipped down to the last detail. Their clothes bore maker's and laundry marks from Lodz and other Polish towns. Their pockets were filled with streetcar tickets, cigarette packets, cinema tickets from Poland, and their wallets bulged with zloty bills. "Everything has been taken care of," Naujocks reassured himself as he waited for the codeword to begin.

All the same he was uneasy. His mind kept jumping back to Heydrich's last words on August 2nd. Then after explaining that he, Heydrich, wanted the "canned goods" to be draped across the entrance of the radio station before they left it again, he had stated with cold frank brutality: "One more thing, Naujocks. If the alarm should be given before you can complete the operation, or if the police are called in before you can get away, *I don't want to see you alive again. The only favor you can do me then is to ensure that your body cannot be identified.*"

At the time, Naujocks had felt that he would most dearly have liked to "jump at this black uniformed devil's ironic mug." But since then he had had time to realize just how great a fix he was in. He decided to be careful — very careful. Then, as he expressed it later himself, "Obviously Heydrich saw in me one of those in the know, who had to be destroyed. I'd already done too much dirty work for him. Wasn't that a particularly suitable opportunity to get rid of me? Then dead men couldn't tell tales."

Thus the days passed that hot August in the provincial sleepy border town in nervous expectancy. Naujocks spent the time by repeated inspections of the Gleiwitz radio station. It was situated outside the town on a secondary road leading to Tarnowitz and was surrounded by a six-foot-high wire mesh fence. Otherwise the station and the two blocks of living quarters for the staff were practically unguarded.

All the same, Naujocks took great care in reconnoitering the place. He surveyed the entrance minutely. He judged the height of the various stories. He assessed the distances between the exit and the fence. A hundred and one minor and major details. And, in particular, he mentally considered all escape routes, as he stated later, "My life depended upon them. I didn't want to be one of the dead, which would be shown to the world press on the day after the raid to prove that 'Polish insurgents' had started the war."

Then on Friday, August 25, 1939, Heydrich called Naujocks from Berlin. It was the order Naujocks dreaded. He was *not* to leave his hotel room from now on under any circumstances. The whole machine had been set in motion. The Führer was to launch his attack on Poland the next day. In the meantime the SS men disguised as Poles were on their way to the frontier, and Mueller was rushing his "canned goods" in the same direction. Heydrich concluded with a strict warning to the nervous, tense, special agent that he must expect the code signal for the operation at any time now. It was *"Grossmutter gestorben"* (Grandmother dead). Then he must act immediately "without fail."[4]

August 31, 1939, the last day of the peace in Europe, was a hot, sticky day. Naujocks looked out the window of his hotel room at the handful of pedestrians on the dusty main street below — men in shirtsleeves and without ties, women, in damp, clinging summer frocks — and thought how unconcerned they were. They were going about the business of living as if they had all the time in the world, as if they were going to exist forever. But he knew differently. For four hours before, just as he had been going down for lunch, the porter at the dusty reception desk had handed him a telegram from

---

[4] It is interesting to note that Heydrich's plans had already been betrayed to the British on that same day by the former's ex-chief, Admiral Canaris. By the early afternoon of August 25, the British Government knew that Hitler was preparing to start a war against Poland by means of simulated frontier incidents.

Berlin. Wiping the sweat from his brow, he had opened it with trembling fingers, knowing already the two words it would contain. He was right. There they were, staring up at him boldly — the signal for the start of World War II:

Grossmutter Gestorben

Now the inexorable machinery of Heydrich's plot was working at full pitch. In nearby Oppeln, "Gestapo" Mueller was already rolling his trucks, with the "canned goods" (meant for both Naujocks and other similar clandestine operations on the frontier) hidden beneath tarpaulins. The SS had taken up their positions in the woods and dirt roads of the area, sealing it off completely from interference by an unsuspecting Wehrmacht. Civilian police stations were already under surveillance in case the uniformed police inadvertently answered the call for help at Gleiwitz. As for Naujocks himself, he had already contacted his men and told them to be ready to leave for the radio station at 7:45 P.M. *Operation Himmler* was under way.

Naujocks and his men took up their positions on a little side road in the immediate vicinity of the radio station just before eight o'clock that evening. Naujocks took a last nervous puff at his cigarette. Somewhere a clock began to strike eight. It was the signal. The big special agent dropped his half-smoked cigarette on the cobbles and instinctively stamped it out. Although he knew he must get his men moving at once, he hesitated. As he stated later: "I had an undefinable and uncertain feeling that I was walking into a trap."

He gritted his teeth and turned to his eager men. "Wait a minute," he ordered. "I'd like to take another security measure."

"Yes?" they queried, surprised.

They were an unshaven, rough-looking bunch in their scruffy Polish clothes. At the same time, they were fanatical followers of the Führer, champing at the bit to get into action at last. Naujocks tried to force some iron into his voice to convince them of the necessity of his new measure. "Three men will remain here," he snapped. "You, you, and you."

"Why?" The three men in question asked in unison, their faces revealing their disappointment at not being allowed to take part in the action. Naujocks didn't give them a chance to argue. "It's an order! Understand? If anyone comes up, give the alarm. If anyone tries to enter the building after us, shoot him at once!"

"*Jawohl!*" the three men said without enthusiasm.

Naujocks jerked his head in the direction of the white stucco, modernistic radio station. "Okay, let's go," he said.

As casually as they could, the remainder of his little force began to walk down the road to the building. A car passed. But its occupants took no notice of the men who moved aside to let it pass. They reached the gate. They were only fifty yards away from the entrance to the station now, but those fifty yards seemed like fifty thousand.

The night porter in his glass cage at the entrance was an old man with sunken cheeks and grey mustache. One of Naujocks' men stuck his big pistol under the old man's nose. The porter's face turned ashen. "Hands up!" he cried in rough Polish. The porter's hands flew up above his head.

Now things happened fast. Naujocks' five men clattered up the stairs. An engineer named Foitzik spotted them. He opened his mouth to protest and found himself staring into the muzzle of a luger. Naujocks, all energy now, his nervousness gone, pushed past him. The staff turned, surprised, their faces suddenly pale and shaken. Naujocks didn't give them time to collect themselves. "Hands up!" he ordered and levelled his pistol at them. Hastily they complied. He pushed them to one side. Telling the story much later, Naujocks explained: "We, then, fired our pistols in the broadcasting room. We loosed off a couple of shots into the ceiling in order to make a bit of a shindy and frighten people."

Swiftly the staff were handcuffed and led off to the cellar. Then Naujocks hit an unexpected problem. He didn't know how to broadcast! As he admitted later, "We had a feverish search before we could get our broadcast through." Frantically he and his men checked through the unfamiliar collection of knobs, dials, controls until finally they came across the so-called storm microphone. This was normally used to inform local listeners that a broadcast might be interfered with by a threatened storm. Hastily Naujocks pulled out the prepared harangue in Polish. He handed it to one of those who spoke Polish. The man grabbed the manuscript.

To the accompaniment of shots and excited German voices, the Polish-speaking trooper said his piece. It lasted exactly four minutes. Then Naujocks snapped an order. His men started to retreat. They clattered down the stairs in their heavy boots, past the scared porter, and out into the open. Dramatically draped across the entrance lay Mueller's "canned goods." Two of the three men posted outside had collected the unfortunate concentration camp inmate from the Gestapo truck and positioned the dead man exactly as Heydrich had ordered. Naujocks gave him a fleeting glance. The gunshot wounds looked realistic enough. There was an ugly red patch at his breast and his hands were stretched out as if he had been done violently to death.

But Naujocks had no time to ponder Heydrich's ingenuity. His one and only aim now was to save his own skin. He gave the prearranged signal. The SS men scattered, running hastily down the road to the waiting truck. They had pulled it off. But as he ran after the others (these men who had started World War II and who would not survive the next six years), he wondered how long Heydrich would allow him to live, now that he knew so much.

Next morning Hitler's own paper, the *Voelkischer Beobachter*, alarmed the nation with the banner headline, "Polish Insurgents Cross the German Frontier," and went on to explain that the "Gleiwitz crime" was "clearly the signal for a general attack on German territory by Polish guerrillas." Hitler followed up the news with his declaration of war against Poland in his speech to the Reichstag a few hours later, declaring there had been fourteen frontier incidents the previous night; whereas Goering told a Swedish mediator that "war had broken out because the Poles had attacked the Gleiwitz Radio Station."

The world press rushed to the "scene of the crime." Here Mueller and Nebe, now appearing in the guise of the "murder squad" investigating the incident, lectured to the attentive correspondents by means of the model of the radio station, which was accurate to the last detail, while in the background the mastermind behind the whole affair, Heydrich, gravely nodded his head, murmuring at intervals. "Yes, yes, that's how the war started."

Thus the war in the shadows began, with its blackmail and brutality, its traitors and its heroes, its tremendous successes and abysmal failures — and its overriding cynical principle that everyone has his price.

It would spread over the borders of Germany to the neighboring countries and from there across the Channel to England. Soon it would slip nefariously across oceans like a plague-bearing rat, dispersing to all four comers of the globe until finally it reached far-off, isolationist America, still at peace. Germany had — as Heydrich assured Naujocks jubilantly — won the first round.

On the same afternoon while Heydrich and his staff celebrated the success of their first major operation of the war, his one-time chief from Navy days and now his major rival, Admiral Wilhelm Canaris, fell into a mood of deep depression.

The 52-year-old little man with the ruddy face and white hair had been in charge of the Abwehr, German Military Intelligence, since 1935, but nothing about him revealed the tremendous power he possessed. He felt the cold even at the height of summer and rarely took off his overcoat when he could avoid doing so. He was an excellent cook, loved his dachshunds, and hated the sight of uniforms. (It is reported that anyone who wanted a favor from him was careful to remove all medals and ribbons before reporting to the little Admiral.)

But in spite of his unmilitary appearance and habits, disdained by his SS and Gestapo colleagues, Santa Claus, as Heydrich called him contemptuously, was reputed to have been the lover of Mata Hari, whom he persuaded to spy for Germany against France in World War I; but when her activities had become dangerous to him, he had betrayed her to the French. It was said also of him that he had once killed an Italian priest while imprisoned in an Allied camp during that same war and had escaped in his cassock; that he had been involved in the postwar murder of German revolutionaries

Rosa Luxemburg and Karl Liebknecht. A hundred and one wild tales and rumors, all of them probably false or at least wildly inaccurate.

For the man who had massive funds at his disposal, who had unlimited power at his command, who knew more that was going on behind the scenes in Germany and Europe than any other living man (including his one-time cadet, Heydrich) was at heart a gentle, moral man who was soon to gain for himself the title, "father of the persecuted."

Now on this first day of the new war, in the German High Command Headquarters, humming with tremendous energy, Canaris drew an associate down one of the dimly lit corridors and, in a voice choked with emotion, said, "This means the end of Germany..."[5]

---

[5] Ex-Gestapo man Gisevius had just informed Canaris that the British were mobilizing.

2 — THE VENLO SNATCH

At a quarter to nine on the night of November 8, 1939, two customs men stood in the darkness of a garden on the German side of Lake Constance. They were listening to the Führer's broadcast from Munich coming to them through an open window of the local reformatory. It was his traditional speech from the beer cellar which had been his main haunt before he had come to power.

Across the lake the Swiss shoreline was ablaze with lights — a ready-made guide for the RAF if it ever ventured this far south.

They did not at first notice the undersized figure some ten or twelve yards away in the dark, like themselves apparently engrossed in Hitler's fiery words. Then one customs man nudged the other. The stranger might be a patriotic German. All the same they were only a hundred yards from the border with Switzerland, the border they were supposed to guard.

The second customs man tore himself away from the speech. "*Hallo! Sie da!*" he called. "*Was machen Sie?*"

Without waiting for an answer, he unslung his rifle and walked over to the man in the shadows, who raised his hands without being asked, as if he had known all along that this would happen.

Minutes later he was standing in the yellow light of the customs post at Kreuzlinger Tor, his pockets ripped out of the cheap suit he was wearing, his pathetic belongings spread out in front of the slightly bored and somewhat puzzled officials: an identity card indicating that he was Georg Elser and a carpenter by trade; a piece of gnawed salami, a bundle of leaflets, a postcard of the Munich Burgerbraukeller (where the Führer was still talking at that moment), and a few pieces of metal. One of the customs men who had served in the army identified the metal pieces as a time-detonator.

"A time-detonator?" the sergeant in charge asked in surprise. He looked at the skinny carpenter with the hangdog face. Then he jerked a fat thumb at the prisoner. "What the devil would he be doing with a detonator?"

The ex-soldier shrugged. The whole affair was apparently just another of the myriad meaningless incidents which made up their life on the frontier. "Don't ask me, Sergeant!" he answered.

It was just about that time; 21:20, half an hour after the man had been arrested, that the Burgerbraukeller was shaken by a violent explosion. A blinding flash of light shot through the air. The great pillar behind Hitler's podium disappeared in an instant. The next moment the roof started to come down on the flushed and excited crowd below.

Six of Hitler's old fighters were killed instantly, as was one of the buxom waitresses. Sixty-three men and women were injured, sixteen severely. Within moments, the cellar which had seen the beginning of Adolf Hitler's rise to power was transformed into a bloodbath. On all sides, the dying and wounded screamed for help while the uninjured frantically fought their way to the doors. "A bomb — a bomb has just exploded — they're dying everywhere in there!" they cried to those who ran to their aid. But the man for whom that bomb had been intended, Adolf Hitler, had left exactly thirteen minutes before, having shortened his speech because of urgent war duties.

The alarm signals went up all over Germany. Heydrich,

Himmler, Mueller rushed to take over. The order went out to every customs post to seal off the frontier. No one must be allowed to leave Germany that night in case the culprit, the instigator of this dastardly attempt on the Führer, tried to get away.

But who had placed the bomb?

By midnight the message reached the fat sergeant at the Kreuzlinger Tor post. He remembered the humble little carpenter's postcard of the beer cellar and the time-detonator. Even his sluggish mind realized almost at once that he had caught a big fish — a very big fish indeed — The man who had attempted to kill Adolf Hitler!

Georg Elser was a loner who felt that the only way the working class could be saved from the horrors of war was to remove the cause of that war — Adolf Hitler. Almost immediately after war had been declared, the skilled carpenter/electrician with the fixed idea had set about finding explosives for his self-imposed task. He took a temporary job in a quarry and there broke into the explosives store to find what he wanted. Then, knowing that it was Hitler's custom to speak at the beer cellar every year, he went to Munich.

He broke into the Burgerbraukeller every night, or hid in the toilet until everyone else had left. Burrowing his way into the big pillar before which Hitler would speak, he planted a time bomb of his own make and sealed up the spot, firmly convinced — as he later told the Gestapo — that in this way "I could get rid of the leadership."

But Adolf Hitler would not believe one man had carried out "the dastardly deed" alone. That same evening when Nuremberg Police Chief Martin stopped the "Führer Special" speeding back to Berlin to inform the shocked leader that an attempt had been made on his life, the thought immediately flashed through Hitler's mind that this was the doing of the British Secret Service. In particular, of their chief agents on the Continent, whose activities he knew, Captain Best and Major Stevens.

Working from the passport control office at The Hague, the British had built up a network of agents in both Holland and Germany to spy on the latter country. For five years they had been smuggling information out of Nazi Germany. In October 1939, however, Heydrich, who admired the British agents' efforts, decided to have a closer look at the PCC network. Using a German emigre in Holland who worked under the code number F479 (his real name was Dr. Franz), he made contact with Captain Best, British Intelligence's representative in Holland. Heydrich fed Best half-truths about the strength of German Army resistance to the Führer, hoping by this means to gain insight into the workings of British Intelligence, the degree of cooperation between the British and Dutch Intelligence Services, and the British contacts with internal resistance to the Nazis inside Germany. It was for this last reason that Himmler had informed Hitler of the Best-Stevens setup.

As Hitler raved about the "machinations of the British Secret Service," Himmler, always eager to please, decided that the contact with the British agents, by now a month old, should be used immediately to support Hitler's fixed idea that Elser was a tool of the British. In the early hours of the following morning, he called the man responsible for directing the operation from his cover address in the Rhenish town of Dusseldorf.

Walter Schellenberg, the smooth young ex-lawyer, was another of Heydrich's intellectual gangsters like Naujocks, only smarter. He had taken a sleeping pill that night after an exhausting day preparing for his next frontier meeting with the

British agents. But the insistent ringing of the special phone to Berlin finally roused him. At the other end he heard a deep, excited voice ask: "What did you say?"

"Nothing so far," Schellenberg said thickly, annoyed at being awakened. "Who am I speaking to?"

"The Reichsführer SS Himmler," came the sharp reply. "Are you there at last?"

Schellenberg sat up sharply and stared at his bedside lamp in consternation. What the devil was this about? "Yes, sir," he said smartly.

"Well, listen carefully. Do you know what has happened?" Schellenberg replied in the negative.

"Well, this evening just after the Führer's speech in the beer cellar, an attempt was made to assassinate him!" Even the drugged young undercover agent could note the real shock and alarm in his chief's voice.

"A bomb went off. Luckily he'd left the cellar a few minutes before — there's no doubt that the British Secret Service is behind it all. The Führer and I were already on the train to Berlin when we got the news. He now says — and this is an order — when you meet the British agents for your conference tomorrow, you are to arrest them immediately and bring them to Germany."

Schellenberg wanted to protest, but Himmler beat him to it. "This may mean a violation of the Dutch frontier, but the Führer says that's of no consequence. The SS detachment that's been assigned to protect you — which by the way you don't deserve, not after the arbitrary and self-willed way you've been behaving — this detachment is to help you to carry out your mission. Do you understand everything?"

Schellenberg, now sitting stiffly upright in his bed, tried to protest, "Yes, Reichsführer, but..."

"There are no buts," Himmler interrupted him sharply. "Do you understand?" Tamely Schellenberg answered "Yes, sir."

A moment later Himmler hung up.

Thus Schellenberg, a slim young man in his thirties with impudent eyes, thick, sleek hair, and a broad sensuous mouth, was confronted for the first time with real danger. Since he had first joined the SD and been given the job of building up Heydrich's own secret service, he had worked up to seventeen hours a day, allowing himself an hour in the morning for riding and a few moments in the evening to dally over his collection of pornographic photos. But in all this time he had never faced physical danger; that had been left to the others like Naujocks. But then Walter Schellenberg, who, far more intelligent than either Heydrich or Canaris, was going to survive the new war: he had plans for himself, which did not include those two men; but to carry them out this university graduate, who was often called "a quibbling lawyer" by his tougher SS comrades, needed the safety of the home front.

He was an intellectual gangster who had soon discovered that Hitler's new "Thousand Year Reich" offered tremendous scope for his almost overwhelming desire for power — and more power. Now he was being forced by that fool Himmler to risk his neck in an operation that could easily go wrong.

It almost had once, less than a couple of weeks before. Then he had met the two British agents, disguised as Captain Schemmel of the German Army HQ, Transport Section. Equipped with a monocle and some carefully doctored "secrets" for their consumption, he had convinced the British and their Dutch helpers that he was a genuine anti-Nazi. He also posed as the confidant of an important group of German generals, who were ready to overthrow Hitler by force if Britain would respect the "new government" they were to form after the coup.

As he had crossed the border, Dutch customs searched his luggage, presumably on British orders. During the search a package of aspirins had tumbled out of his bag (Schellenberg suffered from headaches.) To his horror, he noticed the label — SS *Sanitaetshauptamt* — Main SS Medical Office. Quickly Schellenberg knocked it on the floor and managed to stuff it and the tablets into his mouth before the Dutch spotted them. A little while later, Captain Best, the British agent, had caught him unawares in the bathroom and had asked softly: "Tell me, do you always wear a monocle?"

Schellenberg flushed instinctively. But fortunately Best could not see his face. Knowing that attack was the best defense, he had countered with: "You know, I've been meaning to ask you the same question," and with that the awkward moment had passed.

Now by this time the British, he felt, trusted him implicitly. They had even supplied him with a radio transmitter so that he could communicate with them directly and daily. They had also given him special Dutch credentials which allowed him to cross the Dutch-German frontier without hindrance. In other words, Schellenberg felt that he would be able to lure the British and their Dutch helper to the frontier without difficulty. The trouble would start when they realized that they were being arrested, as Himmler put it. "Kidnapped" would be a better word in his opinion. Obviously they would be armed and would not hesitate to defend themselves once they realized they had walked into a trap. Once the firing started, Schellenberg told himself, anything could happen.

But Himmler had made his decision; there was nothing to do but to carry out the order. Dressing swiftly, he reached for the phone. It was time to call Naujocks, the head of the guard detachment from the SS.

Naujocks and his second in command were doubtful. Always concerned with his own safety and invariably suspicious of Heydrich's motives now that he knew so much, Naujocks felt the operation would be far from easy. The terrain was tough and for days now the Dutch had staked out the whole area around Venlo, where the meeting was to take place. Shooting would be inevitable.

Naujocks made the point that the only advantage they possessed was the element of surprise. Once Best and Stevens had sat down with Schellenberg at their café rendezvous, it would be too late. The time to act would be as soon as Best's ancient Buick drove up.

As Naujocks saw it, he and twelve men of the special detachment would charge through the red-and-white striped frontier barrier and seize the two Britishers, who would be taken completely off guard. The two would be dumped into the SS car, which would not attempt to turn because by then the Dutch frontier guards would be firing at them. Instead the driver, trained specially for this kind of operation, would drive in reverse back across the frontier. This maneuver would be covered by the remainder of Naujocks' detachment hiding in the ditches on both sides of the little country road.

Schellenberg made one or two comments but agreed in principle to the Naujocks plan, especially the latter's suggestion that he, Schellenberg, should not personally take a part in the operation. His role would be to sit in the café and, when he saw Best's Buick appear, he would rise as if to welcome them, and then hurry to his own car and drive off.

Schellenberg, who had a sharp sense of his own value and was highly concerned with his own skin, approved, making only one proviso: that Naujocks introduce him to the twelve SS men of his detachment. As he recalled later: "I wanted all of them to get a good look at me. Captain Best, though he was slightly taller than I, was of about the same build, had a similar overcoat, and also wore a monocle; so I wanted to make certain that there would be no mistake."

Some nine hours later, Schellenberg crossed the frontier and took up his post in the little street café. He ordered an aperitif. But he could not conceal his nervousness and more than once found himself excitedly drumming the table top with his thin fingers.

He had good cause to be nervous. The little town was unusually full of strange civilians, accompanied by savage looking police dogs. The frontier guards were unusually vigilant, too. Normally they went about their routine duties in a slow bored manner. Today they were alert; they carried their rifles slung over their shoulders as if they were prepared to seize them instantly and commence firing. Obviously, as Schellenberg remarked later, "our British friends had taken unusually thorough measures for this meeting."

The long wait in the dreary little café dragged on. The sky over the flat damp Dutch plain grew greyer, and Schellenberg thought it would be soon drizzling again — that cold, miserable, thin Dutch rain which he had grown to hate in these last weeks. He looked at his watch every couple of minutes. Were the British not going to keep the appointment? He glanced at the white customs post, where Naujocks' car was waiting behind the rear wall. Nothing moved. He whispered a fervent prayer that the men of the special detachment were not lulled into a false sense of security by the lack of action.

Suddenly he heard a big car approaching — fast. Almost instinctively he got to his feet. But his companion grabbed him quickly and forced him back onto the hard wooden chair. "That's not the car!" he whispered urgently. "Relax!" With a shaking hand, Schellenberg reached for his glass.

Best and Stevens and their companion Klop, from the Dutch General Staff (who was using the cover name of Lieutenant Coppens), were uneasy too. Dutch troops in their scuttle helmets were everywhere. Something was in the air, and they were relieved when a sentry told them they could go no further. Unfortunately Klop sorted out the problem. He disappeared into the guard house and when he returned, said smilingly in his excellent English: "Everything is all right. The NCO had a message for me which had been phoned though from the office. Carry on."

Best, who was driving, shrugged and carried on. They passed a second sentry post. Now they were proceeding along a straight part of the road from where Best could see the frontier. As Best recalled after the war: "Somehow or other, it seemed different from previous days. Then I noticed that the German barrier across the road which had always been closed was now lifted; there seemed to be nothing between us and the enemy."

The intelligence chief's sense of impending danger heightened. He licked lips that were suddenly dry and surveyed the scene as they came closer and closer to the frontier. It looked peaceful enough. No one was in sight except a plump German customs officer lounging at the side of the road and a little girl in pigtails, playing with a ball and a big black dog in front of the café rendezvous. But still, something was in the air — he felt it in his bones.

Unconsciously he checked his speed.

A nervous Klop called: "Go ahead, everything is all right." The upper-class regular British officer felt a fool for having lost face like this. He let the car move slowly toward the café ...

It was exactly three o'clock. Schellenberg had ordered black coffee to soothe his nerves and had just taken his first sip when he heard the sound of the Buick. He dropped the cup hastily, spilling its contents. He rushed into the street waving his arms, as if the general from the high command, whom Best and Stevens expected, were inside.

Best answered by braking the car and slipping from behind the big wheel. Stevens did the same. Just as the two of them opened the doors, a large open black car hurled out from behind the customs post. With the roar of an engine being driven full out, it filled the street. It was packed with what Best thought were rough-looking men; two of them posted on the running boards were firing machine pistols at the three agents.

Klop reacted first. He threw himself out of the Buick and drew his service revolver — on the first target available — Schellenberg, some ten yards away. Schellenberg jumped to one side. Klop turned his attention to the SS car. In rapid succession he fired four accurate shots at it. The Mercedes' windshield shattered suddenly. Schellenberg, paralyzed with horror at his narrow escape, saw how the "crystalline threads were spreading from the bullet holes."

Naujocks now took on Klop. He leaped from the car and pulled out his pistol. A regular duel started between the two agents. Both men shot deliberately, taking careful aim. Then the Dutchman was hit. His pistol dropped from his fingers, his knees buckled under him, and he fell slowly to the floor in a dark red pool of his own blood.

His opponent taken care of, Naujocks yelled at the mesmerized Schellenberg: "Will you get the hell out of this! God knows why you haven't been hit!"

Schellenberg needed no urging; he fled.

Meanwhile Best and Stevens had been seized. Stevens, London's representative at the talks which had been scheduled to take place this November day, mumbled "Our number's up, Best," and stretching out his hands obediently, allowed himself to be handcuffed. Swiftly Naujocks' men urged them across the frontier with cries of "*Los, marsch, marsch!*" and "*Hup, hup, hup!*" Moments later they were level with the frontier post, and the red-and-white pole descended behind them. They were in Nazi Germany. The operation had been a complete success.

But Schellenberg's problems were not yet over. Leaving Naujocks,[6] he ran around a corner to bump into a huge SS officer, whom he had never seen before. He grabbed Schellenberg by the scruff of the neck and stuck a huge pistol under the pale-faced agent's nose. Obviously he was a newcomer to the operation who mistook Schellenberg for Best.

---

[6] Naujocks survived another two years with Heydrich, but in 1942 he was sent to the front as a private in an SS punishment battalion on Heydrich's express command. The charge was that Naujocks was involved in illegal gold transactions. However, men who knew Naujocks tell me that, in fact, he was fired because, apart from knowing too much, he had listened to one of Heydrich's love-making sessions at the special brothel, Haus Kitty, opened by the latter in Berlin.

Schellenberg pushed him away violently, yelling: "Don't be stupid! Put that gun away!"

The SS man did not react. He grabbed the smaller man again. Schellenberg tried to fight him off. The SS man pulled the trigger, but in the same instant, Schellenberg knocked his hand. The bullet exploded a couple of inches from the agent's head. And then the second-in-command of the operation came running to his aid and explained who he was.

Schellenberg, limp and sweating heavily from nervous exhaustion, crawled into his car and drove off hastily, eager to put space between himself and the trigger-happy SS man.

Although Hitler awarded him the Iron Cross First Class for his part in the Venlo mission and promoted him to major general, Schellenberg was not satisfied. He felt "it would have been better if I could have continued the negotiations as I had wished."

For a while longer at both Hitler's and Himmler's insistence, Schellenberg, Heydrich, and Mueller tried to get Elser to confess that he was in the pay of the British. Gestapo Mueller tried every trick he knew to make Elser talk. Once Schellenberg bumped into the ex-policeman at Hitler's HQ. The latter's face was pale and drawn. He told Schellenberg: "He (Elser) either refuses to say anything at all or else tells stupid lies." Then the police chief massaged his left hand, the knuckles of which were red and swollen. With a malevolent look in his small eyes and his thin lips compressed cruelly, he said quietly: "I've never had a man in front of me yet whom I did not break in the end."

Schellenberg had not been able to repress a shudder of revulsion. But the little Munich policeman who now enjoyed unlimited power was never able to break Elser. He, as well as Best and Stevens, was lodged in a special section of one of

Mueller's concentration camps and forgotten till April 1945 when Elser was killed in an air raid (in other words "liquidated" at Himmler's express order). The two Britishers survived.

But although Schellenberg was not completely satisfied with the success of his mission, his capture of Best and Stevens had achieved — unwittingly — two things. He had broken the power of the British intelligence network in Holland and scared off those in Canaris's Abwehr organization such as ex-Gestapo man Hans Bernd Gisevius, who had been trying to make contact with the British. As for the British, they, too, made no further attempts to negotiate with the German resistance — once bitten, twice shy, they told themselves.

Six months later the German Wehrmacht marched west using, in the case of neutral Holland, "the Venlo incident" as proof that the Dutch had been first to break the neutrality existing between the two states. Swiftly the Dutch, Belgian, and French secret services were rolled up. In the newly captured capitals of The Hague, Brussels, and Paris, specially trained squads from the Abwehr seized huge masses of documents on the activities of the national espionage services. In addition, they captured comprehensive information on these organizations' links with the British security forces.

Thus it was that by the summer of 1940 the intelligence services directed by Canaris and Heydrich were the masters of Western Europe. Not only had the last British soldier been forced out of the Continent at Dunkirk, but the whole of their network built up so hopefully for over five years. Now hard-eyed Reinhard Heydrich was in complete control of the hearts and minds of his sixty million fellow Germans and their hundred and fifty million newly acquired foreign subjects, rapidly being integrated into the "New Order." Now the Reich

Main Security Office dominated and observed every move of its 210 million citizens from the English Channel to the marshes of the Polish-Russian border.

As for the sole remaining enemy, Winston Churchill, he might well tell his cabinet exuberantly: "Gentlemen, we are alone. For myself, I find it extremely exhilarating." But his intelligence chief, Cavendish-Bentinck,[7] a bespectacled immensely tall ex-officer, who invariably wore a bowler and carried a rolled umbrella (years later he would appear at Patton's mud-bound HQ dressed thus in the middle of a battle), was not in the least exuberant or exhilarated.

He knew that terrible summer of defeat that England was devoid of intelligence sources in Western Europe. His eyes and ears had vanished overnight, and now he was like a boxer who has been suddenly blinded and is forced to fight a desperate life-and-death underground struggle with no indication whatsoever of when and how his enemy will strike. The Germans, it seemed, had won the intelligence war.

---

[7] Chief in the sense that he coordinated all British intelligence activities. See British Intelligence organization in chapter 3.

1940-1942: THE BRITISH STRIKE BACK

My experience is that the gentlemen who are the best behaved and the most sleek are those who are doing the mischief. We cannot be too sure of anybody.

Field Marshal Ironside, C-in-C Home Forces, addressing
Home Guard volunteers, England, June 5, 1940.

3 — THE BIG DOUBLE-CROSS

BISCUIT suspected SNOW right from the start. BISCUIT had had a long career of petty larceny, dope smuggling, and confidence tricks; and his long nose told him that the medium-sized, fast-talking Welshman was "dodgy," as he put it in his own particular patois. But MI5 told him that the other operative was okay when they had briefed him in London, so he thrust his doubts to the back of his mind and went along with the scheme.

And what a crazy scheme it was! In this spring of 1940 with German panzers racing through France toward the Channel coast, BISCUIT and SNOW were to set out in a requisitioned trawler, braving both the *Kriegsmarine* and the Royal Navy to rendezvous with SNOW's control *in the middle of the North sea!*

Then two days before, Major Ritter of Abwehr, Hamburg, had radioed SNOW: "Meet me fifty-three degrees forty min. north, three deg. ten minutes east, twenty-six fathoms, midnight Tuesday twenty-first or Wednesday twenty-ninth May." There the German secret agent would come swooping out of the sky in his DO-18 twin-engine seaplane to discuss SNOW's further operations as a German spy in Britain.

But as soon as the battered old traveler had left the Lincolnshire port of Grimsby and BISCUIT had managed to drag his mind away from its all-pervading smell of rotten fish, his suspicions of the other man, who had been working as a double agent for nearly four years, began to grow and grow.

SNOW started to drink hard as the little fishing boat rocked up and down on the grey-green North Sea, and with every stiff drink of the bonded Scotch he became more loquacious. He told BISCUIT of his past; how he had drifted into the espionage game after he had returned from Canada in 1933, needing money for the Scotch he favored and the harem of mistresses he kept; how he had worked for the British for three years, traveling back and forth to the Continent under the guise of an electrical salesman, until finally he had switched sides and started working for the Germans; and how now he was working for both sides.

BISCUIT, of course, did not realize that SNOW was just as scared of him as he was of SNOW. The latter took him for a genuine German agent, while BISCUIT became increasingly convinced that SNOW was the real game. Thus the day passed with the two petty crooks and erstwhile agents glaring at each other over the swaying little table, drinking deeper and deeper into the square-shaped whisky bottle.

On the evening of May 21st, however, two days before the fantastic rendezvous, a German plane swooped down low over the trawler. Both men hit the wet treacherous deck. It was a "Jerry," all right. It turned and came down again, zooming over their heads at three hundred miles an hour, its tail wind thrashing their clothes against their bodies. The panicky BISCUIT could distinctly see the dark outlines of the German aviators. It made a further tight turn and came in again, slower this time. Now the recognition signal — a red and white flare — hissed into the night sky and hung there, bathing them momentarily in its icy-red light. With that the plane disappeared.

BISCUIT found some excuse for remaining on deck, SNOW shivered in the cold night wind and said he was going down below to get another drink, BISCUIT nodded and then hurried to the little trawler's skipper, as scruffy and smelly as his ship, "Turn out the lights. We're going back," he ordered.

The fisherman needed no urging. He did not like the strange job he had been ordered to carry out any better than BISCUIT, who was now convinced that the sudden appearance of the German plane was the final indication of SNOW's treachery; besides, both their time and their position had not been what had been previously agreed upon. That done, he hurried to the cabin and before SNOW realized what was happening, he had snapped the lock closed, SNOW was a prisoner...

That strange little scene of apparent treachery and counter-treachery in the middle of the North Sea was part and parcel of the amazing new secret organization which the British had been forced to build up now that their "eyes and ears" on the Continent had so effectively been blinded and deafened by the Germans. It was the "XX" — for double-cross — or as its players called it — "the twenty game." They called themselves the Twenty Committee.

The "twenty game" had been organized by Major Thomas Robertson, a Scottish major in his late twenties, who saw two advantages in using German agents in Britain: (1) to spy on their former masters; and (2) to feed them with false information about Britain's defenses and resources. As the handsome, intelligent Major saw it, once a German agent had been captured or effectively compromised — if he were in a neutral country, that is — he would be offered the choice of being hanged, or having his treachery revealed to his Abwehr masters, or working for new masters — the Twenty Committee of MI5.

At first no one in authority wanted to buy the young Major's idea. In 1939 Britain had been swept by a spy fever. Unlike the situation in 1914 when Scotland Yard's Special Branch had cracked the whole Imperial German system in Britain in one week, there were now many more Germans of all sorts and shades of political opinion in the country. Many were genuine refugees from Hitlerism. Others were Jewish. Only a few were potential or real enemy agents. As a result, all spies who were caught were executed immediately. The success of the Nazi Fifth Column in Continental countries only served to increase the blind hatred of German spies. But in the end Robertson managed to get his unusual scheme placed in front of General "Pug" Ismay, Churchill's chief military aide.

Ismay saw its value, especially since a cocky final radio message from Schellenberg after the capture of Best had said. "Negotiations for any length of time with conceited and silly people are tedious. You will understand, therefore, that we are giving them up. You are hereby bidden a hearty farewell by your affectionate German Opposition." The malicious message was signed "The Gestapo." Realizing that the whole Dutch organization was finished, as was that in Rome run by irritable Colonel Dansey under the code letter "Z", General Ismay ordered British Intelligence to let the young Scottish major have a chance.

Thus Robertson got his way and SNOW, whose real name was Owens, was recruited into the organization as its first double agent. Almost one year to the day after the war had broken out, SNOW made his first attempt to contact his German control, Ritter, in Hamburg by radio, operating it in — of all places — a dingy little yellow-walled cell in London's Wandsworth Prison.

The Abwehr took the bait, and the Twenty Committee knew that they were in business. Thereafter they kept SNOW busy transmitting genuine and faked messages to his German control in Hamburg, Luftwaffe Major Ritter, alias Dr. Rantzau. Swiftly the masterminds of the Twenty Committee built up

SNOW's reputation for accuracy, allowing him to transmit the true results of German bombing during the Battle of Britain, which of course, could be verified by the Germans through air reconnaissance.

By September 1940, four months after the British Expeditionary Force had fled from France, Major Masterman, former Oxford professor and now head of the Twenty Committee, decided it was time to use SNOW in his most ambitious operation to date. The volatile little Welshman was to plant a new agent on the Germans in an operation which made the mind boggle. As Masterman saw it, the objects of this mission were three-fold: (1) to clarify and report on SNOW's position abroad; (2) to observe and report on the German espionage system in Portugal; and (3) to *enter Germany*, if the Germans would take him, *penetrate the German Service*, and bring back what information he could!

But where would the Twenty Committee find such a man, who would risk his neck on such an amazing mission — and with a man who had proved himself a double traitor a dozen times over the last five years?

That man walked in on the planners of his own accord. CELERY, as he became known, had been an RAF Intelligence officer in World War I. But on volunteering for service at the outbreak of World War II, he had been refused a commission under circumstances which would later enable him to be represented as a man with a grudge against his country. But that was to come later.

In 1940 CELERY was so eager to serve his country that he took to spying on his own volition. Enterprising and observant, he had not forgotten his previous training. When he came across SNOW he took him for a genuine German agent (and he wasn't too far off the mark). Trailing SNOW on his own initiative, he was led to Russell Leigh, SNOW's case officer. Believing that he now had an opportunity to put the finger on two genuine German agents, he reported his findings to the head of RAF Intelligence, Air Commodore Boyle, only to be told gently that both "suspects" worked for the top secret Twenty Committee.

But as Major Masterman observed later: "The obvious policy was to turn the poacher into a gamekeeper." Thus the ex-Intelligence man became CELERY, designed to go on the tremendously hazardous mission; if SNOW betrayed him in Lisbon, he would be a dead man as soon as he set foot on German soil.

SNOW, who was known as "Johnny" to Ritter, arrived first by air. The Welshman and the German met several times clandestinely in various cafés in the Portuguese capital, which was full of spies that year. What they discussed is not known. As Major Masterman recalls: "What exactly happened ... is still to some extent a matter for speculation." But a few days later SNOW went down to Lisbon's harbor to meet CELERY, or "Jack Brown," as he was now known, and whisked him away to the house where Ritter was waiting.

"He was a fairly tall, good-looking chap in his thirties," Ritter recalled much later (he was, in fact, several years older), "with even features. There was something unusual only about his eyes. They were brownish-green and slightly bulging and absolutely cold, without a glint of expression like a blind man's eyes."

SNOW did the introductions. He stretched out an arm in CELERY's direction. "Well, Doctor, this is Jack — Mr. Brown — that is, the RAF bloke I promised you." "How do you do,"

CELERY said and stretched out his hand. It was as cold as his strange eyes.

"Well," the Luftwaffe Major began in his somewhat stilted English, "Johnny has told me all about you — you have been kicked out of the RAF — am I correct?... Do you really think that you want to work with us and that you've got something in which we might be interested?"

"I've no doubt of that," CELERY answered.

"Then we don't have to beat around the bush."

CELERY responded by pulling out his passport and handing it to Ritter. The German pushed it away. "There is no need for such formalities. Your pass may be just as counterfeit as mine. After all, we're in the same business."

Thus on this coldly realistic basis, the three men got down to business, CELERY was a mine of information. He told the silent German about the RAF's purchase of planes in the USA and how they were ferried; the location of rolling stock plants; improvements in British artillery — a hundred and one things of greater and lesser importance. Ritter was visibly impressed, but he was careful.

"I can see that we'll need some time to cover everything, and I cannot remain here in Lisbon any longer. Would you be willing to come to Germany for a few days for a conference with our experts? I give you my word as an officer that I will arrange your safe return to Lisbon."

CELERY was prepared for this question; the Twenty Committee had briefed him on it. Yet although his cold eyes revealed nothing, his palms were suddenly wet with sweat. What if SNOW had betrayed him and this was a set-up job? It would be the Gestapo cellars and the executioner, so he had been told, in full evening dress and armed with an axe.

Before he could answer, SNOW jumped in, "That sounds wonderful, Doctor," he said exuberantly, "when are we leaving?"

"Wait a minute, Johnny," Ritter said, turning his attention to SNOW. "The invitation does not extend to you. I am sorry, but I cannot take you both."

The fat little Welshman's face fell. He sank into a sulky silence. Ritter turned his attention to CELERY again. "What do you say, Mr. Brown?"

CELERY took the plunge. "All right, sir, I'll go."

On February 18, 1941, CELERY arrived at the great port city of Hamburg, the center of German espionage against Britain and the United States. He was put up at the Hotel Vier Jahreszeiten, that splendid nineteenth-century edifice overlooking the Alster. High-ranking Nazi officers strode through its revolving doors, little dreaming that four years later this would become British Military Headquarters. Even the tense, apprehensive CELERY never entertained such an improbable idea.

Ritter went to work with typical German efficiency. A commission of Luftwaffe experts was flown in from Berlin to examine the renegade RAF man, while a couple of leather-coated Gestapo men discreetly observed his every movement when he was not answering the experts' questions.

While Ritter gained much information, the experts could discover nothing suspicious at all in the Englishman's behavior. He exhibited no interest whatsoever in what went on around him in the great port and industrial center. All he ever saw was the Abwehr in operation: its techniques, its personnel, its organization. But unknown to Ritter, lulled into a confident trust in his new agent, it was exactly for this reason that the Twenty Committee had send CELERY to Germany.

On his last night in Hamburg, CELERY was invited to a little intimate Abwehr party by Ritter. Wine loosened all their tongues and their mission was forgotten, save by Frau Ritter who was present. She could not take her eyes off the large signet ring which CELERY wore on his finger. Finally she whispered to her husband, his face flushed with good food and even better Moselle.

"Look at his signet ring, it's the kind you can open — don't you think you ought to examine it a bit closer." Ritter's happy mood vanished almost immediately. Now he, too, became fascinated by the ring. He knew that the Gestapo had examined the Englishman's belongings with their habitual thoroughness, but naturally they had had no opportunity to look at the big ring.

In the end he gave way to his curiosity. "Your ring," he began.

"It's a beautiful one," Frau Ritter chimed in, helping her husband, trying to cover up his naked curiosity.

Later both of them thought the Englishman showed a moment of fear. But he recovered quickly enough. "Oh," he said noncommittally. "It's a family heirloom." He snapped it open and showed them the photograph of the woman it contained.

"Your wife?" Frau Ritter asked.

"Not yet," CELERY answered.

And there the discussion about the ring ended.

But Ritter was not satisfied. A little later he excused himself and called his office. A rapid conversation followed with the specialist he had asked for. Then he returned to the party. It was getting late, and CELERY was beginning to yawn. All the same Ritter insisted that they go to a little bar for a nightcap. CELERY allowed himself to be persuaded.

He should have been suspicious of the German's sudden insistence after the pointed reference to the drink, but perhaps the wine and the fact that he had managed to get through the last three nerve-wracking weeks without difficulty lulled him into a false sense of security. The nightcap served by the technician Ritter had called was very effective indeed. It put CELERY out for twelve straight hours!

As "Mr. Brown's" head slumped on his chest and he began to snore, Ritter went to work speedily. Within the hour he had the Abwehr's experts working on the ring. "Nothing on the picture side," they told Ritter, "but it has a kind of code on the other side written in invisible ink." And that was that. Then their final words put the officer in quandary. "There isn't any more we can do. This is a job for our cipher bureau."

"How long will they take to break the code?" Ritter asked.

"It's difficult to say," was the reply. "Perhaps a week. Maybe longer."

Ritter remembered that he had given "Brown" his word of honor that he would be returned to Lisbon on the completion of his mission, and although he was engaged in the dirty business of espionage, Ritter still considered himself an officer and a gentlemen. In the end he compromised; he found some pretext to keep Brown four days longer in the luxurious Vier Jahreszeiten while the experts sweated over the code.

Finally they made their report. The code was a series of unconnected numbers and letters. All they had been able to discover was that they included a reference to a telephone number and address in Madrid. Ritter decided that this was not enough to detain "Brown" any further. Together they flew to Madrid, where they were to change planes for Lisbon.

CELERY, knowing that his luck would not last much longer and that Madrid was friendly to the Germans, decided he had better cut out while the going was good. At the airport, he excused himself to go to the lavatory. Smilingly Ritter, occupied with his newspaper, waved his permission, CELERY never came back.

He called the number on the photo in the ring, which was that of the Twenty Committee's "man in Madrid." One day later he was on an RAF plane bound for London, carrying with him fountain pens designed to be used in sabotage attacks on British factories and ten thousand pounds in British currency, given him by Ritter, which went into the Twenty Committee's own kitty — or so they said later.

The amazing penetration mission was the end of SNOW's career with the XX organization; CELERY was just as certain that the little Welshman was a German agent as BISCUIT had been. Reluctantly Masterman ordered SNOW to jail, and messages were sent over SNOW's transmitter stating that "the chief was extremely ill; that his nerve and health had collapsed" (to use Masterman's own words), and finally, that "it was impossible to carry on and that the gear would be packed up and hidden." As for CELERY he was sent on another, if abortive, mission to Lisbon.

Then, he too, was retired and went into private business.

But there would be others to follow them: BRUTUS, CARELESS, MUTT and JEFF, LIPSTICK, FIDO, GARBO, SNIPER, SWEET WILLIAM, TEAPOT, WASHOUT, WORM, WEASEL — their names revealing what their new British masters thought were the outstanding characteristics of these former German agents, who were offered the alternatives of dying or changing sides.

Thus the amazing game of double and triple cross went on with great success until finally on May 10, 1945, Masterman brought to an end the last meeting of the Twenty Committee.

But in May 1941, while the British Empire was still struggling for its very survival, "C", as the head of MI6 was known, realized that more offensive action was needed. Up to now British Intelligence had only reacted to the initial German moves. But the success of the CELERY mission had shown that Intelligence could carry out effective original operations.

But "C", the traditional code name for the head of British Intelligence, was a very conventional man. Colonel Stewart Menzies, to give him his rightful name, was a traditional product of the British upper class: Eton, the Grenadier Guards in World War I (in which he had won the D.S.O. and the M.C.), and only very recently Army Intelligence. His thinking was strictly orthodox — though enhanced by a remarkable gift of intuition. Undoubtedly he would have gone on picking bowler-hatted ex-officers, who had gone to the right schools and been in the right regiments, as his predecessor had done, if Churchill had not insisted that he wanted results not excuses. The Prime Minister was determined on a new operational intelligence service. Special Operations Executive — to be run by the labor Minister of Economic Warfare, Dr. Hugh Dalton.

Thus the harassed, relatively new chief of British Intelligence found that he was under attack from both his friends and his enemies. Urged on by Churchill, who was not one to be scared of an intelligence boss, however all-knowing he pretended to be, or by the new blood pouring into the SOE from half a dozen European countries, Menzies knew the time had come for him to *act* and not simply *react*, British Intelligence would have to go over to the offensive at last ...

"SET EUROPE ABLAZE!" were Winston Churchill's bold orders.

4 — WHERE IS RUDOLF HESS?

At exactly a quarter to eleven on the night of May 10, 1941, a middle-aged bachelor farmer, David McLean, was preparing for sleep in the little whitewashed bedroom on the second floor of his modest Scottish farmhouse. But he would get no sleep that night, in spite of his fatigue after a long, lone-handed day in his unfruitful fields.

Suddenly the china ornaments on the mantelpiece started to rattle from the vibrations of an airplane engine somewhere close by. For a moment the noise receded. Then it returned. Very close. He sat up in alarm. Was a bomber going to crash on him, his sister, and their aged mother?

Abruptly the engine cut out. All he could hear was the sinister swish of the plane's wings as it zoomed to the ground. He braced himself for the crash. Nothing happened.

Puzzled, he sprang out of bed and pulled aside the black-out curtain. For a while he could see nothing despite the clear moonlit night. Then against the background of the silvery fields, he spotted a soft white parachute floating down. Someone had jumped from the plane.

Swiftly he pulled on his baggy working pants and tucked in his night shirt, calling to his mother: "It's a pilot come down just outside!... I think he's a German. Get up! I'm going out after him."

And without waiting for an answer the Scottish farmer who had fought in France as an infantry private in the First World War ran out to where he had seen the parachute come down.

He found the German within minutes. The flier was still struggling with his billowing parachute, and he had hurt his leg.

Finally the stranger got to his feet. He was a foot taller than McLean and heavily built. But the Scot wasn't afraid. "Are you a German?" he asked.

"Yes," the other man answered slowly, obviously finding English difficult. "I'm a German. I am Hauptmann Alfred Horn. I want to go to Dungavel House. I have an important message for the Duke of Hamilton."

For a moment McLean stared at him amazed. What did he mean? The Duke of Hamilton? But only for a moment. Suddenly the plane which had crashed several fields away went up in flame. McLean's neighbor awoke. Things happened quickly. The soldiers and the local Home Guard were aroused. The slightly injured German, whom McLean judged to be at least fifty and who wore a very smart uniform, was led away — first to McLean's humble home, where he tasted his first cup of English tea (he did not like it); then to the local Home Guard HQ; and finally to Buchanan Castle, a few miles outside Glasgow.

But back in the area where he had first been captured, tongues wagged excitedly. Far into the night, the RAF, Army, Home Guard officers discussed their captive, who obviously was no ordinary pilot and who had flown so far north. No known German fighter could possibly make the return journey to the homeland; it would simply run out of fuel over the North Sea. Suddenly, one of the puzzled officers, to whom Hauptmann Alfred Horn's darkly handsome face, with its bushy eyebrows, seemed vaguely familiar, turned to the senior RAF officer present.

"You know, sir," he remarked hesitantly. "I believe this man is Rudolf Hess, Hitler's Deputy. I've seen him in Germany, and the more I think of it, the more I'm sure it's Hess."

The mustachioed RAF Wing Commander looked at him contemptuously, then snorted in his fruity upper-class accent: "Don't be a bloody fool!"

But that unknown officer was not a "bloody fool." His assumption was completely right. Rudolf Hess — ex-wartime comrade of Adolf Hitler (in the same Bavarian regiment, though unknown to each other), his faithful secretary during Hitler's imprisonment in Landsberg Fortress when he had written *Mein Kampf*, and now since 1933, his Deputy — had flown secretly to Britain to arrange a peace between the two nations.

When Hitler heard of Hess's flight from Hess's adjutant, he uttered (as Speer who was there described it) "an inarticulate almost animal outcry. 'Bormann!' he roared. 'Bormann at once! Where is Bormann?'"

Thereafter Bormann, soon to become the most powerful man in Germany after Hitler himself, called together the Nazi *Prominenz* to discuss the terrible news. Goering, Ribbentrop, Goebbels, Himmler, they had all to be fetched to the Berghof by the speediest means possible. Never before had Hitler's intimates seen him in such a rage. Later he explained to a special meeting of his *gauleiters* that when he heard the news, he felt like fainting for the first time in his whole life.[8]

What had prompted Hess to fly to England on this impossible mission, which would undoubtedly compromise the Führer with his Italian and Japanese allies? They would undoubtedly think he was trying to establish a separate peace between Germany and England behind their backs. Moreover Hess knew Germany's most important military secret at that

---

[8] Related to the author in 1971 by Herr K. Wahl, ex-Gauleiter of Swabia, who was present.

time — the date of her planned invasion of Russia. What had made him do it? As Hitler told a worried circle of his intimates when it was still not known that Hess had arrived safely in Scotland: "If he would only drown in the North Sea! Then he would vanish without a trace and we could work out some harmless explanation at our leisure."

When it was established that Hess had reached England safely, it became necessary for the Führer to act. On the Monday after he set off on his sensational flight from Augsburg, Munich Radio broadcast the following statement:

> It is officially announced by the National Socialist Party that Party Member Rudolf Hess who, as he was suffering from an illness of some years' standing, had been strictly forbidden to embark on any further flying activity was able, contrary to this command, again to come into possession of an airplane.
>
> On Saturday, May 10, Rudolf Hess set out on a flight from Augsburg, from which he has not so far returned. A letter which he left behind unfortunately shows by its distractedness traces of a mental disorder, and it is feared that he was a victim of hallucinations....

Thus the official explanation of Hess's flight, as suggested by arch-intriguer Bormann and accepted by a grateful Hitler, eager for any way out. From now on Hess was stamped as mad in Germany.

But was he? Anglo-American psychiatrists who examined him at Nuremberg testified he was fit to stand trial. And at the same trial, he astounded his own defense lawyer, the court, and his fellow defendants by suddenly standing up and stating that he had been playing a game — feigning loss of memory and mental illness for nearly five years. Gauleiter Wahl, who had known Hess for many years, was one of the last men to see him before his flight. Wahl recalls: "He did not make the impression of being mentally sick in the least. Messerschmidt,[9] with whom I discussed him just before, and many times after the flight, came to the same conclusion... Hess is more normal than a lot of people I know."[10]

Germany's Munitions Chief Albert Speer, who was to spend twenty years with Hess in Spandau Prison after the war, had another explanation for Hess's flight. He accepted Hitler's theory that the Deputy Leader had flown to England under the influence of his ex-teacher, former general and world-famous "geo-politician" Professor Karl Haushofer. However, he pointed out that, "twenty five years later, in Spandau prison, Hess assured me in all seriousness that the idea had been inspired in him in a dream by supernatural forces."

But if Speer was inclined to pooh-pooh the influence of supernatural forces in 1965, that supreme realist with the hard head, Schellenberg, who was not in the least given to flights of fancy, was not. In a secret report on Hess's flight which Heydrich ordered him to prepare for the Führer, he wrote that "our secret information showed that for some years' he had been under the influence of mystics, astrologers, fortune tellers, etc." (He had even been a "silent adherent" of Rudolf Steiner and the anthroposophists.) "Without being conscious of it, he was led to take this action through the influence of astrological circles and by intimate advisers such as Professor G— and Haushofer."

And who was behind Professor Haushofer and Professor G? Herr Wahl has been kind enough to identify "G" as "Dr Gerl of Hindelang/Allgau who carried out numerous goiter

---

[9] Hess used the airplane designer's own craft, taking off from the experimental Messerschmidt field at Augsburg.

[10] Letter to author, April 20, 1972.

operations. He also practised in England, where he had many friends. A good chap as well as an excellent doctor, he used to be a frequent guest at Hess's home."[11]

Smart SS General Schellenberg did not hesitate to point the finger at them in May, 1941. "They were the British Secret Service and their German collaborators and... they had played a large part in bringing about his decision to fly to Scotland!..."

The chain of events which led to Hess's flight started on September 3, 1940, exactly one year to the day after England declared war on Nazi Germany. On that date, Professor Karl Haushofer, who had once been Hess's teacher in Munich after World War I, wrote to his son Albrecht of a meeting he had had with his former student in Berlin.

> As you know, everything is so prepared for a very hard and severe attack on the island in question that the highest ranking person only has to press a button to set it off. But before this decision, which is perhaps inevitable, the thought once more occurs as to whether there is really no way of stopping something which would have such infinitely momentous consequences. There is a line of reasoning in connection with this which I must absolutely pass on to you because it was obviously communicated to me with this intention. Do you, too, see no way in which such possibilities could be discussed at a third place with a middle man, possibly the old Ian Hamilton or the other Hamilton.[12] I replied to these suggestions that there would have perhaps been an excellent opportunity for this in Lisbon.... In this connection it seems to me a stroke of fate that our old friend Miss V. R. evidently, though after long delay, finally found a way of sending a note

---

[11] Letter to author.
[12] General Sir Ian Hamilton and the Duke of Hamilton.

with cordial and gracious words of good wishes not only for your mother, but also for Heinz.[13]

Address your reply to: Miss V. Roberts, c/o Postbox 506, Lisbon, Portugal. I have the feeling that no good possibility should be overlooked: at least it should be well considered.

A week later on September 10th, Hess wrote to his old teacher:

Dear Friend:

Albrecht brought me your letter, which... alluded to our walk together on the last day of August, which I too, recall with so much pleasure.... Under no condition must we disregard the contact or allow it to die aborning. I consider it best that you or Albrecht write to the old lady, who is a friend of your family, suggesting that she try to ask Albrecht's friend whether he would be prepared if necessary to come to the neutral country in which she resides, or at any rate has an address through which she can be reached, just to talk with Albrecht.

If he could not do this just now, he might, in any case, send word through her where he expects to be in the near future. Possibly a neutral acquaintance, who had some business to attend to over there anyway, might look him up and make some communication to him, using you or Albrecht as reference.... The prerequisite naturally was that the inquiry in question and the reply would not go through official channels, for you would not in any case want to cause your friends over there any trouble.

It would be best to have the letter to the old lady with whom you are acquainted delivered through a confidential agent of the AO[14] to the address that is known to you. For

---

[13] Heinz Haushofer, the Professor's second son.

[14] *Die Auslandsorganisation*, the organization for overseas Nazis, headed by Bradford-born Ernst Wilhelm Bohle, slated to be Gauleiter of a

this purpose Albrecht would have to speak either with Bohle or my brother. At the same time the lady would have to be given the address in L ... or if the latter does not live there permanently, of another agent of the AO who does lives there permanently to which the reply can in turn be delivered.

As for the neutral I have in mind, I would like to speak to you orally about it some time. There is no hurry about that since, in any case, there would first have to be a reply received here from over there.

Meanwhile let's both keep our fingers crossed. Should success be the fate of the enterprise, the oracle given to you with regard to the month of August would yet be fulfilled, since the name of the young friend and the old lady friend of your family occurred to you during our quiet walk on the last day of the month.

> With best regards to you and to Martha.

The result of this interchange of letters, with their poor attempts at security and concealment, was that behind the backs of Admiral Canaris and SS General Heydrich,[15] Albrecht Haushofer sent the following letter to "D" on September 23, 1940:

Even if this letter has only a slight chance of reaching you — there is a chance and I want to make use of it.

First of all to give you a sign of unaltered and unalterable personal attachment. I do hope you have been spared in all this ordeal and I hope the same is true of your brothers. I heard of your father's deliverance from long suffering; and I

---

conquered Britain.

[15] In a letter of September 19th, Albrecht Haushofer wrote: "I do not think that you need much imagination to picture to yourself the faces Canaris or Heydrich would make and the smirk with which they would consider any offer of 'security' or 'confidence' in such a letter if a subordinate should submit such a case to them."

heard that your brother-in-law Northumberland lost his life near Dunkerque. I need hardly tell you how I feel about all that...

Now there is one thing more. If you remember some of my last communications before the war started, you will realize that there is a significance in the fact that I am, at present, able to ask you whether there is the slightest chance of our meeting and having a talk somewhere on the outskirts of Europe, perhaps in Portugal. There are some things I could tell you, that might make it worth your while for you to try a short trip to Lisbon — if you could make your authorities understand so much that they would give you leave. As to myself — I could reach Lisbon any time (without any kind of difficulty) within a few days after receiving news from you. If there is an answer to this, please address it to:[16]

"D" never received the letter. He was too busy helping to fight the Battle of Britain.

But in early 1941, "D" who was an amateur boxer, explorer and Everest pilot, the Duke of Hamilton, a senior officer now in the RAF, was asked to see a group captain in Intelligence in the Air Ministry, London. The Group Captain got down to business at once, while other officers who were present watched the Duke's reaction.

"Now, what have you done with the letter Haushofer wrote you?" he started in a conversational manner, as if it were an everyday occurrence to question a senior RAF officer about his contacts with the enemy.

---

[16] This is Haushofer's draft and does not include an address. The final letter has vanished. Today it probably resides somewhere in the dusty files of RAF Intelligence.

The Duke thought he meant a letter Haushofer had sent him just before the outbreak of war, which he had already shown to Intelligence.

"No, no, not that one!" one of the watching officers, who were themselves Intelligence agents, broke in. "The one you've just received. This one." Swiftly he handed the flabbergasted Duke a photostat of Haushofer's letter of September 23rd.

The Duke read it swiftly and then denied ever receiving the original.[17] The Group Captain shrugged and explained that they had gotten their copy from the censorship authorities. Then he continued: "Well, we're interested in this proposal. We wondered whether you would go out to Lisbon for us and see what it's all about."

The Duke of Hamilton was not too keen. He did not feel it proper to undertake such a mission without the fullest authority; after all he wasn't a spy. In the end, however, he agreed to discuss the matter with the head of RAF Intelligence.

At the subsequent interview, he still hesitated. Finally one of the Intelligence men asked point-blank. "Are you prepared to do it?" Quietly the Duke replied: "I will go if I am ordered to go."

The Intelligence men looked at each other with uneasy eyes: "We don't like to *order* people to do this sort of job," one of them said hastily. "We like volunteers. Then we can brief them." He looked directly at the embarrassed Duke. "So I'm asking you, will you do it?"

"If it's an order, I will," the Duke replied. "But I would like to make some conditions."

---

[17] In his exceedingly well researched book on the Hess flight, *The Uninvited Envoy*, author James Leaser notes: "In fact the Duke has still never received the original: it has disappeared and has never been traced." One does not need to be clairvoyant to understand why. The Duke was obviously being set up as a stooge by the Intelligence men.

In the end the Intelligence men, eager to proceed with their grandiose operation, agreed, telling the highly confused Duke, who now found himself in the midst of a strange world of plot and counterplot, that he must forget the whole interview until Mr. Churchill himself had decided how the operation should be carried out.

A few weeks later, Hess took the ball out of their helpless hands. Shortly before the flight, Professor Haushofer told Hess that he had experienced three dreams on three separate nights; in each he had seen his one onetime student piloting a plane to some unknown yet vitally important destination. In yet a fourth dream the Deputy Führer was walking in some great castle with tartan tapestries on the wall.

That clinched it for Hess. He knew that Haushofer had the gift of accurate prediction and that the Duke of Hamilton was the premier Scottish duke. Encouraged by the professor's dreams, he made his "unusual and dramatic" flight. The rest is history.

Thus in the end the operation (for today it appears, it was exactly that) was only half successful. Churchill was embarrassed by the sudden appearance of "the uninvited envoy" in the island fortress. He failed to react quickly enough to the unexpected windfall and make political and propaganda capital out of it. Indeed he was just as puzzled by the whole affair as was Hitler in faraway Germany. In the end he did nothing, and Hess was allowed to languish in a series of prisons all over Britain until he was finally sent for trial to Nuremberg in 1945.

One of Churchill's problems was that he knew there were enough prominent people in England who would have welcomed some kind of peace with Germany, leaving Hitler to fight it out with the Russians, that these individuals regarded Communism as a greater danger than Fascism. On May 14, 1941, Churchill had a spare lunch with Harold Nicolson of the Ministry of Information, who wanted to know what to do about Hess. After seeing *Comrade X*, a film about a Soviet spy, an expansive Churchill, now replete with plenty of port, white wine, and brandy, told Nicolson that he "didn't want Hess to be made a hero." A surprising statement indeed, but understandable in Churchill's particular position at that time. Then the Prime Minister desperately wanted to know what had gone on behind the scenes prior to Hess's flight. What had made this tall strange man, who was Hitler's officially designated successor, make his bold flight across the North Sea to sue for peace at a time when Nazi Germany was master of the whole of Western Europe and Britain's armies had still not recovered from the shattering blows they had suffered at Dunkirk?

It had all started in Lisbon, Portugal, which together with Spain, formed the British SIS's new "eyes and ears" on the continent. Although as a counterespionage organization, SIS was not supposed to operate overseas, both MI6 *and* MI5 went into action after the fall of France, establishing their own networks, uncovering German attempts to use Spanish Fascists as agents in England, and "turning" German agents in the employ of Canaris's Abwehr.

In particular, Lisbon proved a fruitful field of operations for the British agents. The KO Portugal — the Abwehr HQ — was headed by ex-Austrian Intelligence officer, Major von Auenrode alias Albrecht von Karsthof. This Viennese dandy's main claim to fame was for the huge amounts of money he managed to get out of Canaris for his mostly unsuccessful operations. Within a year the British had managed to set up their own agents inside his organization under the terms of their "double-cross system." HAMLET, MULLET, and PUPPET, the code names of the major British agents, would keep their London masters well supplied with information about the Abwehr's every move.[18]

But there was another German espionage organization functioning in Lisbon (apart from Canaris's Abwehr and Schellenberg's SD, which up to now had not appeared in strength). This was Hess's own *Verbindungsstab* — roughly: "liaison staff." It received reports from Bohle's world wide *Auslandsorganisation*, with which Professor Karl Haushofer was closely connected; spied on many people holding high office in Germany itself, and gave aid to German sympathizers abroad. Naturally the organization provided an ideal cover for an intelligence organization which was constantly on the lookout for fresh agents overseas.

One major source of agents of this nature in Britain was the Link, the Anglo-German friendship organization. Many prominent Britons[19] were numbered among its members, including a former head of British Naval Intelligence — and "Kim" Philby, soon to be an executive of British Intelligence; presently however, he was a pillar of the Link, editing its magazine and all the time working actively as a Soviet agent.

---

[18] Later one of these "masters" came to the Iberian Peninsula to supervise operations personally; he was "Kim" Philby, who by this time had been an agent of the Red Army Intelligence Service for over a decade!

[19] It is interesting to note that five years before, Rosenberg, the Nazis' chief ideologist, had also attempted to make contact with high-ranking Britons. Included among them was the King's youngest brother, the Duke of Kent, who surprisingly enough, was also keenly interested in astrology.

But in early 1940, the imprisonment of the more extreme members of this organization (including one of Britain's greatest military experts) struck a mortal blow to the Link. Yet Hess and his chief advisor Haushofer did not know this. Wasn't Bohle reporting thriving Link groups in Tangiers and Lisbon? But neither Bohle nor Hess was to know that the two overseas branches of the Link were run by the British Secret Service and their double agents!

It was a calculated risk on the part of the British intelligence men. If it backfired, the Germans could easily turn it to their own advantage, announcing to the world's press that there were Britons prepared to make a deal with their enemies, in spite of what Churchill was spouting about "we shall fight on the beaches," etc., etc. But the calculated risk paid off and a report from the Tangiers cell of the Link could state: "Hess is contemptuous of the Abwehr and is pursuing his own ideas of espionage through the Verbindungsstab. For some time he put his faith in the Welsh section of this organization and believed that contacts made in that way would prove fruitful. Now he is inclined to think that the prime target for further conversations lies in Scotland. The Café Chiado in the Rua Gambetta in Lisbon is one meeting place for intermediaries between the Link and the Verbindungsstab, the Hotel Riff in Tangier is another."

Thus contact was established and Hess made to believe that a significant number of important Britons were prepared to discuss peace with him or his representative. But when no reply came to Haushofer's letter, he started to despair of the contact established through Lisbon. As he told his adjutant Pinsch after his abortive first flight to England, when he was forced to return and was confronted by a horrified Pinsch who had opened the letter to Hitler which Hess had left behind for him to deliver: "There have been many attempts to make contact with the other side through Lisbon and elsewhere already, but they had been unfruitful. What the situation needs is a direct approach. Then we can discover how we stand. That's what I am determined to do. If my plane hadn't let me down, I'd have been in Britain by now, perhaps even discussing the matter with the people I want to see."

The question which must be raised here is why did Hess now undertake the flight to make this "direct approach?" First, it was highly dangerous and even Professor Messerschmitt, the designer of the plane he used, could not assure him that the experimental fighter would be able to reach Scotland. Secondly, what would happen if the Duke of Hamilton were not in his country seat in that remote part of Scotland where he had his ancestral home? What was Hess to do then?

Yet in spite of these tremendous imponderables, Hess, the second most important man in Germany, undertook the highly risky flight. Why? Hess's own explanation five years later to Dr. Douglas M. Kelley, American prison psychiatrist, was that one of his astrologers had read in the stars that he was ordained to bring about peace. Schellenberg was more explicit. He reported to Hitler at the end of his investigation of Hess's case (which was soon to result in *Aktion Hess*, in which the Gestapo arrested some eighty German astrologers, soothsayers, fortune-tellers, etc.): "Without being conscious of it, he [Hess] was led to take this action through the influence of astrological circles and by intimate advisers, such as Professor G— and Haushofer. Our investigation has never made clear whether negotiations in Switzerland by Haushofer or by Hess himself preceded the flight. Haushofer has always denied it. However, even if this had been the case, the basic psychological motivation still remains the same…"

Although German astrology had its fair share of cranks, crooks, and charlatans, it had become a fairly "respectable science" by the late twenties, practiced by serious doctors, professors, and scientists, and based on latest research in psychology, typology, and other related disciplines. Hitler showed some interest in it. Goebbels employed a noted astrologer in his propaganda ministry, the Swiss K. E. Krafft, using him and his interpretation of the prophecies of Nostradamus for propaganda purposes. Himmler was a passionate believer in the subject. In 1943 he employed concentration camp astrologers to try to find out the whereabouts of the vanished Italian dictator Mussolini, and as late as 1944, when his own Gestapo was arresting even humble readers of "tea cups" and other variations of the more elegant crystal ball, he was consulting the Hamburg astrologer Wulff.

It is not very surprising to find that Hess listened seriously to Haushofer's interpretation of his own dreams and portents of the future. Hess himself would tell of Haushofer's refusal to use certain trains during World War I when he had been a general on the Imperial Staff because he had a premonition they would be bombed. "And," the Führer's Deputy said once in admiration, "he was always right." It was also not surprising that Hess had on his staff a fully convinced amateur astrologer — Herr Schulte-Strathaus.

Schulte-Strathaus, who worked with Hess in Munich as the head of his cultural department, once gave Hess an impromptu lecture on the subject of astrology. Hess listened smilingly to Schulte-Strathaus with his associate Heinrich Heim, who was responsible for justice and was Hess's oldest staffer after Martin Bormann. "Well, why don't you make a prophecy here and now and we'll lodge it in a safe with a lawyer till the time predicted for it to come true? Then we'll all open the safe together."[20]

Schulte-Strathaus had backed off. But Hess's words had been meant for the sceptical ears of ex-lawyer Heim. He, himself, believed implicitly in Schulte-Strathaus's prediction, as is documented in Dr. Rainer Hildebrandt's biography of Haushofer. He states:

> Hess's astrological foibles strengthened his own conviction that everything possible must be done and hazarded in order to end hostilities without delay, because at the end of April and the beginning of May 1941, Hitler's astrological aspects were unusually malefic. Hess interpreted these aspects to mean that he personally must take the dangers that threatened the Führer upon his own shoulders in order to save Hitler and restore peace to Germany. Time and again Hess's astrological adviser had told him that Anglo-German relations were threatened by a deep-seated crisis of confidence.... Indeed at this time there were very many dangerous [planetary] oppositions in Hitler's horoscope. Haushofer who dabbled a great deal with astrology, seldom left his friend [Hess] without a hint that something unexpected could 'happen' in the near future.[21]

And it was Schulte-Strathaus who told Hess in January 1941 that an unusual conjunction of the planets would occur on May 10th. Then six planets in the sign of Taurus coincided with the full moon. Although Hess attempted to fly to Scotland earlier, the abortive flight of January 1941 resulted in his departure on exactly that day — Saturday, May 10, 1941.

Coincidence or plan? And if it were a plan, who was behind Schulte-Strathaus's amazingly accurate forecast?

---

[20] Rainer Hildebrandt: *Wir sind die Letzten.*
[21] As related to author in 1972 by Herr Heim.

As we have already seen, Schellenberg thought it was the British, working through a Swiss contact linked to Professor Haushofer and the goiter-specialist Dr. Gerl, as well as Schulte-Strathaus. However, the smooth, young, new Major General never explained how this interesting piece of mental telepathy was carried out (if it were carried out, that is). He contents himself with writing in his memoirs: "Heydrich was honest enough to admit to me that my analysis had been correct ... he took up the point about the influence of the British Secret Service and said several times that we had to try to go further in that direction for, if the information proved correct, these circles would be able to inflict additional damage on us. He felt that the British were capable of formulating and carrying out that sort of plan and he would be surprised if we did not have some similar experiences in the future."

It was a prophetic statement. For in exactly one year to the day after he said these words, the British struck again. But this time their method would not be so sophisticated. In May 1942, they would not be armed with crystal balls but with machine pistols ....[22]

---

[22] British writer Richard Deacon has come up with an intriguing explanation of how it was done. According to him in his *History of the British Secret Service*, the SIS employed astrologers of their own to influence Hess's men in their predictions. They worked on Schulte-Strathaus and Haushofer to convince them that Hess's mission in the U.K. would be successful. The name of the young Lieutenant Commander in British Naval Intelligence supposedly behind the plot to lure Hess to Scotland? *Ian Fleming, later to be the author of the James Bond series!*

Fleming is now dead so there is little chance of verifying Mr. Deacon's striking theory. However, none other than Major General Sir Kenneth Strong, head of Eisenhower's Intelligence during the war, and no friend of cloak-and-dagger activities, admits that the War Office had its own tame astrologer on the payroll as early as 1940.

5 — DEATH, OF THE MAN WITH THE IRON HEART

In the first week of September, 1941, Reinhard Heydrich called up his wife unexpectedly at their house in Augustastrasse, Berlin, which by a strange coincidence (or was it coincidence?) joined on to the Dianastrasse, where Abwehr head Admiral Canaris had his home.

Since the start of the war Heydrich had gone from strength to strength. Not only had he managed to lead his tremendously expanded organization successfully, but he had also done several tours at the front, taking "leaves" to go and fly missions against both the Poles and the British.[23] The result was that his right breast was now stiff with newly gained decorations. Another was that he had not seen Lina, his wife, for months at a time.

Now when he told her excitedly that he had been posted to Prague, she burst into tears. The blonde schoolteacher's daughter, who had first met Heydrich when she had fallen out of a canoe and he had dived in to rescue her, sobbed: "I'll never see you again."

The passion that Heydrich always tried to conceal beneath his cold, logical, impersonal manner (Himmler once told him he was "fed up with you, you... and your logic") burst through.

---

[23] Once he had been forced to make an emergency landing behind the Russian lines, but had managed to get back through his own lines. The mind boggles at what might have happened if Heydrich had been captured by the Russians, with his comprehensive knowledge of Germany's greatest secrets. Some associates of his at that time suppose he would cheerfully have gone to work for the Russians.

"Oh, no," he cried, "It's my big chance, don't you see!... Up to now my career has been negative. Now," his thin high-pitched voice rose sharply, "I'm going to do something positive. I'm sick of getting rid of people... putting them behind bars. This is my chance to do something with purpose."[24]

Heydrich had just been appointed Reich Protector of occupied Bohemia and Moravia.

Three days after his arrival on October 2, 1941, Heydrich summoned the German leaders of the country to his HQ. In his speech he made it clear that his long-term aims were to ensure that the "Czechs had no role to play in the future of New Europe." The "racially valuable part of the Czech race could be Germanized," whereas the rest would "be sterilized or placed against the wall." However, his short-term aims were radically different, consisting of vinegar and molasses: he would get rid of the Czech opposition to the Germans by force, but at the same time he would try to win over the workers by bribes.

Within a week, he had set to work, gaining for himself the nickname, "Butcher of Prague," for his ruthless elimination of the Czech oppositional intelligentsia. But while his Gestapo commandos were taking care of this problem, his civilian advisers were working out a completely new deal for the workers. Fat rations were raised for heavy workers. Hotels were requisitioned as holiday homes for Czech workers; and for the first time a comprehensive sick insurance and social security scheme on the German model was introduced.

The results were almost immediate. The Czech workers started to cooperate. Production of heavy armaments needed by Germany to make up losses being incurred in Russia

---

[24] Related by Frau Heydrich to the author, 1971.

commenced to mount. And the great mass of the nation, its leaders behind bars or dead, tamely accepted the dictates of the new Protector.

But although Czech resistance had suffered grievous losses, it was not completely broken. Indeed the exiled Czech government in London still had its key agent functioning in occupied Prague, "A54" or "Rene," who was in daily radio contact with the British capital. "A54", who had been working for the Czechs for nearly six years now, was indeed their best and most reliable agent in spite of his nationality and position. He had informed them of the German plans for the take-over of their little country; the attack of France; Germany's plans to invade Russia; Hitler's decision to postpone the attack on Britain — a hundred and one important, top secret German intentions, vital to the Czechs in their assessment of the enemy. One day after Heydrich gave his speech to his top officials, the Gestapo managed to break Rene's code and passed on the information to Heydrich. As busy as he was with his other duties, the Head of the Main Security Office took over the case personally. He clearly understood its importance by declaring the matter "top secret" and ordering a special team, designated "Traitor X" Group, to find the spy.

Eleven days later the team of spy-hunters seized their quarry. He was no other than Paul Thuemmel, a member of the Abwehr, a founder member of the Saxon branch of the Nazi Party, and to make matters worse, *a first name friend of Heydrich's own boss Himmler!*[25]

The arrest put Heydrich and Canaris in a quandary. Thuemmel had too many friends in high places to subject him

---

[25] Himmler had first met Thuemmel in 1927, when he had gone to make a speech in the latter's home town and stayed the night at the Thuemmel house.

to the usual treatment. Discreetly and politely he was subjected to examination, even being allowed to sleep in his own flat under supervision. (When his guard was asleep at night, he disappeared through the window to continue meeting his Czech contacts in the underground.)

His final interrogator, Willi Abendschoen, sent to Prague specially for the job by Mueller, recalled that during the interrogation of Best and Stevens, they had admitted that a German of high position had come to visit Czech Intelligence in The Hague in 1939. Abendschoen re-examined the two British agents and came to the conclusion that Thuemmel was that German. Checking back, he found that on the date in question in 1939, Thuemmel had passed through the Abwehr's Munster office on a mission to The Hague.

Thereafter, although it took some time to convict Thuemmel, secret arrangements were made at the highest level to remove him from the Party. He was placed in Theresienstadt Concentration Camp under the false name of Major Peter Toman, supposedly a former Dutch military attaché, although he didn't speak a word of Dutch. There he remained till he was shot in 1945.

Naturally Heydrich used the discovery of a traitor within the ranks of the Abwehr for his own purposes. On May 18, 1942, he called a meeting of his own organization and the Abwehr for 10:30 precisely. The invitation cards were stamped "secret" and numbered, and the uneasy guests, who included "Gestapo" Mueller and Canaris, were uneasy and nervous, taking good care to be in their seats at the latest ten minutes before the official start of the great discussion.

At 10:30 exactly Heydrich appeared with Canaris. The former made the opening speech. Then Canaris put forward his suggestions for strengthening the collaboration between the Abwehr and SD and Gestapo. He was followed by Mueller, who unlike Heydrich, could not conceal his contempt for Canaris. He stated point-blank that the Abwehr was an old-fashioned, bureaucratic organization. Canaris's pale sallow face flushed slightly but his veiled eyes revealed little; he knew that Mueller was only a creature of Heydrich. His former subordinate in the Navy was the man who really made the decisions. At the end of the conference, Heydrich laid it on the line. His intentions were naked and brutal. Later they were dubbed "Heydrich's Decalogue" or the "Ten Commandments of the Prague God."

Heydrich declared: "Because of the situation at home and abroad, the organization and personnel of the Abwehr must be changed. The present officers of the Abwehr have shown they are incapable and they must be replaced by new men, trained by the SS. In the interests of Reich security, there must be a centralized Secret Service Organization. Its representatives would have the power to act in all departments and to draw on the total manpower. These men would be responsible to their Minister, to the Minister of State — and to me."

While Canaris's mind reeled at the shock, Heydrich went on to propose his "decalogue" — his ten points for the realization of this aim. But the elderly Admiral need not have feared, for the German double agent from his own organization, who was now on his last journey to the concentration camp, would save him.

Ironically enough, Heydrich's attempts to improve the lot of the average Czech worker would prove to be his downfall. The resultant increase in production angered the London-based Czech government. Week after week, Thuemmel and his "Three Kings" espionage network had passed on the rising figures of war production and in doing so had helped to sign Heydrich's death warrant.

Scared by what Heydrich might do next and angered by the spinelessness of the workers who had to be shocked out of their complacency, the exile Czechs knew they must act. In December, 1941, as a direct result of Thuemmel's reports, the exile government made a decision. It was short and simple: HEYDRICH MUST DIE.

May 27, 1942 dawned cold and a little hazy. But by ten o'clock, when Heydrich said goodbye to Lina at his residence near the village of Panenske-Brezany outside Prague and called for his SS driver, it was warm and sunny. He patted the blond heads of his two children and went outside to where Klein, the driver, was waiting with the open, dark green Mercedes tourer. His advisers had warned him of the dangers of riding without an escort in an open car, but he had laughed at their worried frowns. Didn't the Czechs love him? They wouldn't try to kill him.

Klein, a tall, burly SS man, armed like Heydrich with a revolver, saluted smartly. Heydrich got in and they set off at a smart pace through the dusty village roads towards Prague, with Heydrich sitting next to the driver and closest to the sidewalk. (Before the Germans had come, the Czechs, like the English, had driven on the left-hand side of the road. The Germans had changed that within a week. The change was going to have a decisive effect on what happened next.)

Everywhere the people were going about their business. The men in their fields, barefoot women in their kerchiefs driving geese along the paths, children going to or returning from school, their little foodpails hanging from their leather schoolbags. Occasionally someone would stare at the car speeding by, but the Czechs' eyes were empty of any passion — either hate or love. Heydrich, a keen observer of his fellow human beings, was pleased. Their will was broken.

They passed through the little village of Predboj. Heydrich's eye fell on the dusty road sign, "Praha (Prague) 16 km." At this speed, he told himself, they should be in the capital in ten minutes.

In the Prague suburb of Holesovice, where the Dresden-Prague road took a sharp hairpin turn down to the Troja bridge, the four Czechs[26] who had come to kill Heydrich were also worried about the time. They had taken a long time to select this spot and had been at their posts since 9 o'clock. It was now 10:30, an hour later than they had expected Heydrich to pass.

In particular, the two parachutists Kubis and Gabcik[27] felt that everything was going wrong just when they had finally persuaded the local resistance to let them carry out the plan. Undoubtedly, the assassination would result in reprisals.

Gabcik, his sweaty fingers gripping the English Sten machine pistol beneath his coat, glanced for the hundredth time at the gold hands of the nearby church clock. Kubis, posted on the other side of the bend, where the road from Dresden ran down the slope to the sharp curve, did the same and then stared into the distance where Valcik was hidden. The latter was to signal

---

[26] It is often stated that only two paras dropped on the night of December 28/29, 1941, to assassinate Heydrich. In fact, the RAF Halifax dropped three teams of Czechs: *Silver A*, *Silver B*, and *Anthropoid*. *Silver A*'s mission was to make contact with Thuemmel's "Three Kings" organization; *Silver B*'s to link up with the Czech resistance; and *Anthropoid*'s to kill Heydrich.

[27] They had been trained in England especially for this mission and had been hiding in Prague since December, 1941.

Heydrich's approach down the hill by means of a mirror. But there was no sudden gleam to indicate that the bloody drama could begin.

Another quarter hour passed.

Gabcik was just considering whether they should not call off the operation when he saw it. The signal! A bright flash of light. And again. Then the roar of a speeding motor. A sudden crash of gears as Klein changed down to second at high speed in order to take the bend. And there they were: two very large men, whose pale faces contrasted strongly with the immaculate dark uniforms they wore!

Klein, fighting the corner, rubber and brakes protesting noisely against the strain, did not notice the two Czechs. Everything was as it always was. A streetcar was rumbling towards them. Not far away two Czech police strolled majestically about their lawful duties. Nothing unusual.

Gabcik reacted first. He flung open his old white raincoat and tightened his grip on the Sten, being careful — as they had taught him back in the SOE school in England — not to get his little finger in the way of the ejector; he'd lose his little finger if he did. Then he pulled the trigger. There was no powerful answering jerk. *Nothing!* The green Mercedes was growing larger and larger. He could see the two Germans quite clearly behind the fly-specked windshield. He gripped the trigger again — hard. Again nothing!

Paralyzed he stared down at the machine pistol.

"Josef! Josef!" Kubis screamed in horror.

Suddenly Klein saw the waiting danger. He braked hard. The Mercedes came to a halt, half a yard from the sidewalk. Frantically the two Germans fumbled for their pistols.

Kubis acted. He remembered his grenade. Grabbing it from inside his jacket, he pulled out the detonating pin and flung it as he ran. It exploded against the back of the car. The right tire sank under the impact. The car lurched to one side. The back seat exploded. But the two big Germans seemed to bear charmed lives. As the grenade went off, both jumped out and started firing.

Yelling at the top of his voice and firing as he ran, Heydrich chased the would-be assassins. They fled. Kubis managed to reach his battered old bicycle and escape the "black devil" behind him, whizzing as fast as he could pedal in the direction of the Troja bridge. Gabcik was not able to shake off his pursuer. Klein came on, running and firing, shouting at the top of his voice all the time. Everywhere people were stopping and staring in horror at this Wild West shoot-out taking place before their eyes.

Desperately panting for breath, Gabcik flung himself inside a little store, just as Klein came round the corner after him. Steadying his shaking hand, he took aim. The *Oberscharführer* loomed up large and beefy in his sight. Gabcik aimed at the German's bemedaled breast (Klein had put all his medals on to impress the guard of honor which Heydrich had been scheduled to inspect that day). He pulled the trigger. The big German grunted, threw up his arms, and fell heavily on the hard black cobbles. He was hit in the thigh.

Swiftly Gabcik sprang out of the shop and rushed over to Klein. At close range he shot him again, hitting him in the foot. Klein cried out. He tried to raise himself, but failed. In anger and extreme pain, he threw his revolver at two Czechs watching the scene as if mesmerized, crying, "After him!"

Gabcik turned and fled. The two Czechs, a coachman and a butcher, began to run after him. But without enthusiasm. He pelted out of the side street into the main road. A streetcar was standing there some twenty yards away. It began to move. The conductor, however, saw Gabcik. He left the side door open. Gabcik sprinted and reached it just in time. No one noticed the pistol which he had hastily thrust in his jacket, nor the sweat on his brow and the terror in his eyes. The conductor came for his fare and smiled politely. The other passengers looked unconcerned out the windows at the sunlit street outside. Behind them the cries of the two Czechs grew fainter and fainter. He had escaped. *But had they killed Heydrich?*

For eight days Reinhard Heydrich fought for his life. But the grenade had forced steel and horsehair from the back seat into his ribs and spleen. Blood poisoning set in. Teams of Germany's most skilled doctors tried to save the "man with the iron heart." With all his tremendous strength and overwhelming energy and ambition, Heydrich fought for his life. In spite of great agony, he wanted to live. But in vain. On June 4, 1942, he finally succumbed to his wounds.

And now the Czech exile government in London got what they wanted. A wave of unprecedented terror swept over the country. On the morning of June 9, 1942, ten lorryloads of German Security Police under the command of Captain Max Rostock surrounded the little village of Lidice.

Lidice had long been a thorn in the German side. Indeed the Austrians, when they had controlled this part of Central Europe forty years before, had eyed the villagers with suspicion. Now came the final reckoning. Rostock snapped out the order that no one was allowed to leave. A young boy panicked and tried to make a run for it. He was shot before he had gone a hundred yards. Another woman tried to sneak out by a back road. She too was shot down. The shocked villagers, eyes round with fear, knew that something terrible was going to happen.

It did. The next day from dawn till late afternoon the villagers were taken behind the local barn and shot in groups of ten. A total of 172 men and boys. Their women were shipped off to Ravensbrück concentration camp. Their children — ninety in all — were sent to Germany, where they disappeared, being handed to German families to be brought up as German. Thus today there are men and women in early middle age going about their business in Germany, who feel themselves German, yet in truth are the only survivors of that doomed Czech village.

In the end, according to German sources, some 10,000 Czechs were arrested, of whom 1,300 were shot or killed in retribution for the Heydrich murder. Thereafter cooperation with the Germans ended. As the wave of terror descended upon the Czechs, production figures sank. The Czech "Exile Government's" plan had worked at the cost of thirteen hundred innocent lives — but a small price to pay for their victory over Heydrich's machinations (at least it seemed so to those safe in faraway London.)

But Heydrich's sudden death also brought pleasure and satisfaction to certain quarters within the Germans' own camp. Although Canaris was choked with emotion at the state funeral for the dead SS leader, telling Schellenberg that "After all, he was a great man — I have lost a friend in him," both secret service chiefs knew he meant that the pressure had been taken off the Abwehr. Canaris's organization, which Heydrich had been so eager to take over for his own purposes, would now survive for another two years.

Himmler, too, could not conceal his pleasure that Heydrich, a subordinate who had threatened his own job, had been removed. Maliciously he later told his cronies of his feelings while holding the hands of Heydrich's children at the state funeral: "I can tell you that it was strange holding the hands of those two half-breeds!" Himmler was glad that the "half-Jew" Heydrich was dead, and three months later Heydrich's death mask[28] which had graced the walls of his office after the funeral was suddenly removed. When Schellenberg queried this, Himmler replied cryptically: "Death masks are tolerable only at certain times and on special occasions, either for the sake of memory or example."

And in the background, "Gestapo" Mueller, whom Heydrich had brought into the Main Security Office in spite of Party protests, waited for his own chance, realizing that now the main obstacle to his own rise had been removed...

But the one who profited most was the British Secret Service.[29] With Heydrich's death, the driving force and brain had been removed from the SS counter-organization. Only Heydrich had been able to control and coordinate such varied and difficult men as Mueller, Nebe, and Schellenberg, each eager to advance his own career — and at the same time prevent Himmler from meddling too much in his organization's affairs with his half-baked theories and absurd suggestions for the espionage war. From now on, the German organization would be plagued with interdepartmental warfare, careerism, betrayal, and

---

[28] Heydrich's death mask reminded Dr. Bernard Walter of a church leader from another age. One of Nebe's men sent to investigate the murder, Dr. Walter described the "deceptive features of uncanny spirituality and entirely perverted beauty, like a Renaissance cardinal."
[29] The man who devised the plan was bald, 52-year-old kilt-wearing Col. John Skinner Wilson who, after retiring from the Indian Police, spent most of his life working for the Boy Scout movement. Indeed, he was director of Boy Scouts International before he joined the SOE. From January 1, 1942, till 1945, he was the head of the Danish section of the SOE.

counter-betrayal that no one, including Himmler, was able to stamp out until it was too late and Germany was already losing the war. Heydrich would be sorely missed. Only he would have been capable of sorting out the mess. It was a great — if indirect — victory for the British Secret Service.

And it was a victory that yet another secret service would have liked to have gained for itself. Then on the same day that Heydrich was buried in state, a young Slav was arrested on some trivial offense in occupied Warsaw. Suddenly in the midst of the routine questioning by a subaltern Gestapo official, he broke down. Sobbing and weeping with a typical display of Slavic temperament, he confessed he was not a Pole at all, but a Russian. Almost forcing the surprised Gestapo man to follow him, he made the latter open his case. Neatly hidden away in a secret compartment, it contained a collapsible rifle, equipped with a telescopic sight!

The Gestapo man looked aghast at the young sobbing Russian, his mouth opened stupidly in wonder. "What did it mean?" the unspoken question flashed through his mind.

Before he had a chance to pose it, the Russian answered it for him: "I have come to kill," he said.

"Kill whom?"

"*SS Führer Heydrich!*"

It was clear now that the Russians were as determined as the British to get rid of the man who was the greatest threat to their espionage organization. More so, in fact, for their organization was still functioning in Occupied Europe, and if it was to survive, Heydrich had to be "eliminated". The battle for the survival of the "Red Orchestra" had commenced.

THE RUSSIANS TAKE A HAND IN THE GAME

The Russians are our superior in one field only — espionage!

Adolf Hitler

6 — THE ORCHESTRA BEGINS ITS CONCERT

The master spy arrived in Belgium in the autumn of 1938. In his hand, as he stepped off the ship which had brought him from Denmark, was a Canadian pass, which identified him as Michael Dzumage, a businessman from Winnepeg, born in 1914. But the pass was as fake as the four others he had used in his zigzag course from Moscow to Finland; from there to Sweden and on through Denmark to the Belgian port of Antwerp. The real Michael Dzumage, a volunteer in 1937 for the International Brigade in Spain, was long since dead on some Civil War battlefield or rotting in one of Franco's prisons with other survivors of that bloody catastrophe.

But although the master spy had prepared his cover well, studying, as the Gestapo was later to report, "Canadian industry, economy, agriculture and forestry," he could always shrug it off and adopt a new alias at the snap of his fingers. All his long adventurous life since he had first seen the light of day in 1904, in the little Polish town of Nowi Targ south of Cracow, the medium-sized, heavily built spy had slipped in and out of names as easily as he changed shirts.

Leopold Trepper, as his parents had named him, became "Domb" as a young worker after the Polish town of Dombrowa where he had helped to start a strike. After eight months in jail, he entered Palestine illegally, where he joined the local Communist party under the Domb alias. In the end the British expelled him and he went to Moscow where he trained under another alias at the capital's famous military academy and infamous spy school.

Now a tough-looking determined man of thirty-four, he had arrived in Belgium to set up the greatest Communist spy ring the world has ever known. To the bored passport authorities on that fine autumn day he was known as Dzumage, but to the counterespionage experts of the half-dozen countries which sought him or helped in the search, he would always be known as *Le Grand Chef* — the big boss.

In the months that followed, while the great powers of the West moved inevitably into war, Le Grand Chef built up his network, using old friends from Palestine who were now settled in France and Belgium, local Communist cells, and trained agents, both Russian and German, who had been smuggled west by the same devious routes he himself had used. From his own "command post" as a businessman who ran — with his old Palestine friend Leo Grossvogel — the "Foreign Excellent Raincoat" enterprise, he swiftly established branches in other Belgian cities and France, Holland, and Denmark, using them as covers for his numerous spies. By late 1939, when Hitler marched into Poland, he had a network covering the major West European ports from Antwerp to Stockholm. But there was one difficulty. In 1939, the spymaster's own boss, Stalin, was still allied with Nazi Germany. The pathologically suspicious Soviet dictator reckoned his potential enemy of the future would be "perfidious Albion," the master of the British Empire, and capitalist *par excellence*.

Thus it was that Le Grand Chefs network, still held in reserve and not yet functioning, was directed like the guns of the great British imperial bastion of Singapore, in the wrong direction: not towards the land whence the enemy would come — *but out to sea ...*

But although Le Grand Chef was a loyal subject of his master (in the great purges of 1937-1938, he had seen what had happened to those who had dared to disobey the Georgian dictator), he was also Jewish, as were several of his closest associates in the network; and he was fully aware of what was happening to his compatriots in Nazi Germany. As a result, although Russia was still allied with Germany — indeed the two countries had been partners in the rape of his native Poland — he did begin secretly to build up an organization within Germany. And what an organization it was — for it had links right up to the top of Germany's military machine!

In April, 1933, four months after Adolf Hitler had taken power, two young students stood naked and trembling with cold and fear in the damp morning air. Before them stretched the cobbled courtyard now hastily ringed off with gleaming new barbed wire. But they had no eyes for the courtyard or the wire beyond. Their gaze was fixed almost hypnotically on the line of grinning young men in dark uniforms waiting for them, laughing and joking, occasionally staring across to the two "Red" prisoners.

Then the *Sturmbannführer* snapped out an order. His breath fogged in the damp air. The waiting men arranged themselves in two lines, drawing out their clubs, or if they had no clubs, accepting the lead-tipped whips from the Sturmbannführer. There they stood now, eyes on the prisoners, licking their suddenly dry lips, waiting for the fun to begin.

They did not have to wait long. The Sturmbannführer turned to the two naked men. "*Los*," he shouted. "Three times back and forth! *Verstanden?*"

The taller of the two men, blond and muscular, the image of the new Aryan ideal, hesitated, then drawing in a deep breath, he said, "Come on, Henry, let's show them." He started to run.

The first man hit him with brutal precision across the back of the neck. He staggered but kept on running. The blows started to rain down from all sides. In an instant, his back was a bloody red. And then he was through, his chest rising and falling hectically, his eyes wide with pain and fear.

Henry staggered after him.

The Sturmbannführer gave a moment's rest. He nodded. The big blond man began to run again. Staggering wildly, Henry followed.

When the three rounds were over, Henry fell flat on his face on the wet cobbles. But the big man was not finished yet. His body a myriad bloody weals, the skin hanging off in shreds from his back, he staggered forward once again. For a moment the men of the *SS Standarte 6* who were too amazed to do anything. But then they reacted. The blows began to come down with sickening regularity once again.

At last the big man was through. There was a little to be seen of his once white smooth skin now. His entire torso was a bloody pulp. Swaying badly, he somehow managed to click his heels together in the Prussian Army fashion and cry in a voice which almost broke under the strain: "Reporting three times — and one round of honor!"

"Man," several of the SS men breathed in admiration, "you should be one of us!"

Young, radical, student leader Harro Schulze-Boysen never forgot that beating. He survived it, though it deprived him of half an ear; but his weaker, more intellectual, companion, Henry Erlanger, didn't. Schulze-Boysen swore revenge on the

Nazi system. But how? His first concern was to find some refuge from the new masters of Germany. He found this in the newly created Luftwaffe, in which he became an officer. Even with his bad political record, he was after all the nephew of the Kaiser's nationalist War Minister and the man who had built up the German Navy prior to World War I, Admiral Tirpitz, the former idol of most right-wing Germans. He was helped too by his marriage to Libertas Hass-Heye, the beautiful granddaughter of Kaiser Wilhelm's confidant and adviser Prince Philipp zu Eulenburg, who was a personal friend of Hermann Goering himself. Thus after his marriage to her, at which the fat Air Chief Marshal acted as a witness, the door into the German Air Ministry was opened to him — something which the new Lieutenant was going to take full advantage of.

In the years prior to the outbreak of war, he built up his organization. Some of its members were highly placed government officials like Harvid Harnack, a bald, bespectacled Communist with an American wife. Others were artists like Adam Kuckhoff. But the great majority in his organization (which at this time concerned itself mainly with a lot of highfalutin talk and a limited amount of unsuccessful anti-Nazi propaganda) were members of the old German Communist party which the Nazis had shattered in 1933-1934. Through this basic group, whose members shared Schulze-Boysen's political convictions, the *Oberleutnant* in the German Air Ministry and Harnack, *der Oberregierungsrat* in the Ministry of Economics, built up a large number of excellent sources of information in Berlin in both the military and civilian administration. They even managed to penetrate the Abwehr itself. Captain Gollnow, for instance, who worked for Air Intelligence and Abwehr felt he had to learn English if he wanted to get ahead. On advice from his comrade Schulze-Boysen, he decided to take lessons from a young American woman. Who was she?

Naturally, one of his own group, Mildred Harnack, the former instructor in a Midwestern university! She taught him English — and other things too. He started to share her bed (and if we are to believe the Gestapo, which later, of course, tried to blacken the reputation of the spy ring), as well as those of other women. "As soon as the others learned that Gollnow was pliable," one of them reported, "things happened very fast. In other words, Mildred slept with him. So did Libertas, Schulze-Boysen's wife. In fact, they were both lesbians, so Gollnow was treated to some pretty titillating experiences. They had no difficulty in turning his head completely... just think of it! Two women, one of them, at least — Libertas — a real dazzler, and both of them cultured aristocrats to their fingertips. And here they were, offering themselves to him — showing him pleasures he had never dreamed of!"

Another recruit from the counterespionage sector was Horst Heilmann, an air force corporal who worked in the key decoding department, where his colleagues would soon be attempting to break the Russian spy ring code. Again, if we are to believe the Gestapo, he was seduced into the enemy espionage ring through sex. "Take those two young men in the decoding department, Heilmann and Traxl," the Gestapo witness reports, "Don't think that Schulze-Boysen got them by winning them over to his fairly hazy political doctrines — good heavens, no. He went to bed with them, and that was that. Heilmann was mad about him. He would have followed him to the gates of hell... and he wasn't the only one. Harro was as successful with the men as Libertas was with the women."

But regardless of the methods[30] with which the blond Luftwaffe officer built up his anti-Nazi organization, he had — by the time Hitler started to plan his move east against Russia — a large-scale, well informed *Apparat* at his disposal in Berlin and other large centers of population in Germany ready to move into action, once Le Grand Chef gave the word.

That word came on Sunday, June 22, 1941.

On the evening of June 21st, Le Grand Chef, who was now operating from Paris under the name of "Gilbert," crossed the border between German-occupied France, rushing to Vichy, the new French capital.

Here, although the Director in Moscow had strictly forbidden it, he made contact with the Soviet Embassy, asking to be shown to the military attaché, General Susloparov. The alarmed officials at first refused to allow him any contact with the military attaché. Le Grand Chef, fully conscious of the vital importance of the news he bore, was adamant.

In the end he was shown into the attaché's office where the General, intensely irritated by this breach of security, received him in his dressing gown. He asked him what all the fuss was about. Le Grand Chef replied excitedly that he had a message for immediate transmission to Moscow.

When the spy chief told him that Germany was going to attack the Soviet Union that very night, the General burst out

---

[30] In fact, the truth about the Harnack-Schulze-Boysen recruiting methods lies probably somewhere between the complete libertinism ascribed to them by the Gestapo and the Communist attempt after the war to portray them as true-blue puritans. German writer Ernst von Salomon, who knew them, says: "It is true he and Lib allowed each other complete sexual freedom.... They were merely keeping up with the bohemian style of living which had been so common in Berlin between the wars.... In those days you couldn't even get a kick out of sleeping with your best friend's wife — it was all too easy."

laughing. "Why, you must be out of your mind!" he said. "It's unthinkable, altogether impossible. I refuse to transmit such a telegram. You would simply be making a fool of yourself."

But in the end he gave in and transmitted the message, which followed two others in a similar vein which Le Grand Chef had sent earlier in the summer, both to be ignored by Stalin. But this one was not ignored by the Soviet dictator, who is reported to have sent a special investigator to West Europe to find out who was the originator of "these English provocations." The roar of a thousand German cannons and the rattle of hundreds of enemy tanks were proof enough even for his suspicious mind that Hitler was indeed attacking him.

Operation Barbarossa, the great German plan for the invasion of Russia was underway.

Next morning, Le Grand Chef, was awakened by an excited, flushed, hotel proprietor crying, "Monsieur, this is it! They're at war with Russia!" Trepper-Domb-Dzumage-Gilbert, had been long preparing for this moment, at first unconsciously but then deliberately — in spite of the wishes of his Georgian master. Now he knew that the time had come to turn his whole organization, which stretched from Sweden to Switzerland, against the new enemy.

Soon the whole of Nazi-occupied Europe began to hum with the tap-tap of Morse keys, passing streams of secret information eastward to the Moscow listening stations. Frantically Goering's counterespionage listening service, located in Oslo, Brest, Breslau, and Cranz tried to get a lead on them, while the decoding experts of the Abwehr tried to decipher the pile of records of these illegal messages which started to mount on their desks. In vain! The location of the stations was hard to pinpoint and the code seemed unbreakable.

Thus the *Kapelle*[31] — the German secret service jargon for a spy network — and *rote* (red) because it was Communist, dominated the airways with seeming impunity. The "red orchestra," the greatest Communist spy ring the world has ever seen, appeared to be outfoxing the Germans at every turn.

In June, two days after the offensive against Russia had started, the German listening station at Cranz decided that it would concentrate on only one of the many illegal transmitters which had commenced operating that week — the one which operated under the call sign PTX and which seemed important enough to transmit regularly every day. Enlisting the aid of three other listening posts at Breslau, Oslo, and Brest, the Cranz group managed to narrow down the area from which PTX was operating to a strip of the Belgian coast.

Immediately the news was passed on to Admiral Canaris who ordered his man in Belgium, ex-lawyer and former antitank commander Hauptmann Piepe, a jovial person in his late forties, to start an all-out search for the station. Piepe, who had been transferred to the Abwehr because of his age, his legal training and fair knowledge of French, but who knew nothing of counterespionage methods, did as he was told. Disguised as a happy-go-lucky Dutch businessman named Riepert, he opened an office at number 192, Rue Royale in Brussels, in the same floor as a local Belgian firm Simexco, an import-export business. Then he set about looking for station PTX. Occasionally he would pass the owner of Simexco, who was often away in Paris, and he would raise his hat politely and mutter *bon jour* or *bon soir, m'sieu*, with the best accent he could muster and pass on his way.

The other man would do the same.

---

[31] German for "orchestra."

Thus the spy and the spy-chaser would go about their business, each unaware of the other's identity. By coincidence Piepe had picked an office in the same floor as Le Grand Chef's Belgian cover firm. *Simexco belonged to Trepper!*

Towards the end of November, 1941, Hauptmann Piepe received the technical assistance he had long awaited. A small Luftwaffe outfit arrived in the Belgian capital equipped with the latest mobile directional finding gear. Immediately he put the experts to work. Night after night after the Belgians had been forced off the streets by the German curfew, the camouflaged air force trucks crept along the empty boulevards and avenues, their circular aerials revolving slowly, while in the hot, stifling, yellow-lit cabins the highly trained radio technicians tried to locate the clandestine station.

And German *Gründlichkeit* paid off. The secret operator was obviously staying on the air far too long. (The Germans did not realize the tremendous volume of information that Le Grand Chef was receiving from his Group "Kent" and Group "Choro" that had to be transmitted to the hard-pressed Russians immediately.) Slowly they began to narrow the area from which PTX was operating, moving in from the suburbs through the city's center until finally they had established the general area from which the signals were coming — the Etterbeek district.

Now Hauptmann Piepe took over. Within the confines of a locator truck, disguised as an ordinary civilian vehicle he went out, night after night, combing the narrow cobbled streets and smoky nineteenth-century back alleys of the working-class district. Closer and closer they drew to the source of the signals. Then the transmitter stopped its activities. Piepe knew that they were close — very, very close now! Together with the

Luftwaffe officer in charge of the radio experts, he abandoned the disguised truck and took to the streets himself. The two men were equipped with Siemens's latest development in this field: a radio locating apparatus which could be strapped under a coat with the earphones replaced by an ivory plug somewhat similar to a modern hearing aid.

For three nights the two German officers crept through the blacked-out, deserted streets from curfew to dawn, following the elusive signal until finally the drone of the mysterious PTX station grew so loud that they knew they had found it. It was located in a tall, three-story house located at number 101, Rue des Atrebates.

Thereafter, Hauptmann Piepe moved fast. He got permission from the Brussels Provost Marshal to borrow ten men from the Field Security Police, plus another twenty-five from the local barracks. Preparing for every eventuality, he armed them with axes, fire ladders, and crowbars in case they had to break into the place. Then he ordered them to put a pair of socks over their heavy army boots so that the spies would not hear their approach.

By the second week of December he was ready for his raid. On the night of December 13, 1941, he assembled his command in the shadows as soon as the curfew had driven the last Belgian civilian off the streets. Then he settled down to wait until the Luftwaffe lieutenant who had been his constant companion these last weeks could inform him that the "Red Orchestra" was performing once again from number 101. Even then he did not move. He wanted the spies to be lulled into a false sense of security. The hours passed. The transmission continued with boring regularity. Piepe would have given anything for a smoke. But he dare not reveal his position in case the street was being observed from somewhere in the tall, red brick house. Midnight struck solemnly. Behind him in the darkness he heard a man shuffle his cramped feet. He whispered an order to be more careful. It began to grow very cold. Snow was in the air. In two weeks it would be Christmas.

And then it was one o'clock on the morning of the fourteenth. Brussels lay in a profound silence. There was absolutely no sound save for that persistent buzz coming from the Luftwaffe lieutenant's earphone. Piepe licked his lips and drew his service pistol. "Now," he whispered, hardly recognizing his own voice, and rushed forward together with two Field Security policemen. Suddenly there was the sound of firing. "They're over here!" someone shouted excitedly.

Piepe paid no attention to either the shots or the shouts. He burst through the door of 101. A dog barked at him. He ignored it. He bumped into a dark-haired woman in a dressing gown. He pushed her to one side. Obviously she was not the radio operator. He clambered up the stairs. With a shove of his shoulder, he thrust open a door. The room was empty. But only a moment before someone had obviously been transmitting there. Then as he recalled years later, "There was a still warm transmitter, with a lot of telegrams — all in German."

There were postcards everywhere too, strewn all over the room and again all in German; they had been sent from scores of large and small German cities.

But Piepe had no time for those at that moment. Where was the radio operator? His gaze shot swiftly around the room. The little dormer window was still open. He strode across to it and poked his head through, intending to take a look at the roof. The man in the shadows reacted instantaneously. A pistol shot cracked out. Piepe ducked. In the same moment the man on the roof disappeared. But the man — it was the operator — had not expected anyone to be waiting for him down below. He dropped on to the dark cobbles to be surrounded by soldiers, who wrenched his pistol from him and beat him about the head and shoulders before dragging him into number 101.

Piepe was staring wide-eyed around the secret room behind the place where he had found the transmitter when they brought in the dishevelled, bleeding operator. For a moment he was totally concerned with the modern printing plant, complete with piles of forged German documents which it contained, there were also trays of strange-looking test tubes, plus dead rats.[32]

He dragged his gaze away and started his cross questioning immediately for he knew that this was the best time, while the man was still under shock, to get information out of him. And what information it was! The radio operator identified himself at first as a South American named Carlos Alamo. But the dark-haired, heavy-jawed man soon broke down and revealed his real name. He was Red Army Captain Mikhail Makarov — *nephew of no less a person than Soviet Foreign Minister Molotov!*

Five hours later Captain Piepe, warm with excitement in spite of the bitterly cold wind, left 101, Rue des Atrebates, taking his captives with him. Although he had been up all night, he knew he wouldn't be able to sleep; his discovery was too fantastic. He would have to report his findings to his chief as soon as the

---

[32] They contained — according to Piepe — cultures of various diseases, such as typhus. The rats, again according to the German Captain, were to be fixed up with a small hidden bomb, apparently for use in sabotage operations.

latter came on duty. But in spite of his excitement, he still remembered to post guards in the house, whose job it would be to arrest anyone who came to the place in the next six hours.

Three hours later at nine o'clock, a rather heavy-set man appeared at 101, carrying a basket. He looked like a hundred such humble door-to-door salesmen or hawkers who were commonplace in Brussels in those wartime days when anything and everything was of value.

Piepe's men were taking no chances. As soon as he had rung, they dragged the hawker inside the door, pulled his papers out of his pocket, and pushed him against the wall of the dark landing while they examined them.

They appeared to be in order. So they turned their attention to the man with the basket whose eyes were wide with genuine fear at this strange treatment on a cold winter's morning. Questions rained down on him in bad French.

But in spite of his fear, the hawker stuck to his story. His purpose there was simply to sell rabbits — Belgian giants, he maintained proudly — to the lady of the house. And he couldn't be shaken. In the end the Abwehr let him go.

Understandably the man shot out through the door. Like most Belgians in those days, he wanted nothing to do with the German secret police. Grinning to themselves at the man's hurry, the three Abwehr men lit fresh cigarettes and returned to their dreary job.

The rabbit peddler swung round the corner, then took a quick glance behind him. No one there. He dropped the basket in the nearest alley way. Straightening his rumpled clothes and squaring his shoulders he hurried away. The peddler was Trepper. Now Le Grand Chef knew that the Germans were on to his organization, and he had no illusions about the fact that his agents, now enemy captives, would sooner or later tell the Germans what they wanted to know. The last battle between the "Red Orchestra" and the German Intelligence Services had begun.

7 — WHO IS THE TRAITOR IN BERLIN?

Piepe's sensational discovery caused consternation in Berlin where counterespionage listening stations had already begun to pick up signals from the "Choro" transmitter. *In the heart of the "Thousand Year Reich" there were agents broadcasting directly to Moscow!* Now it appeared that the evil had spread to the occupied territories. Hitler himself was informed and in a rage, he ordered that "this cancer must be burnt out!" Labelled "*Geheime Reichssache*" (Top Secret), the project was put in Heydrich's charge.

The tall, young chief of the Main Security Office lost no time in organizing the search. He founded "*Kommando Rote Kapelle*" which consisted of representatives of the SD, Gestapo, and Abwehr, with Schellenberg as its senior member. It was agreed at the first meeting of this group that the Gestapo would be responsible, under Mueller himself, for finding out who the "Choro" group were. They had already sent 500 reports to Moscow according to German listening stations. The Abwehr, with any assistance necessary from the Gestapo, would be in charge of the search in the occupied territories. The mixed team went to work. In Berlin the hunters were aided in their attempts to find the traitors by the discovery of a half-burned message,[33] which revealed three addresses in Berlin and three cover names "Choro," "Arvid," and "Wolf."

---

[33] The message and key to the code used by Alamo were found in his room at 101, Rue des Atrebates.

The addresses were easily found, but a goodly number of high-ranking Germans lived in the houses in question. Time was of the essence and the Gestapo simply could not arrest every resident of the three addresses without awkward questions being asked. "Gestapo" Mueller wanted the whole organization to be rounded up too. If he approved a wave of indiscriminate arrests, the rest of the "criminals" might be warned and go underground. Thus he ordered that the dossiers of all the residents should be checked for possible clues.

One backroom researcher came up with the first clue. Could "Choro" be the Russian pronunciation of "Harro," the first name of an Oberleutnant der Luftwaffe living at one of the addresses? Mueller ordered that Schulze-Boysen's whole dossier should be brought up from the archives and searched thoroughly for further clues. It told them a lot. "S-B has been known to the Gestapo since 1933." "Prior to 1933 he was involved with an organization which was radically Communist-orientated."

That was enough for the professional policeman Mueller. He set his men to watch Schulze-Boysen, recording all his calls, checking his friends. Swiftly the pieces started to fall into place. "Arvid" was obviously Harvid Harnack, a leading official in the Ministry of Economics. "Wolf" was a little tougher until the Gestapo sleuths discovered another of Schulze-Boysen's friends, an unsuccessful writer named Adam Kuckhoff who had once written a novel which had contained the word "wolf" in its title. "Wolf" was Kuckhoff. Still Mueller did not strike.

Mueller hated the Communists. He had first come into contact with them after World War I when they had set up an abortive republic in his native Bavaria. Regular troops had crushed the republic, but not before the Communists had massacred many of their hostages. It had been the young policeman's first job to investigate the murders. Since then he had pursued them with a zealous brutality matched only by his pursuit of Bavarian Nazis, naturally prior to 1933.[34]

He ordered his subordinates to wait before they struck. He wanted the whole bunch, even though the Führer himself demanded results, and his chief, Heydrich, whom he feared more than Hitler, was breathing down his neck. But in the end he was forced to move by a chance telephone call.

Six weeks after Heydrick had died in agony in Prague, without having had the satisfaction of arresting the "Red Orchestra," Horst Heilmann, the young air force corporal who worked in the Abwehr's deciphering section close to the chief decipherer, 1st Lt. Dr. Wilhelm Vauck himself, fell into conversation with another corporal and a friend of his named Traxl.

Traxl worked in the section connected with deciphering the messages coming through the "Red Orchestra circuit."

Heilmann, who spoke excellent English, dealt with that area of activities. All the same Heilmann kept on friendly footing with his fellow noncom, encouraging him to boast about the achievements of his section. On this particular sultry August day, however, Heilmann realized that Traxl really had hot news. The two fell into conversation about the "Red Orchestra" (Heilmann had already learned from the latter that Vauck was beginning to decipher its messages) and Heilmann egged his friend on to prove that Vauck really was making an effective effort at decoding.

---

[34] Surprisingly enough, the brutal, opportunist head of the Gestapo, with so many deaths and worse on his conscience, was a pious church-going Catholic. Hence his dislike for both Communist and Fascist.

Traxl took the bait. He went back into his section and returned proudly with a decode that "we made months ago."

Evidently he thought it would do no harm to show his comrade the message which dated back to October, 1941. But as Heilmann ran his eye over it, it took all his strength and presence of mind to prevent himself from crying out loud. The flimsy showed that the Abwehr already knew the addresses of "Arvid," "Wolf," and his beloved "Choro."

With a sickly grin Heilmann gave the flimsy back to his friend and returned to his section, his mind reeling at the discovery. Once before he had discussed what he would do if he were discovered with his roommate and fellow conspirator, Rainer Hildebrandt. The latter had advised him to attempt to escape over the Swiss frontier. But the handsome young Corporal had turned that suggestion down. It appeared to him as a betrayal of his idol, Schulze-Boysen. "I can't do that," he told Rainer. "If I did, it wouldn't give Harro a chance of getting out."

Thus on this October 29, 1942, he made the decision which would cost not only his own head, but those of thirty or forty other members of the "Red Orchestra." He tried to warn Harro. Again and again he rang the Schulze-Boysen apartment. In vain. The happy-go-lucky chief of the Berlin group was out sailing with his pretty wife, forgetting the cares of his nerve-wracking secret activity on this glorious summer day. In despair Heilmann left his own number with the maid and asked her to tell her master to call him immediately when he returned from his outing. It was a risky move, because to reveal the secret number of an Abwehr office to a civilian was a punishable offense, but a nervous, tense Heilmann was no longer thinking straight.

Thus while the bronze, handsome Schulze-Boysen and his libertine wife enjoyed their last real day of freedom, a nervous Heilmann paced his tight little office, smoking cigarette after cigarette, his work completely forgotten, waiting for the phone on his littered desk to ring. But it did not ring. Hour after hour he waited. No call from "Harro." Slowly the clatter of the typewriters started to die away. Next door in the washroom he could hear the taps run as people began to wash up before leaving for the day. A head peered round the door of the office, and a fellow member of his section said: "See you tomorrow, Heilmann. Don't tell me you're doing overtime on a nice day like this!"

Heilmann, pale and miserable, muttered something apologetically. The other man disappeared, as did the rest of the section, one by one. The typewriters stopped altogether. The telephones no longer rang. He could hear the door of the big safe, which contained the secret messages and deciphers, being closed. He looked at his watch in alarm. Almost six. Still no call from Harro! What was he to do? If he stayed on after office hours, someone — perhaps the duty officer — might start asking awkward questions. But what if Harro called and he was not there?

In the end he made his fatal decision. He would go and try to contact Harro during the evening. He packed his briefcase and, sunk in thought, left the building. In his gloom and preoccupation he did not notice the yellow light which was still burning under the door of Oberleutnant Dr. Wilhelm Vauck (his room was already blacked out in spite of the bright evening sunshine). Dr. Vauck was prepared for a long evening of work. It was an oversight which was going to cost him his life...

Late that night Dr. Vauck heard the telephone ring in the other room. He took no notice. He was busy with yet another of the "Red Orchestra" messages, in which the Gestapo was exhibiting such an unusual interest; he wanted to get it decoded by the morning. He dismissed the call from his mind. But the phone rang again. And again.

In the end, cursing the uncalled-for interruption, he walked across the hall and down the corridor until he located the ringing. It came from the room occupied by Obergefreiter Heilmann. Hurriedly he switched on the lights and picked up the phone.

"Here Oberleutnant Schulze-Boysen," a deep voice announced. "I was asked to call this number."

Dr. Vauck caught his breath. *Schulze-Boysen!* The man the Gestapo had been shadowing these last nine months. What did he want calling this — of all — offices?

For a moment all rational thought fled from his mind. "Do you write your name with a 'y'"? he stuttered, saying the first thing that came into his head.

"With a 'y'," the strong, confident voice at the other end answered. "Oh, well, I'm afraid that there is no one here," Vauck stuttered, regaining his composure. "Perhaps you could call back tomorrow morning — at say, eight o'clock."

With that the conversation was over, but already Schulze-Boysen's death warrant was signed. Vauck did not reflect very long why the spy suspect should be calling a corporal in his own department. Vauck telephoned Heydrich's Main Security Office.

His information caused a panic. Mueller's long term plan was hurriedly thrown overboard. The Reds, so the Gestapo men told each other, must have known what was going on all the time. A hurried operation plan was set up. They would have to round up the conspirators immediately before they had a chance to get away with their information. That same morning the Gestapo struck.

The leaders were arrested immediately. A week later, most of their closest contacts were in jail. One week after that, the Gestapo spread out its search to the provinces in the Ruhr area — traditionally a center of "red agitation" — and to the more remote Moselle area, which provided good hiding places for people like the Communists who did not want to be noticed or asked awkward questions. By September 14, 1942, "the Harro Group" was broken completely, with nearly one hundred of its leading agents in Gestapo jails.

Three months later they would start going to the gallows, at Hitler's specific wish, that he wanted them all "liquidated" before the year was out. Men and women, they all went to their death, some bravely, others protesting their innocence or crying out in agony at the "shabby way one has to die" for such "a shabby cause." Of the women, lantern-jawed, bobbed-haired Mildred Harnack, the American, cut perhaps the best figure. She walked calmly to her death, muttering: "And I did so love Germany!"[35]

While the "Choro" group blundered blindly to its tragic death in Berlin, Le Grand Chef's organization in the occupied countries suffered one blow after another. First "Kent," then "Hilda," and finally his own "Gilbert" were betrayed to the Gestapo investigators, eagerly assisted by Hauptmann Piepe, who was now generally regarded in Abwehr circles as the best spycatcher it possessed. Thus it was that by the time Schulze-Boysen came to trial, Le Grand Chef's organization was in

---

[35] There were 64 death sentences in all. These included all the leaders of the organization.

ruins and he himself a sick, hunted man.

But Piepe and Gestapo man Giering, very tall and thin (he was to die of cancer in 1943), persisted in their search for him. They arrested his innocent business partner in the Simex raincoat business, which had provided such an excellent cover for the obtaining of information, and threatened the man's wife that she would never see her husband again if she did not reveal Trepper's whereabouts. For days Madame Corbin racked her brains while professional policeman Giering waited, as if he had all the time in the world, for her to dredge up the information from the depths of her brain. But Madame Corbin knew nothing of M. Gilbert, as she called Trepper, save useless trivialities. Even the patient Gestapo man who had spent his whole career waiting for witnesses to break down began to despair. His cancer kept him in constant pain, which he could dampen only by his daily bottle of cognac. Then after three days in a row when the frightened dark-haired Frenchwoman had given him no more than a half-page of notes, she mentioned casually that M. Gilbert was suffering from toothache when she had last seen him.

The German sat up in his chair. *Toothache!* Quickly he asked her if she knew the name of his dentist. Madame Corbin shrugged and said she did. If the Boche were happy with it, he could have it. It was a small price to pay for her husband's life. The dentist was named Dr. Maleplate. She gave Giering his address. Giering left immediately.

Le Grand Chef had been on the run for weeks now. Without either a transmitter or an operator, he knew he was finished. All that was left for him was to get out of Paris and go underground with his American girlfriend, Georgie de Winter, a beautiful blonde half his age, probably somewhere in the remote French provinces. His decision made, he started to make plans.

In a seedy backstreet bistro, he contacted a Frenchman who would provide him with a fake passport — at a price. The same Frenchman would also arrange for his "funeral." Just before his organization had begun to be broken up, he had commenced to spread the word, for reasons known only to himself, that he was suffering from a serious heart condition (at the time of this writing L. Trepper is still alive in his native Poland, hale and hearty and far from dead). Now his French acquaintance was to ensure that he "died" and was accorded a proper funeral, complete with death certificate, black-edged cards, and obituary in the French press. All that remained to be done was to have his teeth fixed before he disappeared into an area where dentists were few and far between.

Thus it was that he decided to go to Dr. Maleplate on November 23, 1942, for a full treatment, after telling his old friends of his Palestine days, Katz and Grossvogel (whom he was soon to betray) that they were to go underground. As he stated in a telegram to Moscow that same day: "The situation is worsening hour by hour. Kent is probably under arrest. Simex has been liquidated...."[36]

Le Grand Chef was uneasy as soon as he opened the door to Dr. Maleplate's office at number 13, Rue de Vivoli; and it was not only the unlucky number which worried him. There was something strange in the air — something which he could not define, but which he knew heralded danger. Dismissing the thought he walked down the long dark corridor, where the dentist, a hearty man with unusually alert eyes, was waiting for him. "*Bon jour, Monsieur Gilbert,*" the latter said, trying to

---

[36] He transmitted this message through the French Communist Party's network which was separate from his own.

overcome his own nervousness at the knowledge that the two German manhunters were hidden in the next room and a whole Kommando of security police were in position outside.

Trepper noted that the door to the rear which was normally open was closed today, but he shrugged the thought aside. Seating himself in the smooth ancient chair, he opened his mouth and prepared for the pain.

"He was extremely relaxed," Dr. Maleplate said much later. "Poor devil." I said to myself, "what point is there in tinkering with his teeth? This is hardly the time to cause him pain. I chatted to him and went through the motions of selecting my instruments."

The spymaster smiled up at the dentist and said: "Things are looking up, aren't they? Did you hear the news on the radio?" He was referring obviously to the news of the German defeats in Russia, the result, in part, of his own work.

The dentist was too much in "a cold sweat" to answer, for at exactly that moment he had heard the jingle of Giering's handcuffs in the next room. Hastily he stuffed a piece of cotton wool in the victim's mouth and fussed around with his drill.

At last Piepe and Giering acted. Through the door which was slightly ajar now — they had opened it once Trepper was safely seated in the chair — they saw that "the dentist was shaking" (as Piepe recalled later). As for themselves, "Giering and I were in a terrible state of nerves." They burst into the room with drawn pistols. Le Grand Chef started up under his cloth overall and then sank back in his chair again. "Bravo," he applauded the two Germans who thought he "was the calmest man in the room." "You've done a good job!"

Modestly Piepe muttered: "It's the result of two years of work."

Slowly the spy raised his hands, adding: "I'm not armed." The Gestapo man motioned him to put them down while he slipped on the handcuffs.

Le Grand Chef waited till the job was done, then he stated firmly: "I am an officer and demand to be treated as such."

Giering nodded his approval.

Dr. Maleplate broke in: "I want you to know," he said to the prisoner, "that this was not my doing."

"Of course not," Trepper said generously, "I wouldn't dream of bearing you a grudge, even for a moment."

Thereafter followed a polite discussion about the dentist's fees, but the latter waved them aside. Trepper shook his hand and disappeared finally between the big dying Gestapo man and the smaller Abwehr officer. It was all very polite, brave, and gentlemanly in the best British stiff-upper-lip tradition.

What followed was neither gentlemanly nor brave. Trepper betrayed one old comrade after another. He, "Kent," and the rest of the professional Russian agents' volunteered to work for the Germans (only two committed suicide rather than go ahead with the double game) in what the latter called the *Funkspiel*, their own version of the double-cross game. Under a Gestapo official, the Germans started their own "Red Orchestra" which supplied Moscow with false information about the Wehrmacht. They continued to do so until in late 1943, Trepper, who by this time was trusted by the Gestapo, asked to be taken into the center of Paris to purchase some medicine for his "bad heart," as well as provide his guard — a somewhat naive official named Berg — with an "excellent remedy" for his bad stomach.

While the sick and trusting Berg remained in the car outside the Bailly Drug Store, not far from the Gare St. Lazare, Trepper strolled into the store and out of the side door.

His disappearance cured Berg's stomach-ache for good!

Thus Le Grand Chef disappeared from the field of espionage, hunted by an enraged Gestapo as well as his former comrades of the Communist party, for they already knew of his treachery. The Chief of Soviet Espionage, Colonel General Feodor Kusnezov, had already broadcast a statement to what remained of his network in Western Europe warning them: *"Avoid Gilbert. Party members will give him no support. He is a traitor..."*[37]

In that same summer when Le Grand Chefs organization was so brutally broken up, a remote Abwehr listening post, some one hundred miles from the Swiss border, was dismayed to find the red monster had sprouted another head in neutral Switzerland, out of reach of the Gestapo and their rough but successful methods. A little while later, it sprouted another — and yet another. The radio experts, hunched over their powerful receiving sets in the delightful Swabian countryside, sighed and then settled down to pinpointing the new enemy. The *"Rote Drei"* (the "red three") was on the air!

---

[37] Gestapo man Heinz Pannwitz, who had been in charge of the investigations into Heydrich's death, was responsible for the "Red Orchestra" operation in France. When he heard of "Willy" Berg's mishap, he finally mustered enough courage to telephone Mueller in Berlin. He prefaced his news with the statement "Now don't faint!" There was no reply. He asked: "Have you fainted?" An oath was his answer. Then he told Mueller. Mueller, in his despair, asked how he was going to break the news to Himmler. Panwitz suggested "not to tell him at all." So Himmler remained in the dark about Trepper's escape.

But this time the Germans were not alone in their search for the Communist spies. The neutral Swiss, playing a delicate game between the Germans and the Allies and determined to be on the winning side come what might, were also interested in the clandestine station, which was harbored like a viper in their neutral and highly prosperous bosom. Brigadier Masson, head of Swiss Intelligence, assigned M. Marc Payot to head the group charged with finding the three illegal transmitters.

It did not take the Swiss long to ascertain where the messages were coming from — nor the Germans, for they obviously had paid agents within the Swiss espionage organization (or conversely the Swiss, eager to be on the winning side "leaked" the information to them). Lt. Maurice Treyet's *Groupe de Lac* special listening service soon pinpointed the three stations, which belonged to the "Red Orchestra's" reserve. One by one the major agents were captured: the chief, a Hungarian named Rado (real name, Colonel Alexander Radolfi of the Red Army); the main radio operator, Englishman Alexander Foote, who had fought with the International Brigade in Spain before entering Russian service; and the 46-year-old German exile Rudolf Roessler, who later was going to give his cover name to the whole ring — "the Lucy Ring."

Lean, bespectacled Roessler had fought in the German Army in the First World War. Thereafter he had worked as a journalist before leaving Germany in 1934, one year after the Nazi takeover, to start up a publishing firm in Lucerne, called Vita Nova. Under this cover he began to work with the heavy-set "Rado," who spoke six languages perfectly and posed as a journalist.

It was Roessler who supplied Rado with most of his information about high-level military and civilian planning within Germany, and it was his code name which appeared on virtually every message meant for Moscow dealing with this sphere of Rado's espionage activities — "*source-Lucy.*"

But where did "Lucy" (and not "Lucie," as he is known on the Continent) get his information? How did he obtain such highly accurate and high-level news? Certainly not from the "Choro" group, which in late 1941, tried to make contact with the Swiss branch of the "Red Orchestra" and failed. Nor from the main "Red Orchestra" organization itself.

After the war many theories were advanced to explain his sources. Two French authors maintained that Roessler got his information from ten ex-World War I comrades who were now all German generals in the High Command! Not a very plausible story. A British author states that in fact "Jim" (Alexander Foote's cover name) was a double agent who supplied the Russians with information that the British had culled from their decoding of top secret Wehrmacht radio traffic. Others believe that Roessler had access to information gained by the Swiss Intelligence Service from their own high-level sources within the German High Command.

Yet others believe that Brigadier Masson, reputably pro-British and pro-French, had leaked the vital information to the "Lucy Ring" himself so that the Allies could be up to date concerning German intentions. Masson hoped that in this way he could help the Allied cause without endangering his native country, continually threatened by their neighbor over the border who had no particular respect for neutrality pacts and pious promises of nonaggression.

But in Germany itself, in that middle year of the war with the defeats of El Alamein and Stalingrad already indicative of the way the wind was blowing, there were those in the highest level of intelligence who were sure that the Communist sources of information *were within their own ranks!*

Thirty-four-year-old Schellenberg, the coming star of German Intelligence, thought the leak was to be found right at the top. In early 1943, he had a strange talk about the now beaten "Red Orchestra" with the man responsible for uncovering the "Choro" group — "Gestapo" Mueller.

One night in that spring, Mueller, who had been drinking, told him: "Men like those you know from Rote Kapelle — Schulze-Boysen or Harnack — you know, they were intellectuals, progressive revolutionaries, always looking for a final solution; they never got bogged down in half-measures. And they died still believing in that solution. There are too many compromises in National Socialism for it to offer a faith like that; but spiritual Communism can."

Schellenberg was amazed. As he recalled later: "I sat opposite Mueller that night deep in thought. Here was the man who had conducted the most ruthless and brutal struggle against Communism in all its various forms, the man who, in his investigation of Rote Kapelle, had left no stone unturned to uncover the last ramifications of that conspiracy. What a change was here!"

But Schellenberg, always able to hold his tongue, said nothing and let the Bavarian continue. "I see Stalin today in quite a different light. He is immeasurably superior to the leaders of the Western nations," Mueller said in that thick Munich accent of his which was made worse by the brandy he was drinking; "and if I had anything to say in the matter we'd reach an agreement with him as quickly as possible. That would be a blow which the West with their damned hypocrisy, would never be able to recover from. You see, with the Russians one always knows where one is: either they chop off your head right away or they hug you."

Mueller went on to praise the Führer's chief aide, Martin Bormann, as "a man who knows what he wants."

Schellenberg was "amazed to hear Mueller express such an opinion. He had always said that Bormann was nothing but a criminal and now suddenly there was this change of attitude." A little afraid, wondering if Mueller was somehow trying to trap him, the ambitious "March violet" (as he was called by old Party members because they thought he had joined the Nazis only after they had come into power in January, 1933) tried to make a joke of the whole conversation.

He said brightly: "All right, Comrade Mueller, let's all start saying 'Heil Stalin' right now — and our little father Mueller will become head of the NKVD."

Mueller looked at him malevolently with his little dark eyes. "That would be fine — and you'd really be for the high jump, you and your die-hard bourgeois friends."

There the conversation ended but Schellenberg started making inquiries and after a "duel in the dark," he came to the conclusion that "he (Mueller) had established contact with the Russian Secret Service." But was he alone? Did his suddenly transformed attitude to the key man in Hitler's HQ mean that Martin Bormann was in the plot too?[38]

Admiral Canaris, head of the Abwehr, seemed to believe so, if we can trust the statement of the cold-eyed "spy of the century," General Reinhard Gehlen, head of the military espionage system in the "Foreign Armies East." In his

---

[38] Naturally we can also assume that this conversation might only be a latter-day attempt to discredit an old rival.

memoirs he records that "the most prominent source and adviser" (to the Russians) was Bormann. We discovered that Bormann was the only person to control an unchecked radio transmitter.

"Canaris explained to me his suspicions, suppositions, and conclusions regarding Bormann's motives for his treachery. He did not preclude the possibility of blackmail, but thought the real motives were his boundless ambition and complexes vis-à-vis his environment — and Bormann's unsatisfied ambition to take over Hitler's post himself."

Thus the two men who thought they knew everything rode together each morning in Berlin's Tiergarten, the ruddy-faced Admiral with white hair, who hated military pomp and lavished his affection solely on his dogs;[39] and the puny-bodied SS General whose weakness was pornographic photographs — Canaris and Schellenberg, the supreme realists.

Knee to knee they rode through the leafy alleyways, never postponing this meeting even when Berlin had suffered an air raid the night before. Canaris invariably called Schellenberg *"mein junger Freund"* (my young friend), or even occasionally *"mein lieber junger Freund"* (my dear young friend), and often he would point to his favorite dachshund Seppi and lecture the SD man on the superiority of the species: "See how superior animals are, Schellenberg! My dog is discreet, he'll never betray me ... I can't say as much about men." And Schellenberg would solemnly nod his head in unspoken confirmation.

---

[39] Canaris always reserved rooms with two beds when he traveled so that his dogs would not have to sleep on the floor; and when he had to leave them behind, he always telephoned Berlin to find out how they were. The Gestapo men who regularly tapped his line must have found it difficult to make anything out of the concerned questions about the dogs' natural functions.

So they would ride on past pale-faced, undernourished Berliners, trudging off to the early morning shift — parents whose sons were being slaughtered by the thousands on the Russian front. No doubt the bent-shouldered workers, lugging along their battered briefcases, which contained their lunches, would look at them and under their breath curse *die feinen Herren*, living the good life in some safe headquarters. Little did they realize that the young man with the skinny shoulders and the ruddy-faced, white-haired gentlemen were mortal enemies, engaging each new morning in a kind of stealthy duel behind the polite chitchat of two friends, sounding each other out for new ways of attack, new weaknesses, new chances to score against one another.

But above all, the two men riding in the park each morning were realists. Both wanted power and the best chance of survival. Both knew in these middle years of the war that Germany was losing. Subconsciously they set themselves four aims — which they would never have dared to express even to their most intimate friends: to eradicate those in their own camp who might endanger their personal plans such as Bormann and Mueller; to continue the war against the "Reds" with every means at their disposal, for both of them hated Communism passionately; to bring the war in the West to an end even if it meant getting rid of A. H.[40] himself; and finally, to "dispose" of each other as soon as the opportunity came along.

Thus they rode side by side, the two strangely divergent men who controlled Germany's intelligence Apparat which now stretched from Japan to America. *From now onwards they would fight a war which they knew they must lose — for both personal and*

---

[40] In his intimate circle Hitler was always known by his initials.

political reasons. But by losing it they would save their own necks and those of their fellow citizens whom they deigned worthy of saving...

BOOK TWO: TRICKS OF THE TRADE

They speak of murder ... I can't trust anyone any more. Assassination awaits me on the least suspicion.

Felix Stidger, *Union Spy*, 1864

1942-1943: THE GERMANS TRY ONCE MORE

Often most valuable clues can be picked up by spies who get beneath windows and peer in at the corners at critical times.

William Le Queux

8 — CANARIS PULLS OFF A COUP

At eight o'clock on the evening of June 12, 1942, the commander of the lean grey German U-boat surfaced opposite the little New York State beach resort of Amagansett. He took his bearings and then ordered the U-202 to submerge and glide in closer to the shore. Lieutenant Commander Lindner was well satisfied with his achievements that summer evening. After a 3,000-mile trip in two weeks, much of it in thick fog, he was right on target. Now he wanted to get rid of his "special cargo" and proceed with his attacks on the fat Allied convoys sailing from New York to Liverpool, laden with men and arms for the boasted Allied "second front."

Ten minutes later the U-202 surfaced again, once more in thick fog, and Lindner started giving out soft orders. The rubber dinghy was hauled on deck, while the four civilians he had brought with him as "special cargo" assembled, waiting for the sailors to inflate it.

When the dinghy was ready and Lindner had given orders to the two *Matrosen* who were going to row the four civilians to the shore (some fifty yards away), he turned to the leader of the team and asked softly: "What do you think of the night, Dasch?" Dasch, a blond man in his thirties with wry, twisted mouth and balding forehead, answered enthusiastically: "Christ, this is perfect!" Swiftly he clattered down the slippery, metallic steps of the conning tower and made his men check through their pockets to see that they had brought nothing from the French port of Lorient that would reveal them as Germans.

Just before midnight, the bearded U-boat commander joined them in a drink to wish them well. Thereafter things moved quickly. They, the two sailors, and four big wooden boxes which contained their supplies and explosives were loaded into the dinghy. A bosun gave them a push from the dripping, barnacle-clad side of the U-boat, and they were alone in the tossing, fog-shrouded Atlantic Ocean.

The waves were higher than they had anticipated and occasionally threatened to swamp the boat. But if they did not do that, the grey-green water succeeded in soaking most of the men before they finally heard the boat's bottom grind against the shingle.

Swiftly the two sailors, who wanted nothing to do with the dangerous mission upon which the four civilians were soon to embark, sprang out of the dinghy and began to unload the boxes. The civilians, having recovered from their fright at the sight of the breakers, joined in, helping to bury the boxes in the dark dunes while Dasch, their leader, carefully staked out the area.

That job done, Dasch shook hands with the two sailors, then turned his attention to getting his men and himself into dry clothes and off the beach.

Leaving his men to get on with it, Dasch walked through the wet sand toward the road to scout around. It was 12:30 in the morning. Everything had gone smoothly. Soon they would walk to the nearest town (he thought wrongly he was somewhere near East Hampton) and get the first train into New York, where they would disappear without difficulty since all of them knew the USA intimately.

Abruptly the German froze!

Someone was walking towards him, slowly swinging a flashlight from side to side.

For a moment Dasch did not move. Then he realized he must keep this unknown person away from where his men were still changing their clothes. The German walked forward. The man with the flashlight stopped and threw a thin yellow beam in front of him. "Who are you?" he asked surprised.

To his horror Dasch saw the man was dressed in the uniform of the U. S. Coast Guard. But he reacted quickly all the same. "Coast Guard?" he queried. "Yes sir," the other man answered and then persisted: "Who are you?"

"We're fishermen from Southampton and ran ashore here."

The young Coast guardsman, who was a little tubby and looked somewhat out of condition, accepted the explanation: "What do you intend to do about it?" Dasch shrugged: "Stay here until sunrise, and then we'll be all right." The guardsman, who was named John Cullen, told the German that if he liked he and his men could spend the remaining four hours of darkness in the local Coast Guard station, less than half a mile away. They could get a cup of coffee there and warm up till dawn.

Dasch was still pondering whether he should or should not, when Burger[41] appeared out of the grey gloom. He was still stripped to his trunks. Over his shoulder he had one of their kitbags. If that was not bad enough, he called out — to Dasch's horror — *in German*!

"Shut up, you damn fool!" he cried back violently in English. "Go back to the boys!"

---

[41] Interestingly enough, Burger had studied under Haushofer, who had taken a "fatherly interest in me," and he had even completed a study on Czechoslovakia for his mentor.

Burger fled. Now young Cullen showed his nervousness. The foreign language, which he could not identify, and the reference to the "boys" hidden in the fog worried him. Dasch did not give him an opportunity to recover: "How old are you?" he demanded.

"Twenty-one," the Coast guardsman replied.

"Do you have a father?... Do you have a mother?" Dasch rapped home the questions.

"Yes," a suddenly frightened Cullen answered.

"Well, I wouldn't want to kill you." He let the words sink in, then continued: "Forget about this and I'll give you some money and you can have a good time."

Dasch held out two fifty-dollar bills. The young guardsman refused. Dasch offered more. "Here, three hundred dollars... take it."

To the German's relief, the young man accepted the money. Swiftly he tucked the bills away in his jacket pocket and attempted to leave, but Dasch, who now knew he was winning, grabbed him by the arm. "Wait a minute," he ordered. He took off his hat. "Take a good look at me." Cullen turned his flashlight on the German. A pale hard face appeared in the circle of yellow light. For a moment Dasch did not speak. He let the American take in the hard look in his eyes: eyes which would kill if necessary. "*Look at my eyes,*" he commanded, gripping the Coast guardsman's upper arm and pressing his fingers deep into the flesh. He repeated the order three times, while the young man stared at him fearfully.

Finally Dasch replaced his hat. "You'll be meeting me in East Hampton sometime. Do you know me?"

"No, sir," the other man sputtered. "I... I... never saw you before in my life."

"My name is George John Davis," Dasch said. "What's yours?"

"Frank Collins," Cullen lied. Then backing away slowly from this strange and frightening visitor, which as a "beach pounder" (as the local Coast guardsmen called themselves) he had never expected to encounter, he fled.

Dasch chuckled and called for the others to come out of their hiding places. Swiftly he told them what had happened and without bothering to answer their scared questions, ordered them to get off the beach at once. *Operation Pastorius*[42] was underway; and Dasch, always a man with an eye for a "quick buck," had plans of his own...

"Operation Pastorius," named after Franz Daniel Pastorius, who led the first group of thirteen immigrant German Mennonite and Quaker families to settle in Germantown (now part of Philadelphia) in 1683, was the major Canaris attempt to take the war to the United States exactly six months and six days after Germany had declared war on her.

Planned by Captain Wilhelm Alrichs, better known to the FBI and the G2 branch of the US Army as "Dr. Astor," the aim was to make Hitler aware that the Abwehr was even capable of taking the war to that remote continent some 3,000 miles away, by landing eight agents in two different spots on the long American east coast. These men, all German-Americans, had spent long years in their adopted country before returning to the Fatherland for a variety of reasons. They were to carry out sabotage against plants in Alcoa, Tennessee, East St. Louis, Illinois, and Philadelphia, as well as the river locks on the Ohio from Pittsburgh to Louisville and on the Pennsylvania railroad at Newark and Altoona, plus

---

[42] Four days later another four Germans were landed on the Florida coast within the framework of the same operation.

137

other targets in New York considered important by the Abwehr.

As J. Edgar Hoover[43], said angrily, when he announced the arrest of the saboteurs to the public in June, 1942: "They would have stilled the machines and endangered the lives of thousands of defense workers... they came to maim and kill."

But both Canaris and Ahlrichs had not reckoned with the venality of George Dasch, for the leader of the New York group had already decided in Lorient (if we are to believe his own statements to the FBI) that he was going to betray the ambitious Abwehr project; and ex-storm trooper Peter Burger was going to help him.

While Coast Guardsman 2/C John C. Cullen's friends in the local station were busy answering question after question posed by Coast Guard Intelligence after their discovery of the cases on the beach. Dasch finally decided to move. Telling his accomplice to stay in their hotel — the Governor Clinton in New York City — he asked the manager to make reservations for him in Washington and went to his room to pack. Carefully, behind the locked door, he took the pile of $50 bills from the still damp canvas bag and placed them in three envelopes he had obtained from the manager. Carefully he wrote a note: "Content $82,350. Money from German Government for their purpose to be used to fight against them

---

[43] Following the war Capt. Ahlrichs passed into the employ of General Gehlen who, after surrendering to the Americans, went to the States to discuss the possibility of working for the Americans in July-August 1945-46. During that period he made his arrangements to become America's "eyes and ears" in Central Europe with, among others, J. Edgar Hoover. Thus Ahlrichs, who was finally captured by the Poles on a sabotage mission in the early fifties, passed indirectly under Hoover's control. For further details see the author's: *Gehlen: Germany's Master Spy* (Ballantine), 1972.

Nazis. George J. Dasch alias George J. Davis alias Franz Pastorius."

That done he wrote another note to Burger: "Dear Pete: Sorry for not have been able to see you before I left. I came to the realization to go to Washington and finish that which have started so far. I'm leaving you, believing that you take good care of yourself and also of the other boys. You may rest assured that I shall try to straighten everything out to the very best possibility. My bag and clothes I'll put into your room. Your hotel bill is paid by me including this day. If anything extra ordinary should happen, I'll get in touch with you directly. Until later I'm your sincere friend George."

Placing the note (which was a direct translation from the German) in a prominent position, he left, his mind full of what he would do with his share of the money "to be used to fight against them Nazis." (Then he was confident the FBI would allow him to keep a large portion of it as a reward for having revealed the plot.) He had been in the United States exactly six days. Now he was on his way to Washington. Operation Pastorius was over before it had started.

The Germans picked up the American newscasters, revealing the failure of the operation (which J. Edgar Hoover made the most of in his inimitable way) on the night of June 28. The result was a wild uproar. General Lahousen, head of Canaris's Group II, recalled after the war: "It was unparalleled confusion. In Berlin everyone started telephoning everyone else. The Foreign Office called the SD. The SD called the Navy, whether they had been concerned in an operation off Long Island. Ribbentrop protested to Dönitz. Keitel joined in and finally, on the following day, Hitler himself."

On the afternoon of June 29, Admiral Canaris was ordered to report to the leader's HQ in East Prussia *immediately*,

Canaris set off at once with Lahousen. Both were nervous and excited, but attempted to justify the unfortunate operation by telling each other that it had been approved by the Party — and after all, Hitler had ordered that the war be carried to America itself.

At precisely 1600 hours on June 30, Hitler emerged from a conference, together with Ribbentrop and General Jodl. Canaris approached him bravely, although he saw to his alarm that the Führer's face had gone white with rage when the leader recognized him.

"*I demand an explanation from you!*" he bellowed even before Canaris could speak. "Why do I have a secret service when they make such completely unqualified mistakes!" He gave Canaris, who was standing stiffly at attention, no time to answer. "A year ago we had the same mess. Will you please explain how this is possible?"

He stared at the white-faced Canaris challengingly, while behind him Ribbentrop, trying to hide his pleasure at the Admiral's discomfiture, peered over Hitler's shoulder.

Canaris sank his head as he always did when Hitler indulged in one of his boundless rages but said nothing; he knew from experience that this was the best method to deal with Hitler.

Froth gathering at the comer of his mouth and flecking his mustache, Hitler ranted on until he ran out of breath. Canaris seized his opportunity. "*Mein Führer*," he said calmly, "every participant in the operation was a party member. All of them were recommended to me by the Party's Overseas Organization as loyal party men. The organizer of the operation possesses the Blood Order."[44]

---

[44] Given only to the Old Guard who had sacrificed their blood or had

Hitler stared at him with those "hypnotic" eyes of his, which Canaris avoided even though he personally felt they had no such effect whatsoever. For a moment, the man who had been known to carry on a four-hour monologue at the drop of a hat, was at a loss for words. Finally he said: "So, and what's going to happen to the poor chaps who volunteered in good faith for this mission? They'll hang them or shoot them." Suddenly, his temper started to get the better of him again. "If that's the kind of work you do, then you should use criminals or Jews in the future!" Then without further comment, he turned and strode away briskly, followed by Jodl and a triumphant Ribbentrop, who hated Canaris. The Admiral was left standing there, white and shaken.

He stared at the departing group of high functionaries for a long time before turning speechlessly and going back to his car. He did not comment to Lahousen, but the latter knew what was going through his chief's head. The "old man" knew he had to pull something out of the hat quickly, or he was finished, and that smart-aleck Schellenberg would take over the whole of German Intelligence. *Canaris needed a coup — and soon!*

In July 1942, Canaris's chief of counterintelligence in France, Lieutenant Colonel Oscar Reile made a start. That spring he had already achieved considerable success in rounding up a major, perhaps *the* major Allied spy ring in France. This was *L'Interallié*, run by an ex-Polish Air Force Captain Garby-Czerniawski, alias Borni, alias Armand. The handsome, dark-haired, intelligent Pole had been hauled off to jail, together with sixty-seven members of his group, plus his mistress and co-spy Mathilde Carré, soon to achieve notoriety under the nickname *La Chatte* — the cat.[45] La Chatte, a small, dark-eyed

---

been imprisoned for their Nazi beliefs prior to 1933.

[45] She gained her name one day when she walked into the Pole's

woman, who wore her hair in long bangs trimmed straight across a beautiful forehead, had been working in Algeria at the start of the war while her husband served there as a French officer. During the subsequent fighting, her husband had disappeared, but that did not worry La Chatte too much. She found solace elsewhere — until she met Armand. Thereafter she became her lover's most aggressive agent, even smuggling herself out of France to meet representatives of the SIS in London. But now she was afraid. What was going to happen to her?

She need not have feared. A German sergeant made an appearance in her cell. He was tall and dark with a firm, determined chin. He was in civilian clothes, which were obviously of German origin, although he wore a French-type beret on his head.

The German — later she found out his name was Hugo Bleicher and he was an NCO in German Field Security — did not waste time. He escorted La Chatte to a large limousine, ordered her to get in the back and pull the curtains, and drove off swiftly.

Colonel Reile had planned the "operation" well. He knew La Chatte's interest in handsome men — and naturally her attraction, in turn, for such individuals. When the Frenchwoman was finally ushered out of the car by the so attentive German sergeant, she found herself in the luxurious villa which had once belonged to the well-known French actor, Henry Baur.

---

office so softly that he said: "You know, Lilly, you walk like a cat, so softly." "And I can scratch as well, if I wish," she replied. "You know I shall call you *ma petite chatte* — my little cat.... It's a good code name too. We shall use it for our radio signals — THE CAT REPORTS."

What happened then was revealed eight years later at her trial in France on the charge of treason. The President of the Court, a M. Drapier, asked her "to tell us exactly what happened."

La Chatte, pale and thin from her years in the British jail, had not lost her courage: "I've already told you exactly," she snapped, "but I'll tell you once again."

So she went through the details once more, but M. Drapier did not leave her in peace: "Good, so you were Bleicher's prisoner. You became his mistress the first night."

La Chatte leaned far across the rail of the pen and looked at the stern-faced judge with pleading in her dark eyes: "Can't you place yourself in my position, *M. le Président?*" she said.

The judge's face did not change: "Answer my question," he rapped sternly. "Did you become his mistress that night?"

"Must I really say what happened?"

"Yes, why did you become his mistress?"

La Chatte gave in. "Bleicher said to me," she explained slowly, "that if I were sensible, then I would be freed that same night." She hesitated and then shrugged in that typically Gallic fashion of hers: "So I became sensible."

But M. Drapier would not let her go: "Wasn't it repulsive for you, the widow of a French officer, to go to bed with a German sergeant?"

She reacted quickly to his suggestion: "Naturally, *M. Président,* it was physically repulsive for me."

Drapier, perhaps motivated by other interests than just legal ones, persisted: "And what else happened that night?"

Silence.

He grew angry. Leaning across his desk, he said: "I want to know what happened!"

Again silence, but there was no need to answer that question.

Early next morning La Chatte and the German Sergeant had left the villa arm in arm and begun to round up the remaining agents of the "Armand" group — one hundred in all! La Chatte had saved her life at the price of a few hours of intensive love-making with Hugo Bleicher and the lives of a hundred comrades!

But that was revealed only in 1949. In 1942, Colonel Reile had used her to break the Interallie and other related networks and then sent her off to England to act as a double agent.[46]

Now he was planning another coup.

In March, 1942, he went to visit the thin-faced Pole in his cell at the Fresnes Prison. As Colonel Reile recalls the conversation today: "I tried to cheer him up, praising the excellent job of work he had done for his Fatherland. Czerniawski then asked about his fellow prisoners. This appeared to me to be an excellent opportunity to discuss the possibility of working for the German Abwehr with him.

"Finally Czemiawski agreed to work for us on condition that his sixty-five fellow prisoners who were in jail with him at Fresnes should not be put on trial. The tall, skinny, bespectacled German with the cleft chin remembers: "It was a strange scene: the prisoner making conditions with the representative of the secret service which had captured him. But I agreed to his conditions and began immediately to discuss the necessary preparations for his flight — to England!"

Colonel Reile had a grandiose plan for the Pole who was now going to become a double agent; and again the French-

[46] She was caught immediately and sent off to a prison specially reserved for people like herself where she spent the rest of the war.

speaking Sergeant Hugo Bleicher, who had "turned" La Chatte so easily in bed, would play an important role.

But let Hugo Bleicher tell the story himself: "At the beginning of July, 1942, I received a strange order. I was told to fetch Armand from his cell at Fresnes and take him to Paris where supposedly he was to be questioned. But on the trip to Paris he was to be allowed to escape — and the escape had to look genuine.

"On July 14, 1942, the French Bastille Day, I drove out to Fresnes, about twenty kilometers from Paris, and fetched Armand. Up to now I had only had orders to catch spies. Now I had the order to let the chief of a big spy organization escape."

But the tall smart sergeant, with the dark penetrating eyes did as he was commanded.

"At top speed we drove from Fresnes to Paris. I drove the car myself. Half way to Paris on the Boulevard Raspail near the Hotel Lutetia, the 'accident' happened. I took a sharp curve to be faced with a truck that was placed right across the road. I braked and jumped out of the car cursing at the other driver. Armand took advantage of the confusion. Although his hands were apparently handcuffed behind his back, he jumped out and took off at top speed. In order to make his flight look more genuine, I fired a couple of shots from my pistol and took up the chase with a few soldiers and my agents. But already it was too late. Armand had vanished. The 'escape' had succeeded."

That was the last the Abwehr heard of Armand until finally in February, 1943, German listening posts in France picked up his first faint message (he had been instructed to build his own radio from parts commonly available in radio and junk shops in London). Delightedly Reile reported his success immediately to his much admired superior, Canaris. Armand was going to be one of his key men. Not only was he to build up a fifth column of disgruntled Polish civilians and military in Britain who did not like the pro-Soviet policy of Churchill and Roosevelt, but he was also to attempt to worm his way into one of the high-level staffs preparing for the Second Front. And in early 1944, the Polish double agent gleefully reported that he had done just that: he had been appointed to the Polish liaison team attached to the key U.S. D-Day force — Omar Nelson Bradley's First Army.

In that year Canaris could confidently assure Colonel Roenne in charge of Wehrmacht combat intelligence in France that he had men like the Pole everywhere in England and that it "is undoubtedly the most remarkable feat in the history of espionage," making it possible for him to order them into action once the danger of an Anglo-American invasion became acute. It was "something to be proud, very proud of."

By that time Armand, or BRUTUS *as he was known now in London, had been working for Major Masterman's Twenty Committee for nearly two years ...*

9 — NORTH POLE CALLING LONDON!

On the night of March 9/10, 1943, ex-sailor Pieter Dourlein of the Dutch Royal Navy was prepared to make his first operational jump, together with two comrades, over his homeland, which he had not seen for more than two years. The heavy-jawed sailor was not unduly nervous, though he did notice that his hands were sweating and he had to keep drying the palms on his grey coveralls every few minutes. But he had been well trained by the SOE and their Dutch Allies in Ringway and Scotland, and he knew that somewhere down below in the darkness comrades were waiting for him to spirit them away before the Moppen and their bloodthirsty search dogs got onto them. PLAN HOLLAND, the SOE plan to build up a Dutch Underground Army and supply it with leaders, radio operators, and arms, had been running for nearly two years, and over thirty-odd agents from England had landed safely before him during that time.

The four-engine British Halifax bomber was now crossing the Dutch coast. It was 0.15 hours and the well-trained pilot had taken the big plane down to avoid the German radar screen. To the rear the sergeant-gunner grinned, raised his thumb at them and released the chattering pigeons which were a cover for the plane's real mission this night. Somewhere in the gloom below was the little coastal town of Harderwijk. A little while later the plane was over the town of Apeldoorn.

It flew in a great circle now and came down even lower. As the bomber eased to the south, the young ex-sailor caught a glimpse of a red beacon. It was their signal. They were right over their drop zone. The jumpmaster called them together. The door was opened. An icy wind whipped against their clothes. But there was no turning back. One-two-three. They all went through the door in so many seconds, the wind clutching them with greedy fingers.

For a novice Dourlein did not make a bad landing — in the upper branches of a leafless winter tree. But apart from a few scratches, he wasn't hurt. Hastily he undid the parachute and slipped down the trunk. Pulling out his pistol and clicking off the safety catch, he dived into the nearest group of bushes to take stock of his position.

As the drone of the plane's engines disappeared and he told himself the crew were well on their way to their special breakfast of bacon and real eggs, instead of the usual rubbery, tasteless, powdered variety, he realized he had landed about one kilometer south of the beacon. As yet there was no one in sight. Neither Dutch nor German.

Then abruptly there was a sound! That of heavy boots walking cautiously through the damp grass. German? He clutched the heavy British revolver more tightly in his big hand. The Germans wouldn't take him alive, he told himself. He started to take aim at the first shadowy figure appearing out of the gloom when he heard someone call his code name softly "Paul... Paul..." He relaxed as abruptly as he had tensed. It was the welcoming committee.

Backs were slapped. Hands were shaken. Whisky was passed back and forth. The conversation was fast and hectic, everyone trying to talk at once, asking questions, answering them. "It was nearly four o'clock in the morning," Dourlein remembered after the war, "before the signal to move off was given. We were divided into small groups, each of us accompanied by two members of the welcoming committee. Then we set off, with about 100 meters between each group. Suddenly after about five minutes my two companions threw themselves on me. They pulled my hands behind my back and I heard the click of handcuffs. The attack was so sudden that I had no opportunity to offer resistance. I thought they'd gone crazy."

"Stop the fooling!" Dourlein snapped angrily.

The only answer he received was the sudden pain as one of his companions thrust a revolver into the small of his back — *hard*.

A whistle blew. Men appeared from the bushes all around him. A tall man stepped over to the completely bewildered Dutch agent. Speaking the agent's language perfectly, he snapped: "You're a prisoner of the German counterespionage." The tall man chuckled for some reason known only to himself. It was not a very pleasant sound. "We have your whole organization in our power. The war is over for you." He paused and let his sentence sink in. "If you do what we want, everything will be all right and you'll stay alive." Then he vanished as suddenly as he had appeared. *Operation North Pole* had claimed yet another victim.

The Abwehr's most successful operation of the war in Holland had started in November, 1941, when Major Giskes (head of the Abwehr in Holland) had been introduced to Dutchman Gregg Ridderhof by his interpreter-sergeant Willy Rupp.

Ridderhof, a large, bloated, professional criminal who spoke an odd mixture of Dutch, English, and Spanish when he was drunk — which was often — volunteered to work for the Abwehr, if they would pay him and get the German currency authorities who held him temporarily under arrest off his back. Giskes, a regular, somewhat snobbish officer, hesitated, but when the fat Dutchman, who was lame in his left leg, said he had contacts to the British Secret Service through their Dutch agents, he agreed. Soon Ridderhof was sending him valuable information.

Later in that same month Ridderhof reported that the British had landed two agents, Hubertus Lauwers and Thijs Taconis, in East Holland to commence building up Plan Holland. Giskes, the middle-aged officer with the rosy cheeks, sparkling blue eyes, and perennially sardonic smile on his thin, rather cruel lips, studied the report very carefully and then wrote in the margin somewhat angrily: "GEHEN SIE ZUM NORDPOL MIT IHREN GESCHICHTEN (Go to the North Pole with your stories)! There is no radio communication between Holland and England. F-2087[47] has three days to clear up the matter!"

Ridderhof was deeply hurt by Giskes's doubts. He set to work "to clear the matter up." In January he explained to the German how the British were using the London-based Free Dutch Radio — Radio Orange — to announce the drop zones and dates of their agents in Holland. One month later on February 27th, the Germans picked up such a message and deciphered it.

Two days later an RAF bomber dropped containers filled with explosives and weapons over the small town of Hooghalen. Giskes did not interfere. He now trusted Ridderhof, who was an intimate of the reception committee which was headed by a tall man named Long Thijs, in reality no other than Taconis of the Dutch SOE. A plan was beginning to form slowly in his mind. While it matured, he contented himself with having Long Thijs watched and

---

[47] Ridderhof's agent's number, and it was this angry remark by Giskes to the traitor which gave the operation its unofficial name, Operation North Pole.

allowing Ridderhof to keep him informed of the Underground's activities.

On the morning of March 6, 1942, he was ready. But as he knew of Canaris's position in relation to Heydrich's Main Security Office, he thought it better to discuss his daring operation with the members of the Gestapo and SD in Holland. There he met first with Obersturmbannführer Wolf and SD man Schreider who was called in later.

Years later Giskes put down his first impressions of the small, almost bald, thirty-nine-year-old policeman with whom he was going to work for the next two years. "He extended a flabby, well-manicured little hand. With a series of small bows, he preceded me... and I had leisure to observe him more closely. Slightly protruding rat-like eyes gave a lift to a pasty face, and the nose betrayed the delights of the bottle. The whole well-fed man exuded joviality, his slightly provincial accents emphasizing the note of southern warmth, as though he was immensely pleased to have found in me an entirely unexpected and beloved old friend. He radiated the well-known benevolence of certain criminal investigators, before which Edgar Wallace murderers are supposed to have dissolved in tears... I was quite sure that he had had my background investigated and that he was fully conversant with my private and political pedigree."

Obtaining the help of the police official, he convinced him that they should arrest Lauwers and Long Thijs, but that they should not be thrown in some Gestapo jail to languish until they were finally "liquidated" in some cold grey dawn. Instead the two SOE men should be "convinced" one way or another to work for the Germans. They would broadcast false information to the British and, at the same time, ensure that they would keep sending planeloads of weapons, sabotage equipment, and money to the "Underground," i.e., Giskes and the pasty-faced SD man Schreider. *Das Englandspiel*[48] was soon to begin.

It was astonishingly successful. By the summer of 1942, the Germans had thirty clandestine drop zones ready for the British planes — they even sent their own Luftwaffe up looking for the most suitable places for the RAF! Agent after agent came floating down — right into the Germans' arms. At first Giskes received each one of them personally, allowing them to drink from the special flasks which they all carried before whisking them off[49] to a converted seminary at Haaren where they were imprisoned; but in the end there were so many drops that it became boring and he left the job of "welcoming" them to his subordinates.

Container after container followed, filled with the latest British equipment necessary for sabotage — plastic explosive, *silenced* Sten machine pistols, special time-pencils, etc., etc. After the war Schreider stated that the Germans received 570 containers and 150 parcels with 15,200 kilograms of explosives, 3,000 Sten guns, 5,000 small arms, 300 Bren guns, 2,000 hand grenades, 500,000 rounds of ammunition, everything from rubber boots to cans of biscuits, plus fifty thousand pounds in Dutch currency and several thousand more in dollars and assorted currencies. In addition some twelve four-engine British and U. S. bombers were shot down.

---

[48] The England game.
[49] In the '60s, he still had these macabre souvenirs in his home in Munich, each one signifying a human life and that moment of utter fear and dejection when the newly trapped agent knew he was lost for ever. When the author visited him (1973), the friendly, highly intelligent counterintelligence man had removed them.

The operation which Giskes had once cursed as belonging with the rest of Ridderhof's tall tales at the North Pole was an astonishing unqualified victory for the German Abwehr and its chief, Admiral Canaris.

Even Schellenberg was forced to send his own men to study it. One of them was his newest recruit, a gigantic, scar-faced ex-Captain of the premier SS Division "Adolf Hitler's Bodyguard" (*Die Leibstandarte*). He had been invalided home from Russia after being wounded and affected with a stomach complaint. His name — Otto Skorzeny.

The six-foot-five-inch Viennese, whose face was marked with the *Schmisse* of his student dueling days, had recently taken over Schellenberg's own sabotage troop, the "Hunting Commandos." It was their job to carry out sabotage and commando operations behind the enemy lines. But although the thirty-five-year-old ex-engineer was a born fighter, he knew little of clandestine operations, and Schellenberg was forced to send him to Holland to study Giskes's *Englandspiel*.

Skorzeny was astounded and pleased by what he found in Holland. "I followed the operation with the greatest of interest."[50] He was so impressed by the Giskes operation that he "ordered" a special, silenced, one-shot British revolver via an agent whose cover name was TREASURE.[51] Fourteen days

---

[50] To the author, 1970.

[51] So far it has not been explained how TREASURE got into this operation; TREASURE was an operative of the Twenty Committee, a twenty-six-year-old Frenchwoman of Russian descent, Lily Sergueiev, who had been in Britain for about a year. Did this mean that MI5 or M16 already knew of the Giskes operation and were using it for their own purposes? Were they deliberately sacrificing Dutch agents for some devious plan of their own? The Dutch always maintained this was the case after the war and even set up a special governmental committee to investigate Operation North Pole. And indeed Lauwers did warn the British right from the start by means of

153

later he received it — courtesy of the RAF. It was a clumsy weapon, but reliable. Skorzeny, never one to put off till tomorrow what he could do today, opened his window and took aim at a duck sitting on the Graacht. He pulled the trigger. There was a slight plop. The duck keeled over. None of the civilians promenading along the waterway took the slightest bit of notice. They had heard nothing.

A few days later Skorzeny left Holland for Berlin where he had his one and only interview with Admiral Canaris, in which he tried to get the Admiral to release to him eleven men of his own special sabotage-commando organization, *das Regiment Brandenburg*. But Canaris was not prepared to surrender his valuable, highly trained specialists to this young upstart. In the end, Skorzeny gave in, telling his adjutant, Captain Radl, that "Admiral Canaris is the most difficult person I've ever met. You just can't get to him. I simply could not make any judgment about him... I'm prepared to let my enemy or a stranger get away with such an attitude, *but not a German!*"

Soon Otto Skorzeny's name would be known throughout the world and Admiral Canaris would never again be able to treat him in such a condescending manner. But that was still in the future. In mid-1943, Admiral Canaris was still riding the crest of the new wave of Abwehr achievements in Holland and France, while his young rival, SS General Schellenberg, was still failing to achieve success in virtually every major operation that his own chief Heinrich Himmler assigned to him.

But slowly Giskes's luck was running out, and the stage was being prepared for Schellenberg's greatest coup.

Young ex-sailor Dourlein had been in prison in the Haaren Seminary for nearly six months now. In spite of what the

---

a prearranged signal. Why didn't they respond?

Germans had told him, he did not believe that they would finally be treated as prisoners-of-war. When the enemy was finished with them, they would be dealt with as agents. That meant the firing squad and a sudden end one cold morning before dawn. And Pieter Dourlein felt he was too young and had too much living in front of him yet to die at this moment. He decided to escape. But how?

The Seminary, he told himself with a slight smile of amusement in spite of his unenviable position, was more like a prison than a religious institution. It was surrounded by high walls, and there were completely open spaces on three sides. In prewar days they had obviously meant to keep their budding priests under strict control. As a result it had not been difficult for the Germans to turn the place into a regular jail. But still the inventive young Dutchman did not despair.

In June, he was transferred to another cell, from which he took up contact with his neighboring prisoner by means of tapping out questions in Morse code on the heating pipe which ran through his and the adjoining cell. The latter — Johan Ubbink — tapped them on to the next cell and so on. Time was passing; as for Pieter, "every morning when I awoke and heard the knocking on the cell door, I asked myself, is this the firing squad?" He knew he must get out soon. Confident now that he could at least trust the men in his block, he asked if any one wanted to escape with him. The only positive answer came from his neighbor Johan.

Together the two men started to plan. As Pieter saw it, the only way to escape was through the barred window over the cell door. But how was he to get through the barred window and into the corridor? "I recalled," he explained much later, "that our instructors in England had said that in many prisons it was possible to squeeze through the bars ... so I took a thread from my mattress and measured the distance between them. Then I pulled my bed from the wall, making the distance from the wall to the bed exactly that between the bars and started to practice. It wasn't easy, but if I took my outer clothing off, I could make it."

That decided, Pieter and his friend Johan commenced fashioning a rope to take them down the 12-meter wall once they were out of the cell. For this purpose they used the underside of their mattresses, which they cut into strips with the razor blade they were loaned twice a week for shaving. "Ubbink was completely unknown to me. I only knew him from his voice... But we decided that the best time to escape was when supper was being distributed. At that time the men dishing out the food made a lot of noise with their little carts. We also decided to select the moment when they were at the other end of the horseshoe-shaped corridor. We knew," he stated later, "that it was regulations to place one's clothes on a chair outside the cell at night so that they could not be used in an escape. We hoped, therefore, that our comrades would help us by placing their clothes in such a way that the fact ours were not there would not be noticed."

In the end the two escapees decided that they would attempt to get out on the night of Sunday, August 29, 1943 — then at the weekend there were not so many guards on duty.

On Sunday, Pieter woke up early. He spent the day in nervous tense expectancy. His two cellmates eyed him every now and again with tears threatening to well up and overcome them. One of them, Van der Boor, said tearfully: "For God's sake, Pieter, don't go. They'll only shoot you!"

The young ex-sailor could say nothing, save grip his comrade's hand hard and mutter unintelligible sounds. He felt he was leaving them for good.

Evening came. The food tray was thrust in through the door. The door was closed again. As soon as the waiter had gone, the young Dutchman took off his clothes swiftly. He knocked on the wall. That was the signal for Johan.

"I sprang on the bed," he recalled later, "pulled the nail out which held up the window and looked down the corridor. Everything clear! A bit further on I saw a blond head looking out too. My future companion ... A few moments later we were both in the corridor. Our pals reached us our clothes and the rope. Together we ran into an empty cell which we knew was never locked. We looked at each other for the first time and slapped each other on the back."

But there was no time for congratulations. Hastily with nervous fingers they slipped into their clothes. Tensely they listened as the guards passed, then they crept in their stocking feet to the toilet.

It was empty!

Swiftly they slipped inside and locked the door. Thus cramped together they waited for six long hours till they thought they would be safe and able to chance getting through the window of the smelly latrine. Twice in those long leaden hours, someone rattled the door, but each time one of them cried angrily, as planned, "*Besetzt, Mensch*! (occupied, man)," and the guard went away.

Finally they made the attempt. They waited till the icy-cold beam of the searchlight had swept by, then squeezed through the barred toilet window. The ground was twelve meters below. Swiftly they played out their rope. Pieter went down first. Johan followed and landed heavily next to him. They had done it with one second to spare. The beam swept back over them one instant later.

Now they were out of the prison. But there were still obstacles. "Now," Pieter recollected, "we had to get over the barbed wire fences some fifty meters away. We approached it carefully up to some five yards when suddenly we heard steps — the sound of heavily nailed boots. A guard! But the man did not notice us and carried on."

Wiping the sweat off their brows in spite of the coolness of the summer night, the two young Dutchmen crawled closer to the last big obstacle. Then pulling themselves upright, they took a deep breath. Johan took off first. He cleared it without a couple of inches to spare and fell heavily on the other side. Pieter prayed that he would not get caught up in the ugly barbed metal and launched himself forward. He did it! He was over and no one had heard him! "*We were free!* Beside ourselves with joy, we fell into each other's arms. But we knew that the end was still not in sight."

They were right. They had a long odyssey before them through the occupied countries with the Gestapo, roused to a frenzy by the escape and alarmed by the knowledge that the two escapees might betray the great plan, at their heels. Giskes recalled: "Everybody at the Abwehr and Gestapo offices was in great agitation. It was clear to me that the bottom had been knocked out of the whole *Englandspiel.*"

But Schreider wouldn't give up. He sent a fake message to England stating "Dourlein (Code David) and Ubbink (Uldenhout) recently captured by Gestapo stop turned round and working for Germans stop they are sent to England pretending to have escaped from Haaren stop caution Germans trying to cause confusion end."

But in the end they got through and after some initial hesitancy and doubt, their story was finally believed. Giskes knew the game was up, but his sardonic humor did not desert him. Together with the SD men he composed one last message for London which read:

"To Messrs Blunt, Bingham, and Successors, Ltd. stop you are trying to make business in the Netherlands without our assistance stop we think this rather unfair in view of our long and successful cooperation as your sole agent stop but never mind whenever you will come to pay a visit to the Continent you may be assured that you will be received with same care and result as all those you sent us before stop so long...."

Soon the successors of Messrs. Blunt, Bingham, Ltd. would be coming; at first deviously and secretly slinking in like grey silent wolves from the forests, later boldly and without fear. But for the time the German Intelligence Services still had a few cards to play and a couple of spectacular games to win. But time was running out swiftly...

1943: THE BIGGEST COUP OF ALL

Your visitation shall receive such thanks
As fits a king's remembrance,

Shakespeare

10 — THE FALL OF AN OLD DICTATOR

It was hot, almost unbearably hot.

In the white glare of the July sun, the streets of Rome were deserted. The citizens had fled the streets and taken refuge behind shaded windows and closed doors. Even the blind lottery ticket sellers and the blue-grey uniformed ex-soldiers, who displayed their stumps with an eloquent plea for alms in then-dark, limpid, Italian eyes, had gone. The capital on the oven-hot Sunday afternoon was abandoned to the lean, hungry dogs, who lay in the gutters, thin-ribbed and panting. After three years of war, even they seemed to sense that there was no use hunting for scraps. Rome was on the verge of starvation. So they lay there, mouths open, tongues hanging out, without enough strength to shake off the myriad humming blue flies.

As undersized, dark-eyed Ercole Boratto steered the black, shining Asturia through the deserted streets, he felt a sense of foreboding. There was not a policeman in sight; and even when the big official car swept smoothly by a barracks, the scruffy under-aged sentry did not present arms when he saw who the passenger was. Instead he yawned and looked the other way. Ercole, who had been driving the "chief" for nearly twenty years now, shuddered in spite of the overwhelming heat. There was something wrong. He felt it in his very bones. Something was going to happen.

But his passenger, clad in a sober blue serge suit, a high-crowned bowler on his completely bald head and pearl-grey gloves clutched in his big hairy hand, did not notice his chauffeur's disquiet. For the first time in months he felt at ease and comfort. Even his long-standing stomach complaint seemed to have vanished. Indeed he felt he might even visit his mistress when he had completed his visit to the King. A few years before he had confided to Ercole after one of his "short stays" with a current mistress (at that time he had at least ten): "A man should have a little engine to wind up his back. That's the only way a man could satisfy them all." Today, he felt really physically fit; he wouldn't need the engine for his "Claretta." "It" would go without that aid.

Naturally there had been that nasty business with the Grand Council. But as he told himself in the hot airless car, he would soon deal with those traitors. As soon as he obtained permission from the King he would throw the whole rotten bunch of them into jail. That morning he had told one of his generals: "Those faint-hearts don't realize that if the man who raised them up (here he had poked himself significantly in his broad chest) wasn't here, they'd be in the gutter with the mob!"

Admittedly, one hour before while he had been eating a hurried bowl of soup at home, his fat motherly wife, Rachele, had been astounded when he told her that he was going to see the King. "You must not go!" she had insisted in that hysterical peasant way of hers. "The King is the King. If it suits him, he'll throw you overboard."

A broad smile had crossed his dark face. He had tilted up that massive jaw which was known to cinema newsreel audiences throughout the world, hated by millions, loved or admired by millions more. "The King is my best friend," he lectured her, lowering his spoon, "perhaps the only friend I have at the moment."

His answer had appeared to appease her, yet when a little later she had told him that the King's secretary had called three times to tell her that he must wear civilian clothes and *not* a uniform, he had felt a little uneasy. The request — made three times — was rather strange. Then he had shrugged it off.

Now on this afternoon of Sunday, July 25, 1943, the broad-chested, big-jawed dictator felt supremely confident. Benito Mussolini, the man who had founded Fascism and shaped it in his own image for the last twenty years, was sure that he could handle the King and the new situation which had risen so suddenly.

As Ercole Boratto reached the gatehouse which barred the way to the Villa Savoia, the King's residence in the outskirts of Rome, he gave the usual signal. Two sharp blasts on the horn. Behind him the two cars containing Mussolini's bodyguard braked hard and then pulled over to the side of the road to take advantage of the shade offered by the carefully tended umbrella pines. Etiquette forbade them to enter the Villa's ground anyway. As the gate swung open noiselessly to admit the Asturia, the sweating gunmen tugged at their tight wet collars and breathed out a sigh of relief. Now they could relax for an hour or so. The King's people would be responsible for Mussolini's safety till he left the Villa again.

Carefully limiting his speed to the prescribed twenty kilometers an hour, keeping an eye open for the King's dogs which sometimes roamed the grounds, the chauffeur drove down the avenue lined with ancient oaks and umbrella pines, licking his dry cracked lips in appreciation for the shade they offered from the white hot glare of the late afternoon sun. He, too, would be glad when they reached their destination and he could relax for the length of the audience. Perhaps one of the royal maids might be persuaded to get him a cool drink.

Admittedly they were snooty, but surely they could not refuse a man a drink on a day like this!

But if the men around Mussolini were considering relaxing at that moment, there were others, not more than five hundred yards away, ready to spring into action — violent, desperate action. They, too, had heard the two short signals on the horn. It was the sound they had been waiting for the last seventy-five minutes.

Under the command of Police Captain Paolo Vigneri, fifty *carabinieri*, the state police, clad today in their grey-green uniforms instead of the gorgeous nineteenth-century ones, complete with sword, they wore in peace time, were hidden from view by a six-foot boxwood hedge.

Three hours before they had left their barracks in Rome, armed to the teeth in expectation of a battle with Anglo-American paratroops, who had reportedly dropped over the capital. Captain Vigneri, a dark, dapper, intelligent-looking man, had also believed that this was to be their mission until he had suddenly been summoned to the office of the new commander-in-chief, General Angelo Cerica.

The high-ranking officer had been pale and tense. Hardly had he extinguished one cigarette, than he lit another with a weak thin hand that trembled ever so slightly. He looked like a man who was being forced to carry a supreme responsibility which was almost unbearable.

The police captain watched the General out of the comer of his eye as he stood there rigidly at attention. He was used to dealing with men at the end of their tether; this man, he knew, was at that stage. It would not take much to break him.

Finally Cerica stubbed out his cigarette violently and leaned across his big desk. His voice almost a whisper, he stared the police officer straight in the eye and gave him his orders: orders of a kind that the stunned captain had never experienced in all his long police career. "Captain," Cerica said, "in a few hours, following the orders of His Majesty Vittorio Emanuele III, you must arrest," he paused momentarily, as if even he were scared to put his next thought into words. Then he pulled himself together. *"You must arrest Mussolini at Villa Ada."*[52]

As the shining black car rolled to a gentle stop, Ercole Boratto noticed with surprise that the diminutive King, his thin face made absurd by a great, sweeping, white, World War I mustache, was waiting for il Duce on the steps leading to the main door. And as if to ensure the superiority of his person vis-à-vis that of Mussolini, clad in his civilian suit, he was wearing the grey-green uniform of a Marshal in the Italian Army, complete with wide red stripe down the pants. Something else struck the chauffeur as strange. The tiny King went down the steps to meet the dictator, a smile on his face, his hand outstretched to greet him. It was something he had never done before since Mussolini had taken over power in 1922.

Boratto shrugged. He pushed home the gear shift. Slowly he drove off in second gear, parking the Asturia near the comer of the steps. Behind him, Mussolini, the King, and two aides disappeared into the villa. Boratto tugged at his collar and tried to make himself comfortable against the hot sticky seat. It was unbearably hot in the car. But he consoled himself with the thought he would soon be home again to a cold shower, a change of clothes, and a long, long ice drink.

---

[52] The king's residence was variously called *"Villa Ada"* or *"Villa Savoia."*

But Ercole Boratto was not fated to go home that particular day. He had just settled down to the paper when there was a tap on the side of the car and a familiar head thrust its way through the open window. It was that of Giuseppe Morazzini, the royal household's chief of police. His face was smiling, but his dark eyes were cold. "Ercole, you're wanted on the telephone... Hurry up!... I'll come with you, I've got a call to make too."

The chauffeur sighed, but got out of the car, feeling his clothes stick to him unpleasantly as he slid from behind the wheel. He stamped his feet to shake the pants free from his damp legs. It was 5:10 P.M. Probably it was Donna Rachele telephoning to the porter's lodge to check when her husband would be free. Time and time again he had been hurried to the lodge just to the left of the Villa's gateway to answer her anxious queries. Breathing heavily in the heat, he followed the official.

In the dark, pleasantly cool audience room, Mussolini was beginning to realize that something was going wrong. Right from the start he had noticed that the little King was nervous and that had heightened his self-confidence. He didn't like the monarch anyway. He found him a nuisance and a political embarrassment. As he had once told his smooth, exceedingly smart son-in-law and foreign minister, Count Ciano, the King was like a "lot of empty train cars which had to be dragged along," but which he would get rid of as soon as was convenient. But now the King seemed to have found his backbone after twenty years of being pushed around by the dictator.

Mussolini had started off by remarking almost jokingly. "You'll have heard, your Majesty, about last night's childish prank...."

The little monarch had cut him off sharply.

"It was not a childish prank," he had snapped, referring to the Grand Council's vote of no-confidence in Mussolini's government which had led to this interview, "*not at all.*" Suddenly he began to pace up and down.

Desperately Mussolini stammered, "Your Majesty, the vote of the Grand Council is of no value whatsoever."

But Vittorio Emmanuele III was not listening. "My dear Duce, things are not working out in Italy anymore. Matters are very serious. Italy is in ruins." He paused momentarily in his pacing and bit his nails nervously. "The Army is completely demoralized. The soldiers have no desire to go on fighting. The Alpine Brigade[53] are singing a song that they will no longer fight for you." Suddenly the little man burst into a snatch of the song, singing in the Piedmontese dialect. It ran: "Down with Mussolini, who murdered the *Alpini!*" Mussolini stared at him open-mouthed. For the first time in his life, the man who lived by the dramatic gesture and the grandiose phrase did not know what to say or do.

Then abruptly the King's twenty years of resentment and anger at this ex-corporal, jailbird, libertine, and son of a peasant who had run his life for so long burst through. "The result of the Grand Council's vote is tremendous!" he said excitedly. "Nineteen votes cast for Grandi's resolution.[54] Don't have any illusions. Don't think that vote doesn't express the

[53] The *Alpini*, one of Italy's elite formations.
[54] Count Grandi, head of the group within the Grand Council who wanted Mussolini to resign.

way the country feels towards you." He gasped for breath. *"Today you are the most hated man in Italy!"*

At that very moment Boratto was experiencing the truth of that statement. Obediently he had followed Morazzini into the telephone box at the porter's lodge. No sooner had he entered when Morazzini and two burly strangers in dark suits, who had suddenly appeared from nowhere, jumped him. Desperately he struggled to escape. To no avail. One of them crooked a thick forearm round his neck. He pulled hard. Boratto thought he was going to choke. He stopped struggling. A rough hand thrust its way into his jacket. It tugged at his pistol. It went and with it the chauffeur's will to resist. There were simply too many of them. But what was it all about?

While his eyes bulged from his head, under the pressure of the burly arm wound around his neck, Morazzini's voice hissed sibilantly in his ear: "Listen carefully."

Boratto nodded his understanding.

"There is no Duce any more. Badoglio[55] is the new head of Government."

Boratto's mind reeled. No more Duce! It ... it could not be possible...

But it was.

Mussolini had just heard the news himself from the little King in stunned silence. "I have come to the conclusion," the monarch lectured him, "that the only person who can control the present situation is Marshal Badoglio. Badoglio is the man of the moment. He will form a government of officers and carry on the war. He enjoys the full confidence of the Army and the Police."

---

[55] Marshal Badoglio of the Italian Army.

"And the Police?" Mussolini echoed dully, staring into space, as if mesmerized.

The little King, savoring his moment of triumph, nodded silently, his hard eyes fixed on the fallen dictator's yellow face.

Now *carabinieri* swung into action. Under the command of dapper Captain Vigneri, three plainclothes policemen, and three noncoms, all skilled in unarmed combat, boarded the ambulance which was going to play such an important role in their coup.

Vigneri tapped hard on the glass partition. The driver put the vehicle into neutral and released the brake. The white-painted ambulance with its twin red cross flags, limp in the hot humid air, began to roll noiselessly down the drive towards the Villa.

There was no sound whatsoever, the carabinieri captain recalled years later. The driver didn't switch on the engine. All that could be heard as they got closer to the royal villa was the faint clatter of china in the kitchens as they cleared away the afternoon tea dishes. Then the ambulance stopped. Not a sound. Bees hummed heavily throughout the white-hot sunlit garden. Vigneri felt his heart beat unpleasantly. Through the glazed window of the ambulance he could see his other men taking up their positions behind the Duce's car. They were armed with machine pistols. Soon he must come out. *Soon!*

It was 5:20 P.M. now. In twenty minutes the King had demolished twenty years of Fascism. But Mussolini, still in a daze, seemed unaware of what had happened. The King steered him to the steps once more. There they shook hands and the former muttered something about the oppressive weather once more just as he had done when he had welcomed Mussolini on arrival. Then he was gone. And the dictator was alone, save for his aide, blinking into the sudden hard white rays of the summer sun. He still was not aware of the danger facing him. As his daughter was to say later, "My father's behavior during those days was completely incomprehensible." In spite of the many warnings he had received these last few days, he had no appreciation of what was going to happen to him. He noticed his car parked farther away on the other side of the drive and not at its usual place near the steps and made a slight gesture of irritation. He did not realize the black official vehicle was giving cover to a group of agents prepared to riddle him with lead if he attempted to get away.

Abruptly a captain of the *carabinieri* appeared from nowhere.

It was Vigneri.

"Duce," he snapped, coming to attention, "by orders of His Majesty we beg you to follow us. We must protect you from possible mob violence."

Mussolini stared at him uncomprehendingly. "There's no need of that," he answered dully after a moment's hesitation. His voice contained neither anger nor surprise, just weariness. "I have my own escort." He brushed the policeman to one side and began to walk down the steps towards the Asturia.

Vigneri doubled forward and stopped in his path. "Duce, I have an order to carry out," he said firmly. Everywhere the hidden soldiers and policemen tensed, their fingers crooked wetly around the triggers of their weapons. Vigneri felt a cold drop of sweat trickle down the small of his back. This is it! What would he do if Mussolini refused? *Would he have to shoot him in cold blood?*

But Mussolini did not refuse. Suddenly his shoulders slumped in a kind of defeat.

The police captain seized his opportunity. "You must come with me," he ordered, in charge of the situation now, and without waiting for Mussolini's answer, he hurried him to the waiting ambulance.

The men hiding within heard their footsteps coming closer, a brisk harsh crush of their boots on the gravel. One of them flung open the metal doors.

Mussolini stopped suddenly so that the captain stumbled into him. The inside of the ambulance stank of disinfectant and the heat waves trembled as the air escaped which had been confined in it. His face blanched. The place was like a furnace.

Vigneri pushed him forward. Suddenly soldiers and policemen appeared from everywhere. They began to press into the ambulance behind the fallen dictator. "But not all these people, too!" Mussolini protested. Vigneri shrugged eloquently, then turning to his men snapped, "Get aboard, boys! And make it fast!"

Watching from a window the little King, who had sworn a few days before, "Never as long as I have breath in my body shall I give an order like that (to arrest Mussolini)," saw how the men hustled him in. The Duce secured his bowler hat absurdly with both hands and then disappeared from sight.

Moments later the steel doors of the ambulance shut hard behind him. Noisily the driver started the engine. The vehicle jerked forward. The noise of the engine grew in volume. Its speed rose. Twenty — thirty — forty kilometers an hour. Well above the maximum allowed in the royal grounds. A minute later it had disappeared from sight behind the ancient oaks.

The King let the curtain fall. It was all over. Benito Mussolini, premier of Italy for the last twenty years, principal ally of the mightiest man in Europe, Adolf Hitler, had been successfully kidnapped. Soon the hunt to find him, which would keep the whole of Europe on tenterhooks for weeks and change the course of World War II, would begin. It would also lead to a great race between the two stars of German Intelligence, SS General Schellenberg and Abwehr Admiral Canaris, to discover the whereabouts of the Duce.

11 — ENTER OTTO SKORZENY

The news of Mussolini's overthrow and kidnapping was received at Hitler's HQ, set in the deep pine forests of East Prussian Rastenburg, with deep shock. Goebbels who telephoned Hitler to tell him the alarming news realized at once that parallels might be drawn with the Nazi state. His first thought recorded in his private diary for that day was, "What are we going to tell them anyway?"

But Hitler, although he was taken by complete surprise by the turn of events in Italy, reacted to them with ice-cold judgment, perhaps for the last time in his career. Immediately he called a conference of his top civilian and military leaders to meet at nine-thirty on the evening of the 25th of June. He knew the Allies would attempt to take full advantage of the situation. Badoglio would, he guessed, try to surrender one way or the other, now that Mussolini was safely out of the way, leaving the country wide open for Allied intervention; and that was something that he, Adolf Hitler, was going to preclude if he could.

That evening as he faced the top men in his state, Himmler and the leading military advisers — Jodl and Keitel — his approach was cold, clear, and calculating. His first words pulled no punches: "The Duce has resigned," he announced solemnly. "Badoglio, our most bitter enemy, has taken over the government."

Swiftly he told the solemn-faced staff members the meager details available before turning the discussion over to them.

Colonel-General Jodl, his extremely cunning chief military planner, was the first to speak. He urged that before they decided upon any form of military action against the Italians they should wait for more complete details from von Mackensen and Kesselring in Rome.

Hitler cut him short. "Certainly," he snapped, acknowledging Jodl's contribution to the discussion, "but still we have to plan ahead. Undoubtedly they will proclaim that they will remain loyal to us, but that is treachery." He ran a pale hand through his dark overhanging forelock. "Of course, they won't remain loyal... Although that bastard[56] stated immediately that the war would be continued, that won't make any difference! They have to say that, but it remains treason. We'll play the same game while preparing to take over the whole crew with one stroke."

He looked hard around the table, his prominent "hypnotic" eyes seemingly sizing up each and every one of his commanders. "Tomorrow I'll send a man down there with orders for the commander of the Third Panzer Grenadier Division to the effect that he must drive into Rome with a special detail and arrest the whole government — the King and the whole bunch — right away."

He turned to Jodl. "Jodl, work out the orders... telling them to drive into Rome with their assault guns... and to arrest the government, the King, and the whole crew." He paused for breath and then added grimly. "I want the Crown Prince above all."

Keitel, towering head and shoulders above everyone at the conference even when sitting down, echoed his master's voice in that wooden stupid way of his. "Yes, he is more important than the old man."

Hitler nodded his head. "Right into a plane and off with them."

---

[56] Badoglio.

General Bodenschatz, the Luftwaffe general at HQ, relieved that the conference was not going to degenerate into another attack on the generals for their stupidity and carelessness, and on the air force generals in particular, grinned and said. "Don't let the *bambino* get lost at the airfield."

Hitler allowed himself a mild smile.

Thereafter the conference broke up, with Hitler issuing a stream of orders to cope with the new situation in Italy: The Alpine passes must be secured; divisions hurried to Italy from France; Field Marshal Rommel, the "desert fox," given command of the whole operation. Someone asked about the Vatican and Hitler snarled: "I'll go right into the Vatican. Do you think the Vatican embarrasses me? We'll take that over right away... The entire diplomatic corps are in there... We'll get that bunch of swine out, and we can make our apologies later."

As midnight approached, a tired but confident Hitler called an end to the preparations, giving orders to arrange another military conference on the Italian situation for the 27th. Now it was time to attend to problem of Benito Mussolini himself.

The six officers, whom he had summoned from all parts of Europe that afternoon, snapped to attention as he entered. Five of them, all field-grade officers, saluted with Prussian precision. Their eyes stared unblinkingly into the far distance, their hands with fingers outstretched, pressed firmly at the sides of their grey field breeches. The sixth, an SS captain, did not salute. Of all things, he bowed instead.

Slightly astonished, Hitler looked at him out of the corner of his eyes. The SS man was worth looking at. He was six foot six at least and broad, too. The side of his face slashed with scars, which could only come from some student dueling, looked as if an unskilled butchery apprentice had done a bad job on it.

The dark-haired giant with the obstinate chin looked — in spite of his awkwardness — a very tough man indeed.

Then Hitler turned his attention to the others, lined up in front of him. At his side the SS adjutant gave a slight signal; and the first officer stepped forward. Swiftly, as he had been ordered earlier in the anteroom, he gave a brief summary of his military career. One after another each of them followed, while Hitler's eyes pierced their faces trying to read what lay behind the unspeaking eyes.

The giant was last. He took a pace forward and clicked his heels. "Skorzeny" he snapped. "Captain of the SS. Detached from the Leibstandarte after service in Russia. Now in charge of the Friedenthal organization."[57] Hitler listened attentively, then nodded. Captain Skorzeny took a pace backwards.

For a moment there was silence. Then Hitler spoke. "Which one of you knows Italy?"

The big SS man was the only one to reply: "I have travelled Italy by motorbike twice — as far as Naples, *mein Führer!*"

Hitler nodded and then asked: "What do you think of the Italians?" There were a variety of hopeful replies. "Our axis partner... loyal ally... member of anti-comintern pact, etc." Hitler looked at Skorzeny.

The latter shrugged almost imperceptibly. He knew that Hitler was an Austrian like himself and probably resented the loss of former Austrian territory to the Italians after the First World War. "I am Austrian, *mein Führer,*" he answered simply, no more.

---

[57] A special SS commando outfit, based on the British commandos, then training for special subversive operations at Friedenthal near Berlin, hence the name.

That answer seemed to convince Hitler. He looked at the big man hard, then ordered: "The other gentlemen can go. I want to speak with Hauptsturmführer Skorzeny."

When they had gone, Hitler turned to him, a little less formal now. "I have a mission of the highest importance for you." Then his voice rose suddenly, as if he were delivering a speech instead of talking to just one man.

"Mussolini, my friend and our loyal ally, has been arrested by his own people. I cannot and *will* not abandon Italy's greatest son. The Duce represents for me the last great Roman. Under the new government Italy will leave the alliance. But I will maintain my loyalty to my ally. He has to be rescued. Otherwise they'll surrender him to the Allies. I order you to find him. This is an all-important mission which will affect the whole course of the war. You must do your utmost to carry out this mission — *and you will succeed!*"

While Skorzeny's head reeled, Hitler continued, "Now to the most important thing. This mission has to be kept absolutely secret. Apart from yourself, only five people will know what is going on. You will be transferred to the Luftwaffe and placed under the command of General Student."

Skorzeny licked his suddenly dry lips. Student was the tough commander of the German paratroops who had captured Rotterdam in 1940 and Crete one year later in two bold actions. The Mussolini mission was obviously going to be something of that kind.

"He's already in the picture. When you leave here you will confer with him, and he'll give you further details. But you will be in charge of discovering where Mussolini is. However, the military and diplomatic authorities in Rome are not to learn of your mission. They are completely misinformed about the situation and consequently will react incorrectly." Hitler paused to collect his breath. Then he gazed hard at the young captain, his eyes piercing him with a look that Skorzeny was going to remember for the rest of his life. "Remember then you are responsible to me personally for the secrecy of this mission. I hope to hear from you soon and wish you all the best."

Skorzeny clicked his heels to attention and looked down at the man whose life was going to be related so intimately to his own for the rest of the war. "I have understood, *mein Führer*," he said. "I will do my best." With that Hitler clasped the captain's hand in both his. Skorzeny saluted, turned, and marched to the door, feeling as he did so as if Hitler's eyes were boring into his back. And he was right. At the door he turned and faced the dictator once more. Hitler's gaze was fixed on him "almost hypnotically" (as he remembered later), as if the Leader was trying to find something in him that lay deep below the surface.

In an anteroom, the SS Captain had just taken out a badly needed cigarette when one of Hitler's tall, black-uniformed SS aides came in and said he was to follow him.

Obediently Otto Skorzeny followed him down the corridor to an office where he was faced by a bullet-headed general in the blue-grey uniform of the paratroops, his broad jovial face scarred by an ugly red weal across the brow.[58] *Kurt Student!*

Skorzeny clicked his heels and introduced himself. Quickly he sketched in what the Leader had told him. But he had hardly finished when there was a light tap on the door and — for the second time that day, an impressed Skorzeny was confronted with one of the "great" men of the Nazi movement: ex-chicken farmer and head of the SS, pale-faced,

---

[58] It was the result of a head wound received at Rotterdam.

178

bespectacled Heinrich Himmler, reputedly the "most feared man in Europe."

He smiled coldly at Skorzeny, then greeted General Student, whom he obviously knew well, a little more warmly. After that, he turned his attention to the waiting SS man, mustering him condescendingly from behind his gold rimmed pince-nez.

He began by telling Skorzeny that nobody in Germany — or in Rome either — knew where the Duce was hidden. However, his own secret service, commanded by General Schellenberg, suspected that the "renegades," as he called the new Italian regime, were preparing to hand him over to the Allies as part of a package deal. He would serve as a scapegoat, who would help to clear their own consciences.

Then he turned his attention to people who might help Skorzeny in his search. In quick time he rattled off a dozen names, of which only a couple were known to the attentive Austrian giant. Swiftly he fumbled in his breast pocket for a pencil and paper to note them.

Himmler stopped in the middle of a word. His dark eyes flashed by the pince-nez. "Are you crazy!" he shouted in his thin voice. "You can't write these things down! They're top secret. You'll just have to memorize them, man!"

Hastily Skorzeny put his pencil and paper away. "This is going to be good," he told himself, as Himmler babbled on, reeling off names and places as if he had known them all his life. He concluded with the words: "Italy's defection is certain. It is only a matter of time. There are Italians in Portugal who are already prepared to begin talks with the Allies."

His eyes heavy with fatigue, his head buzzing with all the new names and places, Skorzeny was allowed to leave. But he knew he couldn't just drop into bed and sleep. There were still things to be done this night. With an enormous yawn, he staggered to the nearest telephone. He had to place a call to his fellow Austrian and adjutant at Friedenthal, Captain Radl.

While he waited, he lit a cigarette to calm his nerves. He puffed away at it nervously as he paced the corridor thinking of the enormous task that had been so suddenly and surprisingly dropped in his lap. "So you can't live without cigarettes!" a voice snapped behind him and startled him out of his reverie.

He turned round.

It was Himmler, his thin face flushed hectically at the high cheeks. "These eternal cigarettes!" He sniffed disdainfully. "*I can see that you're not the right man for this job!*" Then he disappeared as abruptly as he had appeared.

Half an hour later Radl came through, his voice faint and faraway, but clear enough. He was excited. That was evident. Skorzeny smiled at the thought of Radl, who had probably spent the whole day at the side of the phone, wondering what the devil was going on and why his chief had been called to the Führer's HQ so unexpectedly. "What's on?" the adjutant cried, "We've been waiting all day for news!"

Swiftly Skorzeny put him in the picture. "We've got a mission, I can't give you any further details on the phone. I'll fix up the details at this end, then call you again. This is what you can do, however. No more sleep for you and your people this night. Get all the vehicles ready to start. Select fifty men — the best only. All of them will have to be able to speak Italian. Suggest the officers I should take with me." Skorzeny forgot his tiredness in his excitement. The orders flowed from his broad mouth. "We need tropical equipment! Have jump equipment and emergency stuff ready! Everything's got to be ready by five in the morning!..."

Midnight found the giant still working, keeping himself awake with cup after cup of black coffee. Now he was preparing a long list of equipment to be rushed to Friedenthal for the mission. Portable radios. Stick grenades — no — better have British mill bombs. They'd go in the paras' pockets more easily. Rations for six days. Thirty kilos of British plastic explosive, captured from the Dutch underground. Machine guns... Everything might depend upon one single weapon, piece of equipment. Italian *lire*. Priests' cassocks as a possible means of disguise. Dye — black hair dye in case Radl picked too many blond soldiers to go with him. They'd look too obviously German, fake papers ... a hundred and one details to be checked and rechecked.

At 3:30 he finally tumbled into bed, his head reeling with names, places, details. But in spite of his exhaustion he couldn't sleep. The noise of the air conditioner kept him awake. He tossed and turned in the narrow little bunk, trying to force himself to drop off. But to no avail.

He realized that his mission had little chance of success. It was what the Germans called a *Himmelfahrtskommando* (a mission to heaven). Suddenly he realized that he was a father and had not made a will. He turned over and switched on the light. Seizing a pen and paper he set about writing his last "will and testament."

The act of writing his will which had an air of finality about it seemed to settle his nerves at last. Now he turned out the lights, lay back on his hard pillow and fell asleep almost at once. A new phase in his life had begun. If he succeeded in his impossible mission, he would be lifted out of the trough of mediocrity for ever. The mission for Mussolini had commenced ...

In the weeks that followed both the new Italian government under Badoglio and Hitler played a double-game, hypocritically assuring each other of their friendship.[59] Canaris and Schellenberg vied with one another for the prestige of discovering the place where the Italians were hiding the deposed dictator. Twice Canaris gave Skorzeny a false clue and in the end the rising star of the Schellenberg organization had to protest to Hitler personally. Later Skorzeny would write of Canaris's role during this operation: "Was Canaris really interested in carrying out the aims of the German High Command?" Obviously the giant commando leader did not think so.

But in the end Skorzeny found out where the Italians were hiding the sixty-year-old ex-dictator. It was on the very day that Eisenhower announced that the USA and the UK had accepted Italy's surrender while, faraway in Berlin, Himmler was in Schellenberg's Wannsee HQ questioning eighty astrologers, fortune-tellers and clairvoyants fetched from concentration camps all over Germany to divine the Duce's whereabouts.[60] Skorzeny's spies finally established that Mussolini was being held captive on the Gran Sasso: the highest peak in the Italian Apennines, one hundred miles from Rome as the crow flies.

---

[59] By July 29, Hitler knew that the Anglo-Americans were beginning to negotiate with the Italians for the latter's surrender; his engineers had tapped the overseas cable system and "unscrambled" top secret talks between Churchill and Roosevelt who felt their transatlantic discussion was safe via the "scrambler phone." It wasn't.

[60] Later Schellenberg complained: "This affair cost my department a great deal of money because these gentlemen liked good food, drinks, and smokes." But he kept his opinion of Himmler's dealings with the soothsayers to himself. Ever since the Hess flight they had been forbidden to practice their profession in Germany, and now Himmler's recourse to them gave him just one more hold over his master.

In a plane fitted with a special automatic camera, Skorzeny took off with Radl to photograph his objective. As they flew over the Gran Sasso, the automatic camera jammed, so with Radl hanging on to his chiefs legs, Skorzeny hung out of the rear gunner's turret in the freezing cold, taking shots with a hand camera.

The resulting photographs were not encouraging. The hotel in which Mussolini was held captive, had walls like a fortress and, Skorzeny knew from his spies, was garrisoned with at least a hundred armed Italian policemen. Even that was not bad enough; there was no landing place available for the bold operation he was planning other than a triangular patch of grass set among the grey rocks.[61]

All the same Skorzeny, with Hitler and Schellenberg breathing down his neck, set about planning his mission which would become the most celebrated of its kind in the entire war.

While the Viennese commando got on with his planning, Hitler summoned another SS leader to his headquarters that second week of September, 1943. He was tall, erect SS *Obergruppenführer* and *Waffen* SS General Karl Wolff, a favorite of Himmler, who called him most inaptly "Little Wolf." After filling in the tall, distinguished-looking SS General on the situation in Italy, Hitler dismissed the rest of his entourage and then said to Wolff: "I have a special assignment for you, Wolff." He looked at Himmler's intimate with those deep "hypnotic" eyes of his for a moment before adding. "I order you, however, not to speak to anybody about this before I give you permission. I've informed only the *Reichsführer SS* (i.e., Himmler). Do you understand?"

---

[61] Skorzeny was forced to attack from the air; the ground below was held by strong Italian forces.

"Yes, *mein Führer*," Wolff snapped, wondering what was to come.

Hitler nodded and went on: "I wish that within the framework of the present measures being taken against that traitor Badoglio, you occupy the Vatican and Vatican City as soon as possible."

Wolff looked at his Führer wide-eyed, but Hitler did not seem to notice. He knew from his long service at Hitler's HQ that the latter favored Pius XII, who had been Pope since 1939. In earlier years the new Pope had spent much time in Munich and was regarded as a friend of Germany. Indeed in 1941, Wolff remembered Hitler saying[62] to him: If I had to pick a German pope for German Catholics, then I'd pick Engenio Pacelli without any hesitation. Now his regard had turned to hate, for Wolff knew Hitler thought the Pope was mixed up with the plot to overthrow Mussolini. Yet would even he go so far as to order the occupation of Vatican City, the Pope's residence? The Leader's next words told him that Hitler was going to go even further.

"I want you to secure the Vatican's art treasures and archives — *and arrest the Pope and the Curia!*"

Wolff caught his breath.

"I want them brought north. I don't want them to fall into Allied hands... The Vatican is a spy nest anyway and a center of

---

[62] The plot to kidnap the Pope was first revealed in 1972 when Wolff, now in his eighties, told his story. There had been rumors of this amazing plot from 1943 onwards, but the Wolff revelation was the first actual confirmation of Hitler's real intentions.

New evidence just coming to light seems to indicate that Mussolini may have had something to do with the death of the previous Pontiff in 1939. It is alleged that Pope Pius XI was given a fatal "fortifying" injection by a Dr. Petacci, who was the father of Mussolini's mistress, Clara.

anti-National Socialist propaganda." Without giving the SS General time to collect his thoughts, he demanded: "When can you begin this operation?"

Wolff, a cultivated man, left, his head reeling at the monstrous cheek of Hilter's plan. *Arrest the Pope!* It had been six centuries since anyone in Western Europe had dared do such a dastardly deed! All the same he knew it was highly risky to thwart Hitler's plans. On September 12, he flew from Hitler's HQ to Italy and there ordered Schellenberg's representative, Dr. Wilhelm Harster, to recruit Italian-speaking Germans for the planned operations. But at the same time he contacted Dr. Pankratius Pfeiffer, a German priest in the employ of the Vatican, as a first step to arranging a meeting with Pius XII. Wolff knew he must warn the Pope even if it cost his head![63]

In the end the kidnapping was called off, but Wolff need not have feared; Pope Pius had already been warned. His informant was the Chief of the Italian Secret Service General Amé, who had the warning from no less a person than Admiral Canaris himself! The little white-haired Admiral had committed his greatest blunder. Then, in the strange game of treachery and counter-treachery which was being played out in Rome that burning hot summer, Schellenberg's spies were already on to the leak at the highest level. At the express command of the Canaris's "dear young friend" and riding companion, the Admiral was being followed everywhere he went in Rome.

As Schellenberg explained after the war: "The facts of the case came to light in the following manner. One of Canaris'

---

[63] Wolff finally did see the Pope and after his audience about which he will not speak even today, he paused at the door and gave the "Heil Hitler" salute. Pfeiffer who was with him turned to the Pope and excused the oversight: "He's forgotten that we're not in Germany," he told Pius.

assistants, Colonel Helfferich, was on the staff of the German Military Attaché in Rome, General von Rintelen. The Colonel employed two Italian chauffeurs; both were homosexuals and both in Amé's service. I pointed out the dangers of this arrangement to Canaris, but Helfferich was of such high standing that he pooh-poohed my warning: "*Ach*, Schellenberg," he said, "after one's been in our profession a while one begins to see pink elephants!"

Canaris should not have been so confident. Then as Schellenberg noted with barely concealed triumph: "One of these chauffeurs was unwittingly the most valuable source of information for my Political Secret Service, for he repeated all Amé's assignments and conversations to a friend who was in our pay. Thus we were able to piece together a very clear picture of the planned coup and of how far Canaris was involved in the affair."

The man whose faith rested in the loyalty of his dogs was no match for the man who gained his information from the rumpled bed of an Italian homosexual and his German lover....

The start of the great rescue operation had been planned for dawn, but the gliders which were to carry Skorzeny's troops to the top of the mountain were delayed on the Riviera. The giant cursed but then consoled himself with the thought that, by the time they landed on the mountain, the Italians would be resting after a heavy lunch; no Italian in his right senses could expect an attack to come at that holy hour.

In the meantime Captain Radl, using the enforced delay, rushed into Rome and picked up pro-German Italian General Soletti, whom he bustled into the staff car telling him that he was needed for "an important enterprise." The surprised

General did not know what he was letting himself in for, but as Skorzeny explained to him later: he was needed to prevent "any unnecessary shedding of blood."

Finally it was noon and the twelve gliders were drawn up ready to be lifted off the ground into the beautiful bright blue sky. Suddenly the high-pitched wail of the air raid siren sounded. Twin-engine Allied bombers came winging in low over the field at three hundred miles an hour! Bombs started falling at once. Skorzeny and his men scattered hastily. The bombing lasted fifteen minutes, and although the field was badly damaged, a relieved Skorzeny came out of his hiding place, dusting off his parachute overalls, to see that all his gliders were safe.

At one o'clock the brave little armada took off. Skorzeny was in the second flight of gliders with Soletti crouched between his legs. Almost immediately the lead gliders were lost in a cloud bank (they never made it). But Skorzeny had no time for them; it was too damn hot in the canvas-and-wood plane. "I suddenly noticed," he remembered later, "that the corporal behind me was being sick and the general in front had turned as green as his uniform. Flying obviously did not suit them."

Skorzeny realized now that the pilot was flying blind, relying on Skorzeny's knowledge of the Gran Sasso area to guide him to the objective. But he could not see through the glider's thick celluloid windows. While he pondered the problem, the voice of the towing pilot came over the telephone: "Regret flights one and two no longer ahead of us. Who's to take over the lead now?"

"This was bad news," Skorzeny recollected later. "What had happened to them? At that time I did not know that I also had only seven machines instead of nine behind me. Two had fallen foul of bomb craters right at the start."

But he did not reveal his uneasiness to the pilot or the paratroopers. He replied: "We'll take over the lead ourselves." And seizing his knife, he hacked away at the glider's canvas wall until he had carved a hole in it through which he could see. Cool refreshing air rushed in. The General's color changed from green to normal.

A little while later he spotted his objective: the valley of Aquila far down below. "Helmets on!" he roared against the noise of the wind. Obediently his pale-faced paras prepared for action. The fortress-like mountain hotel came into sight. "Slip the tow-rope," Skorzeny commanded.

A sudden silence. They were freed of the roar of the towing plane now. All they could hear was the rush of the wind. Slowly the glider pilot swung his craft round in a lazy circle, while Skorzeny searched for the landing strip. There it was: the triangular patch of grass!

He swallowed hard. He had not expected this. The patch was steep — terribly steep — and littered with boulders! It would be madness to attempt to land there. But there was nothing else available. The glider started to dive rapidly "CRASH LANDING!" Skorzeny cried... "Get as near to the hotel as you can," he added for the pilot's sake. Then he tensed his big hard body for the crash that must come.

It did. At the very last moment Lieutenant Meyer, the pilot, released the parachute brake. The frail wooden plane lurched forward and hit the steep triangular patch of grass. A splintering of wood and ripping of canvas. One last mighty heave and they lurched to a halt. They had made it!

Skorzeny had no time to consider his astonishing luck. He followed the first man out. They were within fifteen meters of the hotel. Above them a lone Italian soldier was standing staring at the unexpected arrival from the sky, his mouth wide open in amazement. The big Austrian did not give him a chance to sound the alarm. He dashed forward, clutching his machine pistol. *"Mani in alto!"* he roared. The Italian's hands shot up. Skorzeny charged through the door. In a little room to the side of the entrance, an Italian soldier was crouched over a radio set. Skorzeny kicked the man's chair from beneath him and while he fell cursing to the floor, the Austrian brought the butt of his grease-gun down on the radio. It splintered and went dead.

He ran on. Before him and the men of his command a ten-foot wall reared up. Corporal Himmel sprang forward. Without being told, he bent and offered his broad back as a ladder. Skorzeny was on it and over the terrace in an instant. The rest followed. Here he paused. Above him he saw a well-known heavy jaw surmounted by a completely bald head. It was the face of the Duce himself — Mussolini!

"Away from that window!" he bellowed, knowing that the Italian guards had been ordered to kill Mussolini if it looked as if he might escape or be released from captivity. The ex-Duce's face disappeared at once.

In a bunch Skorzeny's men rushed into the hotel lobby. They collided with a mass of cursing Italians, struggling with their helmets and weapons. Skorzeny cut right through them. One of his men booted the tripod from a machine gun the Italians were trying to set up. It clattered across the highly polished wooden floor.

Skorzeny clattered up the stairs. Panting heavily he nearly bumped into two young Italian officers. Behind them he saw Mussolini's deathly pale face. He hesitated a moment. The Italians did, too. One of his men, Lieutenant Schwerdt, came panting up to him. Suddenly behind the Italians two grinning faces surmounted by the brimless helmets of German paras appeared at the window. The two men had shinned up the lightning conductor. The Italian officers raised their hands slowly. They knew they were beaten. *In exactly four minutes Skorzeny had rescued the man who was being sought by two German intelligence services as well as those of the United States and Britain!* It was all over — Mussolini was in German hands.

At last Skorzeny had time for the Italian leader. Mussolini was deathly pale and unshaven, dressed in a crumpled, oversized blue-grey suit. But there was no mistaking the joy on his face. Skorzeny was well aware of the importance of this historic moment. Clicking his heels together and stretching himself to his full height, he snapped formally: "I have been sent by the Führer to set you free." Mussolini, a man who had always had an eye for the dramatic, responded in kind. "I knew my friend Adolf Hitler would not leave me in the lurch," he said in German and then reaching up, he pulled Skorzeny's head down so that he could embrace the Austrian with the full fervor of his Italian temperament.

While Skorzeny enjoyed the fruits of his tremendous coup (even Winston Churchill had to admit it "was one of great daring and shows there are many possibilities of this kind open in modern war"), Schellenberg, the Austrian Commando's chief, put the final touches to his secret dossier on Canaris's betrayal. It started with — according to Schellenberg — Canaris's attempts to warn the West of Hitler's intentions in 1940, went on to his traitorous contacts with the Swiss one year later, right up to his dealings with the Italians in 1943: one defeatist or treacherous act after another.

Finally he presented Himmler "with a dossier which included absolute proof of Canaris's treachery." It ended with the sentence, written in Schellenberg's own neat lawyer's hand: "It would have been better for Admiral Canaris to have concerned himself with his own tasks in Italy, rather than carry on such sessions with Amé."

The chief of the Abwehr's days were now numbered...

1943-1944: THE ALLIES START TO GET THE UPPER HAND

And many more Destructions played
In this ghastly masquerade,
All disguised, even to the eyes,
Like Bishops, lawyers, peers or spies.

Shelley

12 — "MAJOR MARTIN" DIES AND IS BORN ONCE MORE

The great deception had started innocently enough in the Junior Carlton Club, in the heart of London's prewar clubland. The young naval officer listened respectfully to the words of the wing-collared, white-haired pathologist who was perhaps the world's leading specialist in his field.

In his long career of criminal pathology and forensic science, Sir Bernard Spilsbury, who one day would die by his own hand, had come across many curious and eerie examples of man's ingenuity in doing away with his fellow human beings. But on this icy winter's day over the coffee and port, he little realized that he was being involved in the most amazing case of his whole long career.

But then Commander the Honorable Ewen E. S. Montagu of the Directorate of Naval Intelligence, an associate of Ian Fleming (who was Admiral Godfrey's righthand man), was a remarkable and cunning man just like Fleming. Patiently and carefully he questioned England's No. 1 pathologist while making mental notes of the good doctor's considered, somewhat pedantic replies. Privately he told himself he wished Sir Bernard would not talk to him, as if he were addressing a jury, trying to impress them with yet another example of his lucidity and brilliant powers of scientific detection. Yet he consoled himself at the same time with the thought that the bespectacled scientist's remarks would help him to present an airtight case to the highly critical Twenty Committee.

Thus while the ancient, tail-coated waiters flitted back and forth among the aristocratic club members, Commander

Montagu persisted with his questions: "What would be the specific characteristics of a body which remained in the water several days after a plane crash... how would they be recognized... what might be recorded as the cause of death, providing the person in question had not died on impact?..."

Sir Bernard's professional ambition was aroused by the young naval officer's questions. "Death would probably result from a lowering of the person's temperature... especially if the man in question were to float by means of a life-belt... first he would fall unconscious... death would occur several hours later..." His voice droned on and on.

Then Montagu posed the key question. "Would there be any outward signs of how the man had met his death?"

Sir Bernard considered for a moment, with his mocha cup poised at his lips. He obviously wasn't given to answering questions of this nature lightly. After all, in the past his answers given before the bewigged, severe judges at London's Old Bailey, not far from where they were sitting now, had meant the difference between life and death for many a pale-faced accused clutching the rail of the oaken prisoner's box. Then he shook his head. "No, in my opinion, there would be no outward characteristics of the manner of death."

Commander Ewen Montagu's heart skipped a beat. It was the answer he had been hoping for throughout the long and intricate lunch. *Operation Mincemeat* was definitely *on*.

The next step for Naval Intelligence's representative on the Twenty Committee was to find his "body snatcher." It was not difficult. Montagu was not a career Naval officer. He had come from the City of London at the beginning of the war, and he knew his way through the mass of red tape which might have baffled another officer. For him it was obvious that if he needed a body in the City of London, he would go directly to the city coroner, the man through whose department passed London's dead.

"But you can't get bodies just for the asking," Sir William Bentley-Purchase told him pompously. The Coroner for the Borough of St. Pancras continued, "I mean, even with bodies all over the place, each one has to be accounted for."

The broad-shouldered Naval Intelligence man persisted. He gave the doctor a little information about "Operation Mincemeat." Not enough to endanger the project, but enough to whet his appetite and gain his support. In the end Sir William gave in and set about his task as official body snatcher. A century after the last body snatcher had been arrested and imprisoned in that same London borough, its coroner commenced a similar macabre job.

It took time. But Montagu had expected that. There were bodies enough in the icy vaults. But their limbs were ripped and torn by German bombs. They were no good for Montagu's purpose. There were also a few who had died from other causes, who would have fitted into his plans, but discreet inquiries among their relatives and next of kin revealed that the latter would not go along with any strange Intelligence plot. In the end Sir William came up with the body they needed: a 30-year-old man who had died of pneumonia in a London hospital.[64]

Thus they met to view the body in the St. Pancras Mortuary: Sir William, Sir Bernard Spilsbury, and Montagu. Behind locked doors, the three of them looked at the deathly pale naked corpse. Then Sir Bernard went to work, his hands and eyes moving quickly and efficiently, thirty years of training and experience behind them. He confirmed what Montagu wanted to hear. The dead man's lungs contained liquid which would

---

[64] The man's name remains a secret even thirty years later.

probably lead any enemy doctor to conclude that he had died of drowning. Carefully he patted and tapped the dead man's skinny chest. Of course, if the enemy cared to carry out a careful, thorough autopsy they would find out that the man had not drowned at sea, but that would be a chance he, Montagu, would have to take.

Montagu, shivering in spite of his thick naval "warm" in the cold tiled mortuary, nodded his thanks and turned to the coroner.

He was not too happy with the whole thing. He was worried about the effect on public opinion if the unorthodox manner of the body's disposal ever came out. But all the same he confirmed that the man's relatives approved the plan as long as he were given a "proper, decent Christian burial" afterward.

For the first time in weeks, Montagu smiled in spite of their eerie surroundings. As he remarked much later when the Government finally gave him permission to reveal the full details of his macabre yet brilliant plan: "At one time we feared we might have to do a body snatch... but we did not like that idea, if we could possibly avoid it."

Now he had his body and in the opinion of the world's foremost pathologist it was in such a condition that they might just get away with it.

All that remained to be done was to dress the man before he was tucked away safely in his vault again till everything was ready. But an unexpected difficulty cropped up. The dead man's feet were frozen solid!

Montagu licked suddenly dry lips and stared at the two doctors. He had been in some strange situations in his time, but never in one like this. But Sir William Bentley-Purchase was equal to it. After all, he had been hardened in the rough and tough school of police surgery where the body was slit

196

open throat to navel with one single stroke so that inner organs could be removed for examination — after all a police surgeon was paid on a "body" basis and he had no time to waste. Swiftly he rapped out an order. One of Montagu's men went up the stairs and returned a few moments later with Sir William's own office electric plate.

The coroner plugged it in and stretched the single burner close to the yellow, ice-hard feet. Swallowing hard and feeling himself about to become sick as the steam commenced to rise from the feet, Montagu turned away.

Sir William did not bat an eyelid. "We'll thaw the feet out," he commented in a matter-of-fact manner, "and as soon as the boots are on, we'll pop him back in the refrigerator and refreeze him."

Montagu pressed his lips together and tried desperately to think of something else. The steam began to rise greyly in the icy air. *Something started to drip on the stone floor...*

On February 4, 1943, the Twenty Committee met at their weekly Monday conference to give their approval to Operation Mincemeat, whose macabre origin and eerie details were now reduced to cold, bloodless officialese. The minutes of that day's meeting ran as follows:

"PLAN MINCEMEAT. The plan is the same as PLAN TROJAN HORSE. The details of the plan were put forward by Commander Montagu and F/Lt. Cholmondeley. It was reported that a body had been procured and it was explained that this would have to be used within three months and that various points of detail would have to be decided before the Plan could be put into operation. The Plan was adopted by the Committee and it was agreed that copies of the Plan should be shown to the Directors of Intelligence; that the Air Military representatives on the Twenty Committee should make the necessary arrangements for the flight during which the body will be dropped... that the Admiralty representative should find out a suitable position off the Spanish coast where the body can be dropped; that the War Office representative should go into the question of providing the body with a name, necessary papers, etc. It was agreed that the N.A. Madrid should be informed of the Plan so that he will be able to cope with any unforeseen repercussions which may come his way."

Operation Mincemeat had been approved and Major Martin, "the man who never was," had been born...

That spring Montagu's first problem was to create a realistic "cover story" for Major Martin of His Majesty's Royal Marines. How could one make him appear genuine once "Operation Mincemeat" got underway? For days and days on end, he and his colleagues of Naval Intelligence talked and talked the problem out. What would a Major normally carry about with him? Money, theatre tickets, bills, letters — they would be obvious things. But how could letters, for instance, contribute to the decision? Under normal circumstances a man carried letters but usually they were puerile and trivial and would contribute little to the person's identification and status in life.

In the end the planners conceived "Martin" as just having become engaged. Accordingly, he would be able to carry out two passionate letters from his fiancée, one containing a worried reference to a "posting overseas." Montagu pushed the results of this sudden engagement a little further. A man who gets engaged usually buys a ring, and because he buys it he falls into debt. Result two more "documents" — a ring ordered and a bill forwarded, plus a discreet letter from "Martin's" bank manager about his overdraft. Parents, too, often object to engagements, especially if they are carried out against the hectic background of war. "Martin" was given, therefore, a somewhat Victorian father who didn't like the idea of this "wartime engagement" but was prepared to accept it. However, he felt that his son should make his "last will and testament" just in case — yet another document in the building up of "Martin's" character and status.

The next step was to prepare the great "plot." As Ewen Montagu recalled after the war: "We drew up a private letter from the Deputy Chief of Staff to General Alexander who commanded our armies in North Africa. This private letter enabled him ... to mention small transparent details... which would make the enemy believe that we were going to land troops in both Greece and Sardinia."

In addition, Montagu convinced handsome Lord Mountbatten, ex-destroyer captain and now Chief of Combined Operations, to allow his name to be affixed to yet another letter, directed to Admiral Sir Andrew Cunningham of the British Mediterranean Fleet. It read:

Dear Admiral of the Fleet,

I promised V.C.I.G.S. that Major Martin would arrange with you for the onward transmission of a letter he has with him for General Alexander. It is very urgent and very "hot" and as there are some remarks in it that could not be seen by others in the War Office, it could not go by signal. I feel sure that you will see that it goes on safely and without delay.

I think you will find Martin the man you want. He is quiet and shy at first but he really knows his stuff. He was more accurate than some of us about the probable run of events at Dieppe and he has been well in on the experiments with the latest barges and equipment which took place in Scotland.

Let me have him back please, as soon as the assault is over. He might bring some sardines with him — they are "on points" here!

Yours sincerely
Louis Mountbatten.

The string was in the tail of the message. It built up "Martin's" cover, but the apparently innocent remark in the last sentence about bringing back the rationed "sardines" was cleverly worked in so that some enterprising Abwehr officer poring over the message would believe that he had been astute enough to read through and beyond the Chief of Combined Operations' reference. *Natürlich*, he would congratulate himself on his smartness: "*sardines*" *could only mean Sardinia*!

On April 18, Operation Mincemeat was finally ready. "Major Martin's" body, carefully packed in dry ice in a container labeled "optical instruments" was loaded on to *HMS Seraph* in the Scottish port of Holy Loch. Commander N. L. Jewell, the captain of the British submarine, solemnly receipted the "optical instruments" and quietly passed on the word to his Number Two, beside him on the conning tower supervising the preparations for departure, to tell any of the crew who asked that the container enclosed an automatic weather station.

Then he went down to his cabin, where behind the curtain, his only privacy during the long, dangerous voyage ahead, he exchanged a few whispered words with Montagu and his companion Archibald Cholmondeley. Then the conspirators shook hands. The two men who were to remain behind left, and the submarine slid from her moorings into the grey mist. The two Intelligence officers watched her until they could see her no more, the thin cold rain dripping silently from the peaks of their caps; then they turned and made their way back to the khaki-colored Humber staff car with slow weary steps. Their job was over. They had worked seven months on it. Now it was up to Commander Jewell.

Everything went all right the first and second days. Although they were in "U-boat alley," where Allied planes automatically bombed everything that moved on or below the surface of the water because the British Admiralty had declared this area of the Channel as being reserved exclusively for enemy shipping, Jewell knew they were safe. All Allied aircraft had been ordered to keep an eye open for a British submarine which was on a special mission in that area.

The third day passed peacefully enough. There was plenty of enemy shipping about — mostly French and other Continental fishing boats — but no one spotted them. On the fourth day, Jewell received a radio message from the Admiralty to change his course and tackle a group of ships heading for the general direction of the North Spanish ports along the Bay of Biscay.

Jewell changed course immediately and sped after them at a steady twelve knots an hour, occasionally coming up to periscope depth to check whether they were in sight. Suddenly on one such occasion it happened. The periscope had just been raised when a trio of fat-bellied Hudsons of Coastal Command swooped down and commenced dropping depth charges all around the lean grey sub.

A sweating, angry Jewell hit the alarm button. His Second shouted "Dive! Dive! Dive!" Abruptly everything was hectic yet efficient action. The sub submerged sharply. The vibrations of the depth charges decreased. While the crew held their breaths as if the pilots so far above them could hear them, Jewell cursed fluently and easily, using cuss words he did not even know he knew.

A little while later, *HMS Seraph* surfaced once more, but was met again with the same reception. Jewell decided he would relinquish the chase and concentrate on the major task on hand: disposal of "Major Martin."

One day later the little submarine surfaced off the mouth of the Spanish Rio Huelva. It was still daylight, and although Spain was a neutral country, Jewell knew the coast was infested with Abwehr and their Spanish "V-men," who would report their position to the German Admiralty. Swiftly he checked his position and then submerged again till nightfall.

As soon as it was dusk, Jewell commenced to move ever closer to the shore, running his diesels at half speed so that he would not unduly alarm any German paid coast watcher. Again he ran into trouble. Suddenly a swarm of Spanish fishing boats appeared from nowhere, the only indication of their presence their carbide-lit bow lanterns. Cursing, Jewell submerged and cancelled the operation for the night. Then he changed his mind and tried again. Once more he hit a swarm of Spanish fishermen searching for the sardines which were a staple part of their diet. He dived under them and groped forward in the gloom until he finally came to a rest just off the Punta de Umbria. He was ready to discharge the body.

Now he moved swiftly. He ordered the bearded submariners off the deck and conning tower, leaving only the officers with him. Bewildered and grumbling about what had "got into the Old Man's head," the seamen and the petty officers clattered down the metal ladder while the officers, dressed in a picturesque variety of clothes, ranging from greasy old naval overalls to baggy civilian corduroy pants, stared at him puzzled. Jewell checked that no one was listening at the bottom of the ladder, then turning to his officers, filled them in briefly about their strange mission. Together he and two other lieutenants opened the case of "optical instruments" and pulled out the body.

It was an eerie scene, as they checked whether "Martin's" papers were still there and the briefcase were securely attached to his wrist by the little chain. Then in the yellow light, which wavered in the hand of the nervous young man who held it, they fitted "Martin" with his "Mae West." It was difficult. The body was frozen stiff and unyielding, but finally they managed it. The ceremony was not, however, over yet. Devoutly the skipper clasped his hands together. The bewildered officers knew what that gesture meant. They followed suit, lowering their eyes. Swiftly, in a low voice, Commander Jewell murmured the committal ceremony for the stiff body lying there on the wet dripping deck. It must have been one of the most amazing "burials" in the history of the Christian Church.

That completed, the body was slipped gently over the side. Jewell's voice changed. It rose a couple of levels as he started rapping out orders. Once more he was the typical Royal Navy sub skipper. The engines commenced to chug as the lean grey boat swung around. The ripples grew into waves and slowly but surely "Major Martin" was driven toward the faint outline of the Spanish coast and the waiting Germans...

Early on the morning of April 30, 1943, the body was found by a Spanish fisherman who dragged it on board his little boat and landed it at Huelva harbor. While the Spanish harbor authorities seized the dead Briton's papers, the local doctor Fernandex Contioso carried out a post-mortem. His findings were that the mysterious soldier had been in the water five or six days and had died of drowning. This checked with the items found on the body — theatre tickets dated April 22, plus

Montagu's carefully forged bill from the London Army and Navy Club, which gave the 24th as "Major Martin's" date of departure.

The finding of the body was now reported to the local British representative who ordered a gravestone immediately and passed on the news to the British Ambassador in Madrid, Sir Samuel Hoare. Hoare requested the Spanish authorities to release the body for burial at once. The Spanish Navy Minister Salvador Moreno-Fernandez refused politely, but firmly. His excuse was that his Ministry had to check the dead man's papers thoroughly.

Back in London Montagu and the members of the Twenty Committee rubbed their hands in glee when they heard the news. That meant the Spaniards — and, of course, the Germans too — were beginning to bite. The bait had worked.

Sir Samuel Hoare stepped up the pressure. He *insisted* that the dead man's briefcase should not be opened, but forwarded — *unopened* — to nearby Gibraltar at once! The Spanish declined, but the briefcase was forwarded to Madrid where the Naval Chief of Staff Alfonso Arriega passed it on to the local Abwehr office. The Germans went to work swiftly. They opened the case without leaving the slightest trace, removed the vital papers, and forwarded them immediately to Berlin.

One day later Adolf Hitler himself was reading the translations of the two vital letters, which were accompanied by the Abwehr's own interpretation of their meaning. It read: "There is no doubt about the genuineness of the captured documents. We are checking, however, whether they have been played into our hands deliberately and whether the enemy is aware of their loss or that we have gained possession of them. It is possible that the enemy has no knowledge of this fact."

One day later the documents were back in the briefcase in Madrid and thereafter passed into the possession of the British Ambassador. A few hours later they were on their way to Gibraltar. After that they were flown immediately to London, where experts went to work trying to ascertain whether the Germans had opened the briefcase. Meanwhile, "Major Martin," accompanied by a couple of solemn, sad-faced Naval officers from the Embassy, was laid to rest in the ornate little cemetery in Huelva. His grave may be seen there to this day.

In the end, Montagu, who had even thought of placing a notice for "Capt (A/Major) W. Martin" in the *Times* under the "List of Missing" — just in case the Germans had ordered an agent in London to check up on him — was informed by the experts that the briefcase had been opened. The proof was the marks of the drying chamber on the outer surface of the envelopes it contained. Apparently they had been eased open in a complicated process using sea-water; thereafter they had been dried in a drying chamber. Hence the faint marks.

Montagu was ecstatic. But his happiness was dampened by the thought: would the Germans "buy" the idea and react accordingly?

The first proof came exactly fifteen days after "Martin" had been found. One of the enemy's crack tank divisions — the First Panzer — was moved from Southern France to Greece. Thereafter things moved fast. Keitel himself ordered the strengthening of the German garrisons of Corsica and Sardinia. Admiral Dönitz also ordered fresh naval units into the area and the increased mining of those waters. The great deception had worked. OPERATION MINCEMEAT HAD BEEN AN UNQUALIFIED SUCCESS!

Operation Husky, the Allied invasion of Sicily, came as a

complete surprise to the Germans and their Italian allies! Fourteen days later Hitler still did not believe that this was the main Anglo-American attack. Fourteen days after Husky had commenced, the Führer ordered his favorite general, Field Marshal Rommel, to leave Vienna and fly immediately to Greece to supervise German preparations for the invasion of that area, which must come at any moment. With him was the man whom Commander Montagu and the Twenty Committee had duped so thoroughly — the head of the Abwehr, Admiral Canaris!

The long and complicated operation to fool the Germans as to the location of the Allies' first landing on the European Continent, after being chased from it three long years before, had worked. Now the planners of the Twenty Committee, operating from their obscure offices in the heart of London, had to meet the greatest challenge of all — the full-scale Allied invasion of France.

13 — TREASURE BRINGS HOME THE BACON

Lisbon in March, 1944, presented a vastly different picture from worn-torn London. There was no rationing. The shops were full. If you had money enough — although prices had gone up tremendously due to the war — you could purchase all those luxuries and delicacies absent from the English stores since 1939. But TREASURE was not too interested in the silk stockings, latest lipsticks, colorful Latin clothes, in spite of her French appreciation for such things. What she enjoyed most was the warmth of the Portuguese spring. It did her poor, worn, dying body good to feel the sun's rays penetrate through her thin dress after the long icy English winter.

The food was tremendous too, after the austerity of the English restaurants with their "whalemeat" steaks, powdered egg omelets and inevitable boiled Brussels sprouts. As long as she lived — and her English doctors had assured her gravely that would not be long — she would always associate the London of 1944 with the smell of boiled Brussels sprouts and the thick, brassy sound of Major Glenn Miller's Air Force band.

But in the second week of that balmy March, London had receded to the back of the twenty-six-year-old's mind. It was replaced by knowledge of the paramount importance of her mission here in neutral Portugal. Would she be able to pull it off?

On the night of March 13, she decided to find out. She took up the meeting place *they* had assigned to her, knowing in the back of her mind that she was risking a date with death; for in the Lisbon of 1944, the greatest spy haven in the Western world, agents came and went suddenly without too many questions asked. And if, on a grey morning, one of them was found floating in the harbor, a neat red bullet hole through the back of his head, the Portuguese, so concerned with their fragile neutrality, would shrug their shoulders and ask no questions.

One minute after nine that fine warm spring evening, with the air full of the scent of tamarisk and jasmine, TREASURE waited, her alert eyes searching the length of the Plaza Pombal. Her contact was exactly sixty seconds overdue, and the Germans were notoriously a very punctual people. Had they already lodged in one of the dark eighteenth-century hallways, clad in those absurdly long leather coats they always wore, wide-brimmed felt hats dragged deep down over their narrow foreheads, hands gripping their revolvers? When would — what the British called "fun and games" — begin?

Suddenly she was alerted by the sound of a speeding car. It came in fast down the length of the Plaza, its headlights dimmed. She just had time to identify it as a Citroën when it squealed to a halt. In the same instant, its lights were extinguished. A door was flung open. A large hand reached out. Before TREASURE knew what was happening, it had grabbed firmly and dragged her inside. The lights flashed on again. As she fell back against the cold leather of the seat, the ancient French auto swung round and shot off back into the direction from which it had come, TREASURE had made contact with *I LUFT* (Paris) who still knew her as TRAMP...

TREASURE was Lily Sergeiev, a young Frenchwoman of Russian origin, whom Ladislas Farago has called "one of the great ladies of espionage in World War II."[65] Major Masterman of the Twenty Committee whose remarkable organization "ran" her as one of their chief double agents was less flattering. For him she was "an intelligent but temperamental woman."

Lily Sergeiev was a strange husky girl whose component of male hormones perhaps explained her somewhat unfeminine behavior. As a sixteen-year-old she had stowed away on a German freighter commanded by a Captain Bueking and, when she had been discovered, she had contrived to so upset the crew that the Captain swore he would remember her to his dying day. One year later she was hitchhiking her way from Paris to Warsaw.

The outbreak of war in 1939 found her in Beirut, the capital of French-occupied Lebanon, on the second leg of her long journey by cycle to faraway Indochina; and it was in the Middle Eastern country that she made a conscious decision to enter the secret service, regardless of what power employed it. She craved adventure. As she wrote a little later in her diary (TREASURE is unique in that she kept a diary which has been preserved): "The idea had come to me one night in Beirut. I turned it over for two days. At night in bed with the lights out, it all seemed so simple! But in the morning in broad daylight, my scheme seemed mad and childish — the sort of thing one reads about in books, but which does not happen in real life."

But the square-jawed young French girl, whose appearance was definitely masculine, recalled a journalist she had met on her first trip to Estonia to visit an uncle. She had bumped into him once again in Berlin — he was a German — and had discovered by accident that the somewhat seedy "journalist" was in reality one of Admiral Canaris's Abwehr agents. That had been in 1938. Now in 1940 after the fall of France, she wrote to him in Paris asking him (as she noted in her diary)

---

[65] In *The Game of Foxes*. New York: McKay, 1971.

"could I through him get enlisted in the German secret service and then *perhaps be able to help those who were carrying on the fight.*" And for Lily Sergeiev "those who were carrying on the fight" were her newly occupied compatriots. Lily was deliberately attempting to join the Abwehr so that some as yet unknown spymaster in London would one day be able to use her as a double agent!

Her amazing attempt to penetrate German Intelligence paid off. Felix Dassel, the German journalist, took her up on her offer. In Paris he introduced her to moustache, Major Emil Kliemann, a big bluff Austrian who liked the good life and was a leading figure in German Air Force Intelligence. At first Kliemann did not quite know what to make of this strange recruit who had attempted to enter the Abwehr in such a strange manner. But in the end he sent her for training; and for two long years she was taught coding, the use of invisible ink, recognition of different Anglo-American formations etc., etc. By the spring of 1943, she was ready for her first assignment, suggested naturally by herself; she would go to Madrid and apply for a visa to enter England. Kliemann thought her crazy. But he had nothing to lose if she wished to stick her head in the lion's jaws. He gave his approval. One week later tramp, as he called her in a moment of drunken inspiration, was on her way to the Spanish capital. "Now my holiday is over," she confided to her diary in a highly indiscreet manner, "and I must start on my enterprise. If I succeed, from now on I shall be alone, utterly alone...."

The dim lights of the ancient Portuguese street lights were not powerful enough to illuminate the face of the heavy-set, middle-aged man who had dragged her so suddenly into the Citroën. Was he a Gestapo man? TREASURE asked herself, her heart beating frantically. But the young Frenchwoman, who had already done so much that was simply "not done" in those days, was not going to give up without a fight. They wouldn't liquidate her so easily; her mission was too vital. As soon the man in the shadows spoke, asking her how she had managed to get out of England, she knew he was not Kliemann.

She snapped in return that she was not answering any questions till she was confronted with Kliemann himself.

The man in the shadows persisted while the driver roared through the deserted streets. He asked if her name were Nina and whether she had been in the Russian town of Kiev.

She replied in the negative.

The man was not put off. "It's strange," he continued unperturbed in a voice that seemed obscurely familiar, "I once met a girl who had the same name as you. She was very gay. I brought her from Danzig to Rouen."

TREASURE knew who the man in the shadows was now. "Take your hat off," she commanded in that masculine way of hers.

"Why do you want me to do that?" he asked in surprise, but he obeyed her command.

She looked at him hard in the gloom of the back seat. "You see I wanted to know if you've changed at all — *Captain Bueking.*" And before the man who had once transported her unwittingly from the Baltic to the North Sea could reply, she added: "What have you done with the *Adel Iraber?*"[66] The ice was broken. The sea captain who was also now working for the Abwehr grasped her hand enthusiastically. It was a strange coincidence after all these years and under these strange circumstances, but TREASURE knew with a sudden lightening

---

[66] Bucking's ship in the thirties.

of her heart that it meant she was safe: she had fooled the Germans.

Five minutes later she was climbing the rickety stairs of the sleazy, smelly little place at 23 Traversa Sao which Kliemann was using as his "safe house" while in Lisbon.

Kliemann was apparently ill. He lay on the bed in the dingy, little, bug-infested room as she came in and made hardly any attempt to rise in that *Wiener-Kavalier* manner he usually affected in the presence of *Damen*. Now his gallant mustache drooped and he was obviously feeling out of sorts with the world and himself.

"I've been ill," he said after they had exchanged greetings. "But how are you?" The big florid Air Force major, who lived it up in Paris, dining at the best of French restaurants, knew that she was suffering from a serious case of uremia. "You wrote and said you were in bad shape. Are you better?"

TREASURE shrugged: "It seems I've had it," she answered casually, as if she were talking about someone else. "The doctors in England gave me another six months to live. I must hurry up and live them."

Kliemann twisted his face sympathetically. "Do you want to go back to France?" he asked.

TREASURE replied in the negative, asking whether he were not satisfied with her work up to now.

Kliemann said naturally he was.

TREASURE now explained that she had obtained a job in the British Ministry of Information, working for the documentary film producer Sydney Bernstein. [He] "is the head of the Films Division," she added. "He sent me to Lisbon to contact script writers and novelists who've escaped from France. The British intend to make propaganda films to be shown in the European countries once they have been liberated... Right after the invasion, Bernstein wants to outdo the Americans."

Kliemann smiled at the "Jew's" ambition and congratulated her on an excellent excuse for visiting Lisbon. Then finally he came round to the subject which was the reason the British had really sent her to the Portuguese capital. "Excellent," he said in his thick Austrian-accented French, "if this comes off, I can send you as many script writers as you want. And how about the radio?" TREASURE's heart missed a beat. He mentioned it so casually. "How are you going to get it into England?"

She knew from her training in France that transmitters of the type she wanted — a high speed AFU set — were usually hidden within the framework of the normal pear-shaped *Volksempfaenger* ("people's radio") which the Boche had imported into France. The crystals which were an integral part of the transmitter would then be hidden in one of the tubes whereas the whole set would have to be taken to pieces before any suspicious counterintelligence agent would be able to find the socket for the morse transmitting key.

"I've thought of a plan," she said hurriedly before the Austrian could suggest any other alternative. "Tomorrow morning I'm going to see a young man I know at the British Embassy. His name is Stewart. I'll ask him to get me a second-hand radio. You can't get them in London. Two or three days later I'll tell him I've found one — *yours*. But I'll pretend I don't want to pay duty on it, and ask him if he wouldn't send it for me through the diplomatic pouch."

Kliemann had nothing but admiration for his female agent — so much in fact that he had hired her in spite of Admiral

Canaris's dislike of women in the spy game. He smiled for the first time that evening. "Excellent," he congratulated her.

TREASURE breathed out a sigh of relief. He had swallowed the bait. Thereafter the German agent and the British double-agent got down to discussing the intimacies of frequencies, call signs, and transmitting times. Finally Kliemann gave her the details of her mission (she knew it already from the Twenty Committee but naturally she did not tell the Austrian that). She must concentrate all her activities on the Anglo-American preparations for the coming invasion, in particular troop movements in Bristol-Salisbury, the major troop concentration area. Its location in the south of England would indicate that the Anglo-Americans intended to land in the Normandy or Pas de Calais area, the two obvious spots for the cross-Channel invasion.

A few days later on March 23, 1944, TREASURE flew back "home to England" with nothing more lethal in her luggage than a huge basket of oranges, pineapples, and bananas (rarities in the embattled island in those days). But somewhere in the bowels of the same plane in the "diplomatic pouch" was the AFU set, which would mean sudden death for many thousands of German soldiers while saving those of many British and American ones. As an admirer wrote later of this woman who would not live to see the victory which she was so instrumental in bringing about: "All around her she could sense the invisible army of the Allied soldiers whom she would save from death on the bloodstained beaches of the Normandy landing."

The first move in *Operation Fortitude* had been won by the British.

The plan behind Operation Fortitude as conceived by the Twenty Committee, was to create two army groups — the real one under Field Marshal Montgomery — and an imaginary one, entitled the First United States Army Group (FUSAG). When Montgomery's men hit the beaches, FUSAG would be left behind to persuade the Germans that the real attack was still going to come through the Pas de Calais. They would not then throw in the full weight of their forces in France; some would still be held back to meet the second and "real" invasion.

Thus in that tremendous spring of 1944 while Montgomery's British and American assault divisions collected in the British Midlands, the West, and Southwest, fake information had to be sent to the Germans to indicate that the Allied order-of-battle placed its main emphasis on Scotland and the East and Southeast of England. The conclusion German Intelligence would draw — so the British and American spymasters hoped — would be that the Pas de Calais was the place to watch.[67]

To carry out this scheme, the Twenty Committee employed its best two double agents, BRUTUS and TREASURE, BRUTUS, the former "Armand," had had a tough time since he had "escaped," courtesy of Colonel Reile, in 1942. At first the British were suspicious of him, not because they did not trust him but, as Masterman explained after the war: "We could after a time be sure of BRUTUS and his motives *but could we also be sure that the Germans really trusted him?*... If they convinced themselves that he had thrown them over, his traffic from this country would be a source of great danger to us." In the end the devious, almost Oriental minds of the members of the Twenty Committee were convinced that the Germans trusted BRUTUS, and they put him to work. Because of political difficulties with the Poles — and potentially also the

---

[67] A German map of the British order-of-battle captured on May 15, 1944, in Italy showed that the enemy "bought" the scheme.

Russians — the latter knew nothing of the activities of the double agent. Narrowly escaping a court-martial at the hands of his fellow countrymen, BRUTUS moved up the ladder of promotion at a miraculous rate even in those wartime days of rapid advancement. By the spring of 1944, attached as a senior liaison officer at Bradley's First Army HQ, he even gained access to the Supreme Commander's own Forward Command Post — courtesy of the Twenty Committee.

Day after day, week after week, he transmitted information to the German Abwehr in France, convincing the enemy that the German Seventh Army would not bear the brunt of the major attack in Normandy; that pleasure would be reserved for the Fifteenth Army in the Pas de Calais. As the pleased spymasters in Paris noted on his reports: [they were] "uniformly excellent," and "the intelligence supplied by this agent is contributing materially to the clarification of the enemy's order of battle."

They were no less pleased with TREASURE's work, especially as she could relay it directly to them now, thanks to Kliemann's transmitter. Night after night she would make her way to the address in the London suburb of Hampstead, the exact number of which was only known to her conducting officer. There, she, her conducting officer, and the FANY officer[68] would set up the AFU set and begin transmission to the faraway German listening posts.

For TREASURE these nocturnal sessions in the strange decrepit old house were a torture. She was constantly in pain

---

[68] British female auxiliaries. The Twenty Committee used them in their radio work and in the supervision of their double-agents' transmissions. In addition they were expected to learn "the hand" of particular agents on the Continent, i.e., the individual manner of transmitting, unique to each agent.

and thought she was going blind. Her doctors warned constantly she had only a few more months to live. Her bosses in the Twenty Committee were becoming increasingly "displeased" (as they put it with typical understatement) with her displays of temperament (TREASURE had a formidable temper); but they knew they could not bring off Operation Fortitude without her. So they tolerated her moods, her scenes, her drinking bouts, her hypochondria, and forced her to work on.

Soon they would get rid of her and send her back to France to die. By that time Kliemann would have been captured, the tremendous ruse successfully brought off, and her services no longer needed. On that day, the dying woman, who had been the most important cog in the great deception would make one of her last entries in her diary. It would read: "I'm Number 75,054, I've lost my personality. With it, I've lost my solitary state. I'm no longer alone. I've got the whole army with me ..."

While the anonymous masters of the "Double-Cross" game played out their strange roles in the depths of a bombed, decrepit London, other no less curious figures made their contribution to the great operation soon to be launched across the Channel. In this case it was made deep below the green-grey waves. Night after night they would come up from the depths in the midget submarine that had brought them this far and plod awkwardly along the shingle in their flippers, searching for the information that might cost them their lives at any moment.

The information they sought was varied. It might range from the position of a certain lone German gun overlooking an important beach through the composition of the clay at a certain level above the water line up to the strength of the "Rommel Asparagus," as the Germans called the underwater sea defenses which the new Commander-in-Chief in France, "Desert Fox" Field Marshal Erwin Rommel had initiated. And all the time the men who risked their lives nightly on these lone patrols knew they might be doing so for nothing.

The men who swam in on these patrols were highly intelligent and were well aware that their chiefs back in Portsmouth might be acting on orders from some obscure Intelligence office in a London backstreet to allow them to be captured while surveying an unimportant beach! The backroom boys knew they would talk once the Gestopo had been given full opportunity to work them over; and the information beaten out of them would be passed over to the German Army, which would concentrate forces on the *wrong* beach.

By the spring of 1944, most of those working closely with British Intelligence realized that their masters were prepared to sacrifice individual lives if by doing so they could save those of the thousands in khaki and olive-drab who were soon to storm across those lonely Norman beaches. All the same they swam in, night after night, to face not only treachery and betrayal, not only the Führer's Most Secret Order No. 00/3830/42 which ordained instant death upon capture, but a whole range of automatic killers — flamethrowers and machine-gun nests, land mines and booby traps, barbed wire, and mantraps.

Just before dawn on May 18, 1944, thin-faced British officer George Lane and his friend and companion, Roy Wooldridge, had finally managed to get beyond the breakwaters at Cayeux-sur-Mer after a night of reconnoitering the beach there. There was the sudden noise — still faint, but definite — of a motorboat.

At first the two men, their faces still blackened with the grease they had slathered on the previous night when they had gone ashore, were unconcerned. They thought it was the Royal Navy boat come to pick them up. Then Lane saw the flag it bore. It was white — just like the Royal Navy ensign — but instead of the Union Jack, the left quarter was decorated with the black and white swastika of the *Kriegsmarine*! The two Britishers kept their heads, although they knew what would happen to them if they were taken alive. Lane whispered to Wooldridge: "Perhaps we can capture it and sail it home." He drew his Colt .45. The little German motorboat circled them cautiously, and they could see that three crew members were covering them with machine pistols. Lane and Wooldridge raised their hands — slowly and carefully.

Things happened quickly after that. They were brought into the little harbor they had left only a few hours before and thrown into a cell. Lane did not see Wooldridge[69] again after that. On the next day he was blindfolded, thrust into a car, and driven at high speed through the still Norman countryside. Half way there he managed, however, to jerk his blindfold up a little and spot the name on a signpost just before the car stopped. It was "La petite Roche Guyon."

A while later his blindfold was removed, and he was thrust, blinking at the unaccustomed light, before an obviously high-ranking German officer. "I have something important to tell you," the German said in excellent English. "You will meet an important personality, but you must give me your word as an officer and gentleman that you will behave accordingly."

Lane, who by now was completely mystified by the whole procedure, (he had been encouraged by his superiors to believe

---

[69] He was, however, also brought to Le Roche Guyon.

he would be tortured and shot almost immediately after capture) pretended to be hurt. "But of course," he answered shortly, "I never do anything else but behave like an officer and a gentleman."

The German seemed satisfied. But the preparations were obviously not finished yet. The bedraggled English captive was let into a large room which was well furnished, a fire burned in the large grate. An elegant, high-ranking officer rose to greet him. He too spoke excellent English. "It must be very nice in England," he said in a conversational manner.

"Do you know England?" Lane asked.

"Yes, I know England very well — my wife is English."

Again the German stated that he would soon meet an important personality. Suddenly he stopped in the midst of his conversation and looked at Lane's nails. "I should imagine you'll want to clean your nails before you go in," he said, completely out of the blue.

The Britisher stared at him thoroughly perplexed. What was this — a drawing room party or a German Army lunatic asylum? "Yes," he managed to say, "but who am I going to meet?"

The German — he was Colonel Hans-Georg von Tempelhoff — drew himself up to his full height, as if the very mention of the name deserved respect. Proudly he announced: *"You will meet his Excellency Field Marshal Rommel."*

Thus the dirty, bedraggled British undercover soldier met the man whose empire he was helping to destroy, and one of the war's strangest conversations commenced.

Rommel told the British officer to sit down and then began to ask questions through his interpreter. It was all very friendly. Some time after the conversation, the broad-faced Swabian who had gained such a great reputation in the desert asked: "And how is my friend Field Marshal Montgomery?" Lane answered: "To the best of my knowledge, he is well. He's planning an invasion." Rommel smiled and fingered the knight's cross which dangled from his neck: "So, you believe that he is planning an invasion and the British will at last start to fight."

Lane attempted to smile though he did not feel one bit like smiling. This was only the first act. "Yes," he answered, "it says so in the *Times*, the best newspaper in the world — it has everything."

Rommel laughed and asked a few more questions. Lane's confidence began to return. As he remembered after the war: "This man was all soldier, I thought, and I began to enjoy the situation." He turned to the interpreter and said: "Would you please ask the Field Marshal if I can ask a question now?"

The question was translated and Rommel gave his approval. Madly, Lane racked his brain for a suitable question. Finally he asked: "Do you think that a military occupation and government are an ideal situation for a conquered people?"

Rommel seemed to like the query. He went into a long explanation. Lane listened carefully to the translation, then couldn't help saying: "That's all well and good, but, Your Excellency, you can't maintain that the people like being ruled by a military government in this way!"

Rommel's face hardened a little. "Of course, they can," he said firmly. "You should see how happy and contented people are all over France, because now they know what they've got to do. We showed them it and they like it."

Suddenly Lane laughed. Rommel looked puzzled. Lane explained: "I can't see that, Your Excellency, because every time *I* travel your people cover up my eyes and tie up my hands."

For a moment Lane thought he might get away with having his eyes left uncovered when he left which would be soon. But he had not reckoned with Rommel's staff. One of them bent down and whispered something in the Field Marshal's ear. He caught the words *Befehl ist Befehl.*

He knew what that meant: "Orders are orders." He'd had it!

But the meeting with the Field Marshal had saved his life. On Rommel's express order he was removed to a concentration camp (together with Wooldridge) where he survived the war instead of being shot.

But now while the car which was to take him to Neuengamme Concentration Camp sped through the "peaceful" French countryside, those "happy and contented" people of Rommel's were preparing to fight. They were no longer happy to play their own particular role in London's attempts to fool and bewilder the Germans. Nor were they happy reconnoitering and passing on information across the Channel. Now they wanted blood and revenge. They wanted to strike back. The SOE and the new American giant with which it was now to work, the OSS, had perforce to embark on a new intelligence role — the inciting of bloody, violent revolution.

14 — "ORGANIZATION SHUSH-SHUSH"

In 1940, Mussolini had joked that the U. S. Secret Service was "the best in the world because no one knows where it is!" In other words, there wasn't one. And one year later when President Roosevelt asked "Wild Bill" Donovan, the much-decorated World War I soldier, to form one, he had confessed gloomily to the New Yorker: "Bill, you will have to begin with nothing. We have no intelligence service."

Major-General Donovan, the New York Irishman who was one of only three soldiers to hold all three top decorations, including the Congressional Medal of Honor, was undismayed. With a will he set about the task of forming the organization which later became known as the Office of Strategic Services — the OSS.

Scholars and adventurers, crooks and cops, men and women of a half a dozen national backgrounds rallied to his strange banner. Some were out for an unorthodox war; others for a quick buck or a safe billet. Many were talented men and women who felt they could best use their particular gifts in the pursuit of victory under Donovan's command.

But at first the OSS was plagued with undesirables and dead beats. There were the Ph.D's who felt their degree qualified them automatically for a major's leaf and a chauffeur-driven vehicle. There were the crazy inventors with explosives which could be baked into bread and eaten if the possessor felt he was under suspicion (though it wasn't thought advisable to smoke a cigarette immediately afterwards); or a noisome chemical named *"Who-me?,"* which duplicated the smell and consistency of a loose bowel movement. Its purpose was to be sprayed on the pants of high Japanese officers so that they would lose "face" before the "natives."

It was not surprising therefore, that by 1942, when Donovan was getting really under way, he was still being mocked by the press as "Hush-Hush Bill;" while his organization filled with Ivy League graduates and such Social Register names as Dupont, Vanderbilt, Morgan, Roosevelt, etc., etc., was made fun of on the cocktail circuit in Washington as "oh, so secret" or "oh, so silly," or even worse, "organization shush-shush."

The Germans picked up the gossip about the new American secret service, which combined the same functions as both the British SIS and SOE, and commented over their radio broadcasts, beamed to the United States that Donovan's organization consisted "of fifty professors, twenty monkeys, ten goats, twelve guinea pigs — and a staff of Jewish scribblers!" The reference to the animals was explained by the fact that Donovan had to locate some of his offices in the National Health Institute, where they shared quarters with the latter's experimental labs.

In the spring of 1942, when the main body of the OSS moved to London under the command of Ivy Leaguer David Bruce, now a colonel, things changed. The OSS agents from the Social Register who had survived the course up to this time now found themselves confronted with the grim and violent realities of their new profession. The days of the cocktail circuit, the brittle chatter, and glamorous uniforms were over. They were pushed into the British SOE training schools. They were forced to take the eight parachute jumps just outside Manchester under the critical eyes of shaven-headed RAF jump-masters. They had to undergo survival training in the harsh bogs and bare hills of the far north of Scotland. They were chivvied and bellowed at from early morning to late at night by lean, trim — even sadistic — Commando instructors, occasionally only too pleased to have a little fun at the expense of these "Yanks" who were — as the saying in 1942 had it — "oversexed, overpaid and *over here*!" And they were confronted with the really harsh truth when they met their agent-instructors in the SOE training schools — whose twisted postures, missing fingernails, and scarred backs spoke eloquently of what happened to the agent who missed out and fell into the hands of the Gestapo!

Slowly the dross was abandoned. The ones who could not make the grade were sent back to Washington to complete the war within the safety of the United States. (No reject was ever allowed to re-enter a theater of war lest he be captured and reveal the secrets of the new U.S. intelligence service.) The OSS started to shape up and become a trim, professional organization.

With unlimited money at its disposal and an ever expanding number of personnel (by late 1944 it had some 30,000 operatives all over the world), the OSS started to outstrip its mentor and older brother, the SOE. The British did not like it. They regarded the "Johnny-come-latelies" with a certain amount of suspicion and resented the order from higher headquarters that they had to share all information and intelligence resources with these brash young "cousins" of theirs (as Churchill insisted on calling them) from over the seas. But in the end Gubbins's men and women had to give in and cooperate.

Now the Americans started to inject new blood into the clandestine operations which the SOE had been conducting in Occupied Europe for nearly four years. The "Yanks" brought with them a new approach. It was neither sophisticated nor subtle, but brash and direct, supported by the overwhelming weight of American weapons and money (at first the OSS had relied almost completely on British weapons, radio sets, procedures, planes, etc.). As was to be expected of a "young" nation which had been calling for an invasion of the European Continent ever since they had entered the war, in spite of British objections, the Americans wanted their operatives to conduct all-out war against the "Nazis." Spying and sabotage would now have to take second place; direct violent action against the enemy would be paramount. The idea of *Operation Jedburgh* had been born.

The Jedburgh teams most often consisted of a British SOE officer, an American from the OSS, and a French officer from the SOE French Section. This little team — usually called in secret service circles a "Jed" — would be parachuted into France, amply supplied with gold and local currency. There they would form their own little army from the local French *Maquis*, who would be trained and supplied from the air with American and British weapons. Once the signal for D-Day had been given, these "Jeds" would spring into action and start actual physical operations against German troops hurrying to support their comrades facing the Allied invasion forces on the beaches. The days of sabotage were over. In their place had come the "hit and run raids" based on the Maquis guerrilla principle of *"surprise, mitraillage, évanouissement"* — "surprise, shoot, vanish." There was only one catch — the Germans would reply in kind, and if they could not find the "Jedburgh" team responsible, they would wreak their revenge on the innocent...

The first "Jeds" left the United Kingdom for North Africa in

May 1944, just prior to D-Day. From the long-standing Allied airfields on the African coast they were flown in over the weakly defended area of Southern France and dropped in remote wooded parts of Brittany. From there they started to harass the German divisions streaming from the easy life in the South to support their hard-pressed comrades in the North.

It all worked according to plan. Time and time again in those first days, the Anglo-American-led Maquis sallied out of their mountain fastnesses and lonely forests to descend upon some unsuspecting German column, shooting it up, killing half a dozen enemy soldiers, blocking the road with one of their destroyed, flaming vehicles, and disappearing back the way they had come even before the Germans had time to realize what had happened.

There was 23-year-old Navy Sp/1C Edwin Poitras, who was assigned to a "Jed" as a radio operator. The plane carrying him to his team was shot down, but Poitras managed to parachute to safety and join a Maquis group, directing their operations. One day their HQ was dynamited and they had to flee to the hills. On impulse Poitras decided to drive into the nearest town, have a look round and buy a few supplies, but unfortunately — for the Germans — he hit trouble. As he explained it later himself: "One day I drove into town to get some cigarettes and a carload of Gestapo chased the truck I was in and opened up with submachine guns. I put a live grenade into an empty briefcase and tossed it out, and they stopped to pick it up. Maybe they thought it was my codebook or something, *but anyway there were four very dead Gestapo a moment later!*"

There was the unknown OSS agent who tipped off Bruce in London where Rommel's HQ was to be found. This resulted in what could be described as the first aerial ambush, when in

July 1944, a lone British spitfire came zooming out of the clouds to shoot up the Field Marshal's staff car as it sped along a lonely French road. The "Desert Fox" suffered severe wounds which took him out of the German command in France for good — and, incidentally, also out of the plot to assassinate Hitler.

Some of the more experienced British officers of the SOE, operating independently of the Jedburgh teams were horrified at the latter's cool disregard for their own lives and those of the French men and women working with them. Others were frankly contemptuous of the Americans' inexperience and what appeared to them clumsy methods.

Denis Rake, ace SOE agent, a mild-mannered man who loved cats and who must have seemed a very strange Secret Service man to the Americans, if only because of his somewhat bizarre sex life and habits, recalls meeting a Jedburgh team commanded by elderly Prince Obolensky, a relative of the Russian czars and now a naturalized American citizen. To him they appeared very well dressed — straight from one of those London tailors who supplied handmade uniforms to wealthy officers. In fact, the whole team was composed of rich American businessmen's sons and lawyers. One of the elegant lawyers told the ragged SOE agent, who had been in and out of France several times in these last years and had had some amazing escapes, "We're one-dollar-a-year men, you know." He meant that the group was accepting only nominal pay.

Rake's comment summed up what he thought of them. "*One dollar a year! Blimey, that's exactly what they were worth!*"

Later the eighty-two Americans connected with the Jedburgh operations became the most highly decorated group in the entire war. Fifty-three received the Distinguished Service

Cross, the Croix de Guerre, Legion of Merit, Silver or Bronze Star, or Purple Heart. But in the summer of 1944, their efforts caused an immediate reaction in the German camp. Nazi troops struggling vainly to reach the battlefront in Normandy, but frustrated by the American-led Maquis groups, struck back with the utmost brutality.

The elite SS Division *Das Reich* hurrying up "Route Nationale 20" in the direction of Normandy had been harassed by ambushes and attacks ever since it had been given the order to move. Its pace had been slowed down to a walk, and its brave but inexperienced commander, SS General Lammerding, eager to prove himself in battle, was furious. He raged at both his own officers and the French "gangsters and criminals" who were preventing him from winning the "Knight's Cross of the Iron Cross" which every self-respecting SS General should have. He ordered the utmost brutality in pushing forward, echoing Himmler's recent words that SS divisions should give command to officers who were *"brutal und forsch"* — brutal and pushy.

Meanwhile, thirty-five miles north of the location of his division, news of the local Maquis' triumph had reached the little provincial town of Tulle. Encouraged by the victories of their compatriots farther south, the locals swamped out onto the streets to support the town's Maquis group. Together the civilians and the Maquis, armed with American submachine guns and carbines, attacked the small German garrison of second line troops and *Wehrmacht* civilians who had barricaded themselves in the Hotel Lattremolière, a college of education, and a local factory.

Both the college and the hotel were taken by storm and Colonel Bouty, the mayor of Tulle, proclaimed its liberation to the cheers of the power-drunk civilians and Maquis, standing among their own and the German dead. Some of the latter had been shot when they had tried to surrender. But in the summer of 1944, the French were not about to make any fine distinctions between Germans who were still fighting and those who had already surrendered. "They were Boche, weren't they?"

At dawn the SS came. The lead companies of the Lammerding division battled their way into the rebellious French town, determined on revenge, and urged on by their commander who had proclaimed that Tulle would pay with "blood and ashes" for its bloody act of defiance.

It did!

The Maquis and the armed civilians, who had been so successful against the German second-line troops, were no match for the crack SS troops. Five-hundred men and several women were rounded up. All were to be publicly hanged on Lammerding's own order.

SS Stunnführer Walter, a Catholic from the Rhineland, did not like the idea one bit. He disobeyed Lammerding's orders and selected instead one hundred twenty hostages. The local priest, Abbe Espinesse, pleaded with him for the life of one of the hostages, a mentally retarded eighteen-year-old boy, saying he was innocent. Walter replied: "I know, they're all innocent, but they have to pay for the guilty." Finally the SS Captain released twenty-one prisoners, but the rest were taken to the Place de Souillac.

From every tree in and around the little square, from every lamppost and iron-barred balcony, the nooses were waiting, swinging slightly back and forth in the slight summer breeze. Next to each rope were two ladders and two SS men in their camouflaged battle jackets. One by one, the deathly pale, sometimes weeping French men and boys were shoved up the ladders. As they did so, one SS man placed a noose around the man's neck and pulled it tight. In that same instant, the other soldier kicked the ladder away. There was a stifled scream, the clatter of the ladder, and the victim swung back and forth, his tongue hanging out.

In the end ninety-nine Frenchmen, between seventeen and forty-five years of age, were executed that day, while (if we are to believe local reports) Fraülein Geissler, one of the German secretaries, sat in the blue dusk watching the hangings, drinking and chain smoking, and listening to popular songs on the gramophone. Thus they died, the men of Tulle, to the tune of the sad little German melody which was so popular with the war-sick defenders of the Reich:

"Es geht alles vorüber,
Es geht alles vorbei,
Nach jedem Dezember,
gibts wieder ein Mai."[70]

But the Maquis did not give up. That same night they kidnapped one of Lammerding's officers. *Das Reich* went to work once more. On the following day they rounded up the entire population of another village on their route — Oradour-sur-Glane. Old people were routed out from their beds as were black-smocked, cropped-hair school children from the local école where the schoolteacher had just scrawled on the blackboard:

"I make a resolution never to harm others." The pathetic children and their schoolmaster were never again to harm anyone.

---

[70] "Everything passes. You get over everything. After each December, there's always a May."

As soon as the 200-odd citizens of the villages had been herded into the dusty square, the SS machine gunners opened up. Methodically, as if in a training exercise, they swung their thin-barreled weapons from left to right, mowing down the men and boys. Then they moved through the heaped bodies, pouring gunpowder over them. Satisfied with their work, they set fire to them. Only five of the wounded, who had pretended to be dead, escaped.

In the local church, where they had imprisoned most of the village's women and small children, the SS men ignited special smoke grenades. Some of the women died at once. Others panicked. Screaming and coughing, they tried to run out the one door. The waiting machine guns burst into their harsh melody of death. Two hundred forty-one women and two hundred two children died either in or outside the little church. Again the SS set fire to their corpses as well as to the village itself.[71]

Thereafter they left the still burning, silent village behind. Soon they arrived at the Normandy front — ten days late. But at what cost in human life, innocent and guilty, American, French, British, and German!

Thus the Battle for Normandy was won. The SOE and OSS had successfully completed their bloody work. The Allies were firmly established on the Continent of Europe, thanks in part

---

[71] Today Oradour-sur-Glane is still as it was. The French have retained it as a monument to the horrors of war. General Lammerding disappeared after the war. When the heat was off, he reappeared although he had been sentenced to death by a French court in absentia. Soon he become a successful building contractor in Dusseldorf. In 1971, worried by German inquiries into his past, he turned his business over to his son and "retired" to a border village near Austria (an obvious escape route). French ex-Resistance workers threatened to kidnap him à la Eichmann, but Lammerding died (presumably) before they could put their plan into operation.

to their efforts. As Eisenhower, the Supreme Commander himself, was to remark soon: "I cannot overemphasize the decisive value of this most successful threat (the Fortitude deception), which paid enormous dividends, both at the time of the assault and during the operations of the two succeeding months."

It was fulsome praise indeed, but supported by Field Marshal Keitel's own statement at Nuremberg the day after he had been sentenced to death for "war crimes": "German military intelligence knew nothing of the real state of Allied preparations. Even when the craft carrying Allied troops were approaching the coast of Normandy, the highest state of alert was not ordered."

Indeed Schellenberg's intelligence service had predicted the date of the invasion in spite of what Keitel said (his operators had discovered the key code word which heralded the start of the invasion[72]). However, the SD was entering the last round, and as the events at Tulle[73] and Oradour showed, it, like the rest of the German Army, was beginning to lose its nerve.

---

[72] The key sentence sent over the BBC — "soothe my heart with monotonous languor" (the second line from a poem by the French poet Verlaine) — had been interpreted by a sergeant at the Fifteenth Army's listening post. His commander Col. Meyer had taken the news immediately to the Fifteenth's commander, General von Salmuth who was playing bridge with several other officers. He murmured the usual "state of alert," then continued with his game, telling the others: "I'm too old a bunny to get excited about that."

[73] Otto Weidinger, a regimental commander in *Das Reich*, who was imprisoned by the French from 1947-1951 in connection with the Tulle massacre, but was released after the proceedings had been stopped, recently wrote to a German newspaper *Die Welt* to give his side of the events. Among other things, he states: "On the morning of June 9, *Das Reich* found fifty-two German bodies at the school, with cracked skulls, their eyes gouged out and other terrible mutilations. According to local statement the Maquis had driven over

BOOK THREE: THE END OF THE ROAD

He, the trained spy, had walked into the trap
For a bogus guide, seduced with the old tricks.

W. H. Auden

the bodies with trucks... the soldiers had had their sexual organs cut off and thrust in their mouths. The female companions of the Maquisards had urinated and defecated on the bodies. In a kind of frenzy, they had lit a fire and crazy with wine, they had played football with German steel helmets between the corpses."

1944-1945

They are not fools, however much we try to persuade ourselves of the contrary. But supposing they had got some tremendous sacred sanction — some holy thing, some book or gospel... something which would cast over the whole ugly mechanism of the German war the glamour of the old torrential raids.

John Buchan

15 — A MISSION IS PROPOSED

On Sunday afternoon, the 4th of August, six weeks after the events at Tulle, SS General Schellenberg, who had succeeded Admiral Canaris in February when the latter had been removed from his post as commander of the Abwehr, was working in his office at Military Intelligence.

Schellenberg had been overjoyed at his new command, which now combined the old SD and the Abwehr under one master — himself. But it had meant a lot of extra work. The Abwehr agents all over Europe were scrambling over each other to defect to the enemy or go underground like rats leaving a sinking ship, and Canaris's old organization was in bad shape. Even those who had remained loyal such as Giskes and von Feldmann had got themselves posted as the heads of the new *Frontaufklärungskommandos*[74] (combat intelligence units) where their valued talents and long experience were being wasted in routine day-to-day intelligence missions. And although his own organization had remained loyal, there were signs that there were waverers within its ranks too.

Thus Schellenberg worked this warm summer afternoon at his desk, outlining his plans for a reorganization and fighting against the nagging thought at the back of his mind that it was all for nothing: Germany was nearly beaten and the only solution to his own personal and Germany's problem was a quick peace with the Western Allies.

---

[74] There were four of these organizations in the West: Nos. 306, 307, 313 and 314. Lieutenant Colonel Giskes commanded the most successful, No. 307, soon to be stationed on the German border with Luxembourg and Belgium.

Suddenly the train of his thoughts was disturbed by the ringing of the telephone. He reached for it with a pale, well-manicured hand on which he wore a big blue ring that concealed a gold capsule containing cyanide poison.

It was Mueller calling. In the last months their relationship had grown progressively worse. Since Kaltenbrunner had taken over Heydrich's job he had wormed his way into the confidence of Mueller's friend and patron Martin Bormann. Both Kaltenbrunner as head of the Main Security Office (who had been a schoolmate of Skorzeny's and was, like him, huge and tough — at least on the surface — his face also a mass of duelling scars), and Mueller, the chief of the Gestapo, had taken it upon themselves to put the smart young ex-lawyer in his place.

Now in a sharp voice "Gestapo" Mueller ordered Schellenberg to drive to Admiral Canaris's home — at once. Schellenberg asked why and was told that, at Kaltenbrunner's own orders, he was to arrest the old man. Apparently Canaris was implicated in the July plot to assassinate Hitler. The ex-Abwehr chief was to be taken to Fuerstenberg in Mecklenburg and "not to return with him to Berlin until everything had been cleared up."

For Schellenberg, Canaris belonged to the past. He had had his triumph in February when Canaris had been removed from his post. He wasn't interested in inflicting any further injury on the old man. He protested, therefore, that he was "not an executive officer and would not dream of carrying out such an assignment." "Furthermore," he added sharply, "I shall telephone Himmler. This is an imposition."

Mueller was unimpressed. "You know that Kaltenbrunner has been put in charge of the investigation of July 20th," he said calmly. "*Not* Himmler!"

Schellenberg knew. Kaltenbrunner was now trying to imitate Heydrich and assure himself a completely independent position, free of Himmler's restrictions, although he had not half Heydrich's intelligence and flair for police work.

"If you refuse to comply with the order," Mueller went on, "which I herewith repeat, you will have to suffer the consequences."

Schellenberg realized immediately what Kaltenbrunner's and Mueller's game was. If he refused to carry out the order, they would somehow or other implicate him in the July 20th assassination plot. Then he, too, would end up in the Plotzensee cellar, being slowly choked to death with a piece of thin piano wire attached to a hook, while a movie camera recorded his last agonies for the benefit of Adolf Hitler. He hung up without another word.

When he arrived at Canaris's home with his assistant, Baron von Voelkersam, one of Skorzeny's men, to arrest the Admiral, Canaris was very calm. His first words were: "Somehow I felt that it would be you. Please tell me first of all, have they found anything in writing from that fool Colonel Hansen?"[75]

Schellenberg nodded gravely: "Yes," he replied, "a notebook in which there was among other things a list of those who were to be killed. But there was nothing about you or your participation."

"The dolts on the General Staff can't live without their scribblings," the white-haired Admiral snorted contemptuously.

Schellenberg explained his mission to Canaris.

---

[75] An officer in charge of Military Intelligence, who was involved in the July plot.

He took it calmly, though the younger man could see he was worried. "It's too bad that we have to say good-bye in this way. But — " he hesitated, then bit his lower lip, as if he were trying to repress some emotion unknown to the SD man — "we'll get it over with." Then he pulled himself together. Something of the old Canaris came through: a man confident of his own ability to explain, appease, solve problems. "You must promise me," he said, "that within the next three days you will get me an opportunity to talk to Himmler personally. All the others — Kaltenbrunner and Mueller — are nothing but filthy butchers, out for my blood."

Schellenberg promised. Then he said in a completely official voice (as he wrote in his memoirs after the war): "If the Herr Admiral wishes to make other arrangements, then I beg him to consider me at his disposal. I shall wait in this room for an hour and during that time you may do whatever you wish. My report will say that you went to your bedroom in order to change."

The Admiral understood at once. "No, dear Schellenberg," he retorted speedily, "flight is out of the question for me. And I don't want to kill myself either. I am sure of my case and I have faith in the promise you have given me."[76]

Half an hour later they set off from Berlin in Schellenberg's big tourer which, like so many of his possessions was a showy affair, complete with short-wave radio for keeping in touch with his HQ. It was a vehicle he was inordinately proud of. Conversation was difficult. According to Schellenberg, "Canaris assured me several times that he knew very well I had

---

[76] Naturally we have only Schellenberg's word that the escape offer was a genuine one. Perhaps this was a way he had thought to get rid of Canaris in a quick efficient manner without bringing himself into conflict with Mueller and Kaltenbrunner.

no share in bringing about his dismissal. He hoped that fate would be kinder to me and that I would not one day be hunted down as he had been."

Schellenberg must have smiled to himself at that remark. That clever young man had no intention of allowing that to happen to him. When he died, he would do so in bed. (*He did!*)

Some while later the two of them arrived at the Border Police School in Fuerstenberg, where twenty high-ranking officers were being held in connection with the plot against Hitler. Here he drank a last bottle of red wine with his old rival. The latter gave him a few final instructions on how he was to conduct the promised conversation with Himmler. Then they parted. Canaris embraced him, tears in his eyes, saying "You are my last hope... Good-bye, my young friend."

Schellenberg walked out. He did not look back. Canaris was as good as dead.

One hour later, he was back at his bullet-proof office desk, equipped with twin sub-machine guns which he could fire while seated if attacked by one of his visitors. He looked at the handful of flimsies which had come in during his absence, then ordered a teletype message sent immediately to Mueller. It read: "I have carried out the order which you transmitted to me by telephone today. Further details you will hear through the Reichsführer SS Schellenberg."

"Case Canaris" was over. The white-haired Admiral, with the passion for dogs — the only animal which would not betray him — had been betrayed to his executioners. His long intelligence career, which had started as a young lieutenant on the German cruiser *Dresden* back in 1915, was at last completed. Soon he, too, would be a victim of the monster he had helped to create...

In 1938 when he was still only twenty-eight, ambitious young Schellenberg had written: "An intelligence network has to be built up gradually. In alien soil it must be fed like a plant and be given plenty of time to take root. Only then will it have a healthy growth and bear fruit in abundance... Useful contacts should be maintained for years if necessary and only be exploited when the time is ripe ... In intelligence work one must never be in a hurry." Now in 1944, Walter Schellenberg, who had made a remarkable career since he had joined the SS in 1933, realized that he had to throw his old principles overboard. In 1944, with Hitler's "Thousand Year Reich" promising to last only a few months more and with Germany's enemies hammering at the door, he knew he had to hurry. If he didn't, there were those who would not hesitate to get rid of him in exactly the same way that they — with his help — had gotten rid of Canaris; and his own end promised to be more immediate and violent than that of the wily old fox Canaris who knew too many secrets to be done away with just like that.

There was his new Chief, Heydrich's successor, Kaltenbrunner. He was a giant of a man, whose rotting teeth had occasioned Himmler to "order" him to go to a dentist and have them taken care of; his foul-smelling breath made it difficult for anyone to hold a conversation at close range.

At eleven o'clock each morning Schellenberg was forced to report to this brutal-looking giant whose face twitched nervously all the time. He knew that Kaltenbrunner, just like his crony Mueller, hated him; yet the visit gave the former an opportunity to start the day's drinking. As soon as Schellenberg came through the door, the bottle of cognac and two glasses appeared on the table in front of the Austrian as if by magic; Kaltenbrunner lit one of the hundred cigarettes he smoked every day, and the drinking started.

During these impossible conversations, Schellenberg could never resist looking at Kaltenbrunner's hands. To him they looked like those of "an old gorilla;" Canaris had called them "the hands of an assassin... real assassin's paws." They made him shudder involuntarily, for he could always imagine them clasping around his own neck.

In fact, the chief of the Main Security Office, whose small brown eyes made Schellenberg think of a "viper seeking to petrify its prey," was a dullard who had no stomach for violence. But he was — probably under Mueller's influence — developing a taste for power and had established direct contact with Hitler through the good offices of Martin Bormann, another of Schellenberg's pet hates.

For Schellenberg, however, Kaltenbrunner was suffering from what he called a "Heydrich complex." By this he meant Kaltenbrunner hated Heydrich so much that he committed one stupidity after another. Now he felt this "Heydrich complex" had been transferred to him and that, as he put it, "I suddenly became the object of all the animosity he had previously entertained against him (Heydrich)."

But it was not really Kaltenbrunner who scared the SD chief. That honor was reserved for "Gestapo Mueller," the ex-Bavarian plainclothes detective, who remained such an enigma for Schellenberg. In spite of Mueller's rough-and-tough talk about "driving all intellectuals into a coal mine and blowing it up," there was something shrewd and devious about the man, which was perhaps revealed by his nervously twitching eyelids. Had he gone over to the Russians? Was he playing a double-game? What was his real relationship to Bormann and Kaltenbrunner? What did they have up their sleeves for the day when Hitler should be removed? *And where did he, Schellenberg, fit into the plans of this unholy threesome?*

This was the most important question for the man who was determined to survive, come what may. A lot of questions, but few answers. For the time being, however, the only surviving member of the intelligence trio — Heydrich, Canaris and Schellenberg — who had begun World War II on Germany's behalf, knew that while he developed his own particular form of life insurance, with the unwitting aid of Heinrich Himmler, he must play along with Kaltenbrunner and Mueller. And he knew, too, that in their continuance of the war against their erstwhile enemies — Russian and Anglo-American — they would have no time for the type of subtlety he had outlined so confidently in 1938. They would want immediate, direct action — and violence, plenty of it...

In November, 1944, the "Führer's favorite commando," Otto Skorzeny, was called away from his private last gamble which he was planning at his HQ near Berlin, to a conference at Himmler's headquarters near Hohenlychen.

Things had changed a great deal since that summer day in 1943 when Himmler had doubted he was the man for the Mussolini job. Now he was received as an honored guest at the simple wooden hut in the forest which served as the Reichsführer SS's HQ, despite the fact that everyone else in Himmler's office outranked him.

Quickly he "made his report" in the German fashion and shook hands with the others — his chief Schellenberg, whom he did not like; his old acquaintance from their student days together, Kaltenbrunner. The other man present was only vaguely familiar to him, and the man in the uniform of an SS general had to mention his name before the Commando could place him. It was Pruetzmann, who had been running police work in Poland and Russia before the advancing Soviet armies had chased him out. From all accounts Obergruppenführer Pruetzmann, a man in his mid-forties who had been a member of the Party ever since his days as an apprentice in a North German bank, was not exactly brilliant.

As usual, Himmler was somewhat long-winded before he came to his reason for having called the conference and inviting Skorzeny, whose mind was still on the great project with which Hitler had entrusted him one month before. Finally the Reichsführer SS took off his pince-nez and wiped it carefully while everyone waited in silence. Kaltenbrunner took out yet another cigarette and Himmler glared at him. But the head of the Main Security Office no longer cared what Himmler thought. Skorzeny smiled to himself. The "Reichsheini," as Himmler was known behind his back in their circles, was keeping them in suspense.

Finally Himmler replaced his pince-nez and faced Skorzeny. "Skorzeny," he said, "I want you to take over the *Werewolf* and knock it into shape."

Before Skorzeny could reply, Himmler launched into a detailed account of what he intended to do with the new organization, of which both he and Bormann, his greatest rival at Hitler's HQ claimed to be the father. The "Werewolf Organization," named after the mythical medieval creature which could transform itself into a rampaging wolf, had been born that first week of November when Himmler, carried away with his own oratory, had proclaimed to a meeting of *Volksturm* men that soon the Germans would be able to strike the enemy in their rear, "coming and going like wolves."

In essence the new organization, which was in the process of being formed, had the job of sabotaging the enemy's rear and carrying out assassinations of "undesirables" and "traitors," i.e., Germans who were prepared to cooperate with the Allies crossing Germany's frontiers in East and West.

General Gehlen, Commander of German Army Intelligence in the East, had first drawn up the plan for this organization, based on what his own double-agents had learned about the Polish "Home Army" (a similar set-up). Schellenberg had forwarded it to Himmler: "This is madness," had been his first reaction, and he had raged against staff officers in soft jobs. Now, however, he had accepted the idea, and had begun recruiting the first of the five thousand volunteers the organization finally contained.

Already the organizers had introduced the full range of conspiratorial devices: secret passwords, clandestine arms dumps built up *behind* the Anglo-American and Russian lines, and training schools, where the volunteers who came mainly from the Hitler Youth and Maidens and SS would learn to "consider it our supreme duty and right to kill, to kill, and to kill, employing every cunning and while in the darkness of the night, crawling, groping through towns and villages, like wolves, noiselessly, mysteriously" (as Goebbels's *Radio Werewolf* would soon announce shrilly).

Now he wanted Skorzeny to take over, for Himmler had not too much confidence in Pruetzmann's ability. The latter had the reputation of being careless and lazy. Under other circumstances, Skorzeny would have been prepared to take up the challenge offered by Germany's first resistance organization. Prior to the German withdrawal from Belgium and France, he had set about building up a clandestine organization which would commence to operate once the Allies had taken over, sending information to the Germans and sabotaging Allied installations behind the front. But now, racing against time to carry out Hitler's secret order of the month before, he had no time for additional duties.

Himmler must have noted the look on the Austrian giant's scarred face, for he said: "I know this job would fall into your competences, Skorzeny, but I think you've got enough to do at the moment."

Skorzeny picked up the chance offered by Himmler's words. "Certainly, Reichsführer, I've more than enough to do, and I'd like to make the suggestion that I take over all operations (of this kind) outside Germany's borders."

Himmler nodded his approval and thus it was agreed that Pruetzmann would continue to run the "Werewolves," while Skorzeny would take responsibility for all sabotage and clandestine operations outside the borders of the Reich.

Watching them carefully, Schellenberg breathed a sigh of relief. With his subordinate Skorzeny safely out of the affair, he could now wash his hands of the whole stupid business. Although he had passed on Gehlen's plan for the *Werewolf* to Himmler, he had protested against it.

As he wrote later in his memoirs: "I then pointed out to him the senselessness of the Werewolf organization which was being forced to carry on the struggle against Germany's defeat. This plan, I said, would bring nothing but suffering to the German people. Opportunities would arise for every sort of crime to be committed." Himmler had waved aside his protests, merely saying: "I will try to think of some way to finish this business."

But his protest had been motivated not by humane interests alone; but also by fear of what would happen to him if he were connected with such a suicide operation, the leaders of which would undoubtedly be executed by the Allies once they were caught. Hadn't Goebbels already announced that the

"Werewolves" would repudiate the Hague convention? This, in his opinion, was tantamount to sentencing oneself to death before some American or British firing squad.

Thus while Himmler droned on, Schellenberg relaxed. He was not involved. He let his chief's talk submerge him, only half-listening to the man's grandiose ideas — flying bombs, submarines discharging missiles at New York, new wonder weapons, and jets. Did the Reichsführer really believe in Goebbels' propaganda lies, he wondered?

Skorzeny looked at him with contempt. He had very little respect for his chief, nor for Kaltenbrunner, who showed no emotion whatsoever, neither disapproval nor approval of Himmler's impossible plans for the continuance of the war. He did note, however, that Kaltenbrunner's typical nervous twitch was absent as he watched Schellenberg out of the comer of his eye.

The big Commando followed the direction of his gaze, while pretending to give his full attention to Himmler who was still rambling on about "bombarding New York in the near future with V-1's." As he later described the scene: "Here decisions of the greatest political importance were to be made... but Schellenberg remained silent. Naturally he had the ability to give his opinion on the problem, but he was scared to do so until he was certain about the attitude of his superior (i.e., Himmler). He called this hesitancy himself his 'diplomatic ability,' which ensured that he did not put his foot in it."

Little did the Austrian giant know what was really going on in the head of Walter Schellenberg at that moment; for as that long grey afternoon drew to an end in the cold little wooden hut, Schellenberg already knew that he had come to make his separate peace before these madmen, with whom he had to associate, pulled him down with them to that bloody, burning final destruction which had to be their fate, as in some primitive Teutonic legend.

Thus Himmler and his still loyal subordinate Skorzeny (who would soon start on the last of his amazing exploits, full of faith in the *Endsieg*, final victory) continued their dialogue, as if this were 1940 and not 1944; describing the technical innovations necessary for the successful bombarding of New York; considering whether a submarine or a bomber would be a better vehicle for launching the V-1 missile which would "bring about the decisive change in the war," as soon as "America started to feel the impact of the war itself...."

And all the time the scar-faced chief of the Main Security Office chain-smoked in thoughtful silence, while his subordinate Schellenberg, coldly aware of his chiefs scrutiny, smiled politely at the fool of the Reichsführer, who paraded up and down in front of them in his highly polished jackboots, planning impossible operations with weapons which did not exist and commanders who were long dead.

Frozen into attitudes like characters in some second-rate melodrama, the fools (some might call them patriots) talked and talked as the grey winter light faded while the realists (some might call them opportunists) planned how they would rescue their own skins, each engrossed in his own thoughts. That November afternoon marked the prelude to the last desperate act, which would bring to an end the "Thousand Year Reich" that lasted exactly twelve...

16 — THE LAST GAMBLE

Up to now, twenty-one-year-old Lieutenant Bouck's recon platoon of the Ninety-ninth Infantry Division, dug in on a pine-covered hill at the edge of the village of Lanzerath overlooking the German-Belgian border, had not been attacked. Like the rest of the long Ardennes front, it had been startled almost out of its wits by the dawn bombardment. Intelligence back at divisional headquarters had always maintained that this was a safe front and that outfits like the Ninety-ninth, as yet unblooded, were sent here for a kind of realistic training before they went out to the real "shooting war." But after the horizon had lit up so dramatically and so blood-red for half an hour on that grey December 16, 1944, morning, nothing had happened.

And it was that unnatural calm that worried the young tousled-haired infantry lieutenant and his men. Below the little group of white-painted stone houses, now pocked with the leprous marks of the intermittent machine gun fire which had been going on since the Americans had first arrived in the previous September, was absolutely quiet — too quiet.

Bouck decided to act. Instead of pulling back as the tank destroyers of the Fourteenth Cavalry had done, scuttling for cover as soon as the heavy German cannon had destroyed the dawn calm, he decided to enter the village himself with three of his best men.[77]

Ten minutes later the four, spread out at the regulation distance, clutching their weapons nervously, started to

---

[77] Letter from Dr. Bouck to author, 1971.

approach the village. It seemed empty. Either the German-speaking villagers, who had not been particularly friendly to the Americans in the past few days, had fled as soon as the bombardment had started, or they had buried themselves in their stout stone cellars. Furtively picking their way over freshly snapped branches of trees which lay in the muddy road, they advanced towards the little house which had been used by the tank destroyermen as their observation post. Everything was silent, save for the chatter of a German machine gun, high pitched and angry, and the slow pock-pock of an American gun answering the challenge.

Bouck raised his free hand, the little patrol dropped to the ground. Cautiously he surveyed the house. Its door was swinging wide open — evidence of the hasty retreat of the cavalrymen — and he could see the crucifix fixed to the kitchen wall. But there was no sign of life, enemy or otherwise. He'd risk it. Gripping his carbine more firmly, he signaled to his men. They got up from the ditch. Now they did not need to be told what to do. Now was the time for action — quick action!

Hastily they clattered up the cobbled path. Someone kicked an American helmet liner out of the way. They were inside. The place was strewn with U.S. equipment which the men of the Fourteenth had abandoned in their hasty retreat. Bouck had no eyes for it. He wanted to get upstairs where he knew one of the tiny bedroom windows overlooked the German frontier. Followed by the next youngest man in the platoon, after himself, Private Tsakainkas (because his name was so difficult, he was called "Sak"), he scrambled up the narrow dark stairs. The house smelt of unwashed humans and animals. The door to the bedroom was closed. Lieutenant Bouck booted it open. He stopped in his tracks.

The room was occupied!

A big man in the dark clothes common to that area was speaking in low hurried tones over the public telephone — in German!

For a moment Bouck did not react. Sak reacted for him. He drew his bayonet and called out, "Reach!"

It was all a little absurd, Bouck thought later, but the man, who obviously did not speak English, understood well enough. His face went pale, and dropping the phone his hands shot up in the air, while the young private glared at him aggressively.

Bouck did some quick thinking. He knew the inhabitants of this border area between Germany and Belgium had been German until 1919 when the Versailles Treaty had given the three East Cantons of Malmedy, St. Vith, and Eupen to the Belgians. In 1940, when the Germans had returned, the three ex-German areas with a population of some sixty thousand citizens had been incorporated back into the Reich and the menfolk conscripted into the Wehrmacht.

In recent months those menfolk had crossed the long, thinly defended front repeatedly, *actually going on leave from their Wehrmacht units to their families in American-controlled Belgium!*[78] Was this tall, scared man one of those? Or was he a German spy?

Bouck decided to give him the benefit of the doubt. Besides if they killed him and his body were found by the Germans before they managed to get away, there would be hell to pay.

Making a snap decision, he ordered: "Let him go!" Sak jerked his head toward the pot-holed, cobbled street. The German (or Belgian) needed no urging. His broad pale face broke into a

---

[78] One of my own informants in the area states that such a group of local men actually crossed the front just before the Battle of the Bulge started and "stole" a U.S. Sherman tank.

grin of pure relief, and he shot down the stairs. Seconds later he was running off towards the German lines, as if the devil himself were after him...

All along the thinly held Ardennes front that day, the first of the great attack which later became known as the "Battle of the Bulge," after Churchill had described it in this manner to the British Parliament, similar agents were at work, as they had been for the last few months, pumping information back to Colonel Giskes's 307 *Frontaufklärungskommando*; just as had the many "escapees" from the former German occupied territories who had supplied so much welcome information to Allied Intelligence about German defeatism and war-weariness. Giskes' *Operation Heinrich* was paying dividends.

It had all started just over two months before — on the afternoon of October 21st to be exact, when Otto Skorzeny had been ushered into the presence of the ailing, aging Adolf Hitler at his headquarters deep in the pine forests of East Prussia.

But in spite of his poor state of health, due to drugs, overwork, and the effects of the July attempt on his life, the Führer greeted his "favorite Commando" warmly and with a firm double-handed handshake. "Well done, Skorzeny," were his first words. "Now come and sit down and tell me about it" (Hitler was referring to Skorzeny's most recent exploit — *Operation Mickey Mouse* — kidnapping the favorite son of Admiral Horthy, ruler of Germany's ally Hungary, who had intended to break away and go over to the Russians.)

Skorzeny filled in the details, while Hitler watched him in admiration. Finished with his narrative, he rose to go; he was well aware that Hitler's time was precious.

But the Leader detained him. "Sit down, Skorzeny, and stay a while." His yellow, sick face suddenly filled with fresh life and enthusiasm and to Skorzeny, he appeared to have recaptured some of that old look which he had seen in 1943, one year before, when he had first met Adolf Hitler. "I am now going to give you the most important job of your life," were his opening words. "In December, Germany will start a great offensive. It may decide her fate."

Swiftly, carried away by his own enthusiasm, Hitler sketched in his plan for an attack on the Allied "ghost front" in the Ardennes, defended by only four divisions: two badly mauled by the fighting of the previous months and two completely green and inexperienced. Consisting of some eighty thousand fighting men, they were to be attacked by a quarter of a million Germans, supported by two thousand German jets and other new or secret weapons, who would rush to cross the River Meuse and then split the British and American armies before capturing the key Allied supply port of Antwerp.

Concluding his introduction to the strategic and political background of the new offensive, Hitler said: "I have told you so much so that you will realize that everything has been considered very carefully and has been well worked out." He paused and looked hard at his fellow Austrian.

"Now you and your units will play a very important role in this offensive. As an advance guard you will capture one or more bridges on the River Meuse between Liège and Namur. You will carry out this operation in British and American uniform. The enemy has already used this trick. Only a couple of days ago, I received the news that the Americans dressed in German uniforms during their operations in Aachen."

Skorzeny accepted the information which he knew was calculated to ease any doubts or fears he might have about his

253

own and the fates of his men, should they be captured in American uniform.

"I know you'll do your best," Hitler continued. "But now to the most important thing. Absolute secrecy. Only a few people know of the plan. In order to conceal your preparations from your own troops, tell them that we are expecting a full-scale enemy attack in the area between Cologne and Bonn. Your preparations are intended to be part of the resistance to that attack." "*Jawohl, mein Führer,*" Skorzeny snapped obediently. Then remembering all his other missions, especially those which select groups of his men were conducting hundreds of miles behind the Russian lines at the request of Schellenberg and Gehlen, he said, "But time is short and I have other tasks."

Hitler nodded. "Yes, I know time is short, but I know you'll do your best. For the period of the offensive, I am sending you a deputy. But one thing, Skorzeny," he raised a thick forefinger in warning, "I do not want you to cross the front line personally. You must not run the risk of being captured."

Then he rose. The interview was over. *Operation Greif* (Grab) had been born and with it, Giskes's *Operation Heinrich.*

Almost immediately Skorzeny started to look for volunteers who would join his Panzerbrigade 150, forming at the German Army training ground of Grafenwoehr. With Hitler's permission he was able to recruit from all three services plus the Waffen SS; but although he was flooded with volunteers, attracted by the adventurous nature of the secret mission or simply wishing to escape the boredom of routine military duties and inspired by the name Skorzeny, he found to his disappointment that only a handful of the three thousand-odd men he finally collected spoke perfect English. Indeed he was lucky if a day brought him two good speakers of the language.

Still he persisted with the operation, animated by that great energy and talent for organization which Hitler liked so much, dividing his motley recruits of all ages and backgrounds, dressed in half a dozen different uniforms and ranks, into three language categories: the one hundred or so perfect "native speakers;" the two to three hundred who spoke passable English; and the great majority whose English might fool *"a raw American recruit on a dark night who was hard of hearing."*[79]

In particular, he aimed to produce a change in the military psychology of his recruits. Although by this time most of them were dressed in captured GI uniforms and carried American weapons, they still reacted like members of the Wehrmacht, jumping to attention when he approached "making their little men" (as the German Army slang had it), with their faces rigid and palms extended parallel with the seams of their trousers. Skorzeny felt they were obviously Germans in American uniforms.

Within the short time Hitler had granted him, he instructed them how to slump in that typically American way; how to chew gum incessantly; and walk with that easy unmilitary sway that the GIs affected. Some of his best men he sent off to U.S. POW camps to mix with genuine GIs. The rest had to attend daily lectures in military English and view captured U.S. war films so that they could familiarize themselves at least with the rudiments of GI talk. In the meantime he had been perfecting his plans to spread alarm and disquiet behind the American front as well as capture one of the three bridges across the Meuse.

For the latter purpose he divided his command into three armored columns which, equipped with American armored cars and tanks (he never managed to get enough of these and

---

[79] To the author.

had to make do with camouflaged German vehicles), would accompany the lead squadrons of the Sixth SS Panzer Army in their task of breaching the U.S. Fifth and Eighth Corp fronts. For the former purpose, he gathered together the best of his English speakers under Captain Stielau, the last of six company commanders for this special group who had followed each other in rapid succession between November and December.

The *Stielau-Einheit*, as it was called, consisted of about eighty men divided into two groups; the sabotage group, of eight jeep teams; and the reconnaissance group of six teams, which a few days later was subdivided into four short-distance reconnaissance jeep teams and two long-distance ones.

The crews consisted of four men[80] — a driver, a commander, a saboteur/radio operator and an interpreter who spoke perfect English and, in most cases, had spent some years in the States. In a few cases, these men had actually served in the prewar U. S. Army. Besides their normal equipment, Skorzeny's men also carried a cyanide flask concealed within a typically GI Zippo lighter. And although they never spoke about the reason for its presence in their equipment, their intelligence told them why it had been included. In spite of what Skorzeny's lawyer had told them about their position in wartime if found behind the enemy line in enemy uniform, they knew there would be only one outcome: death by firing squad.

Suicide was perhaps a better way out!?

Thereafter the individual jeep teams trained together and were cut off from any contact with their fellows. Indeed they were guarded at their training camp by SS men, not to keep strangers away from this strange operation, but to keep the

---

[80] Skorzeny later discovered to his consternation that Americans usually had only three men to a jeep.

jeep-team members inside. Their paybooks had been taken away from them so that they couldn't desert easily; and a rumor went round the camp that one of their members had been shot because he had written a letter home describing their training.

It was only a rumor. But then rumors flew round the camp daily; they were part and parcel of their strange isolated existence. And Skorzeny encouraged them actively. If later one of the teams was captured, its members could relate the wildest of tales to American Intelligence.

Some of the Stielau unit thought, for instance, that they were going to strike through Belgium into France and link up with the German garrisons still trapped on the Channel coast. Others thought their task would be to assassinate some top Allied general.

On November 20, 1944, when Skorzeny paid his one and only visit to the Grafenwoehr camp, a Lieutenant N asked to see him. The young, fresh-faced officer was one of the commando team and with the energy and dash to be expected from a commando, he launched into his explanation for the interview straight away. "*Obersturmbannführer*," he said, looking Skorzeny straight in the eye, "I think I know the real target of the Brigade."

The Austrian started. He sat upright behind the desk. Had one of his three battalion commanders, the only ones to know their real objective besides himself, blabbed?

The young officer was pleased with Skorzeny's reaction. "Yes," he continued eagerly, "the Brigade is to march on Paris and capture the Allied HQ there."

Skorzeny relaxed as suddenly as he had grown alert. He could hardly hold back his laughter. "Swiftly, I considered the story," he wrote later. "Wasn't this a wonderful rumor!" He murmured a few words and let the man get on with it.

The Lieutenant took his "so-so" as confirmation of his supposition: "Can I offer my services to you, *Obersturmbannführer*? I've spent a long time in France and know Paris like the back of my hand. My French is good too. You can rely on me. I'll be as silent as the grave."

Skorzeny played him along. "Have you considered how the mission could be carried out?" he queried. "Isn't it a little too bold?"

"Of course it can be carried out," the other man shot back. "I know you'll have made your own plans, *Obersturmbannführer*, but I have considered the mission myself and come to the following conclusion." Swiftly he launched into a long and detailed explanation of how he would get the Stielau men to Paris, and it was only with difficulty that Skorzeny could stop him. All the same he had to admire the young officer, who seemed to have used his very vivid imagination to good effect.

As the latter saw it, they would be divided into two groups: one the GI guards, who would be the English-speaking group, in charge of taking German prisoners — the rest of the outfit — back to Paris. They would even be able to take with them "captured German tanks" meant for the U.S. Ordinance inspection. "I know Paris exceedingly well," the man said enthusiastically at the end of his outline. "I know the Champs-Elysée and the town — and I've often eaten at the Café de Paris."

Skorzeny was puzzled by the reference to the Café de Paris, but he realized it was time to bring the conversation to an end. "All right, then, Lieutenant," he said, "sleep on it and work the plan out in more detail. We'll talk about it again later." Then he held up one nicotine-stained forefinger in warning. "But I want you to be as close as the grave with the rest. You understand?"

The Lieutenant understood.

As he went out, Skorzeny burst out laughing. Another hot rumor had been born. Little did he realize that November afternoon, however, how valuable to his operation that rumor was going to be. But he had no further time to spend on it now, he told himself. There were still a hundred and one things to be attended before the December deadline set by Hitler; and at the back of his mind there was still that nagging fear that Keitel's order[81] had already revealed the secret of the whole operation to the Allies. He need not have feared. Giskes was taking care of that particular problem.

Operation Heinrich was Lieutenant Colonel Giskes' last great ruse. The man who had proved himself the Abwehr's greatest spycatcher in Holland knew that Germany had lost the war, yet the veteran Intelligence man could not resist the bait offered by the new assignment. From October till early December, 1944, he and his six combat intelligence sections stationed in the Prum-Bitburg-Trier area worked assiduously to convince the Allies that the Germans were beaten — and that the new troops appearing behind the front in that rugged forest country were meant for defense and not attack.

The Eifel-Ardennes border area in which Giskes operated is ideally suited for clandestine operations. But whereas Allied security on their side of the front was very loose and they had the disadvantage of not being able to communicate easily with

---

[81] Field Marshal Keitel had given a "top secret" order asking for volunteers for the Skorzeny operation. It had sent the big Commando into a great rage, and he had considered calling the whole thing off; he felt the order would fall into Allied hands. It did, but by then it was too late.

the locals who spoke German on *both* sides of the border, Giskes had at his disposal the highly alert German Field Security Police who did speak the language. In addition, he employed local people from both sides of the border in both his espionage and counterespionage work.[82]

Thus it was that during the two months prior to the great offensive, he sneaked a large number of bedraggled, broken men from the German forced labor camps across the border into Luxembourg and Belgium. Most of them were natives of those two countries who had been conscripted into Germany. They were only too eager to gain their freedom and pay for it by passing on false information to Allied Intelligence who usually picked them up as they came trudging through the lonely shell-shattered woods or down the abandoned streets of the little border villages.

Some of these pathetic wretches did not even know they were the unwitting purveyors of Giskes's carefully doctored "news," all of it calculated to lull the suspicions of the Allied Intelligence men. The bits and pieces of information found in their sugar-sack rucksacks and black-dyed coats made of old blankets had been planted upon them before they had made what they believed was a genuine "escape" from the work camps, which were usually guarded by a handful of old men or wounded veterans.

---

[82] The author has learned of only one Allied agent who was discovered by farmhands in the neighborhood of Oberkail, some thirty miles from Trier. He was beaten to death by them before the police could intervene. Naturally none of the locals are eager to talk about the incident.

Colonel Giskes invented a red agent, "Otto from Saxony," who was supplying the Belgian escapees with information. As he told the author in 1973: "I tried to convince U.S. Intelligence that if we attacked, we would attack Aachen, well away from the Ardennes, the real point of attack."

Bit by bit the veteran spymaster fed his opposite numbers working away at Luxembourg's Hotel Alpha, less than forty miles from his own HQ in Trier as the crow flies, the information which was calculated to make them believe that the Germans had no intention of attacking, this month or any other month.

And the operation paid off.

Intelligence work had never been rated very highly in the U.S. Army. Prior to the outbreak of war, officers assigned to the G-2 or S-2[83] branches of the Army had never really had an opportunity to use their training; they were usually stationed in the States, remote from the prewar espionage war being fought behind the scenes in Europe. As a result they were burdened with other duties such as "post exchange officer, club officer and *officer for the control of social diseases*" (as Eisenhower has written).

When the war had broken out, they had been forced to take what information the British gave them and learn their craft "on-the-job." It was not the best way of doing things and the American Intelligence officers, trying to cope not only with the intricacies of their new metiér but also foreign languages, did not always give of their best. Indeed Eisenhower himself used a British officer, General Kenneth Strong, as his chief-of-intelligence throughout the campaign.

As a result, American Intelligence, ranging from General Luther Sibert, an ex-West Point professor, who was now Bradley's Chief of Intelligence in Luxembourg, through Colonel "Monk" Dickson, who had been recalled to duty in 1940, and had become G-2 for the First US Army (which would bear the brunt of the German initial attack), down to

---

[83] Army Intelligence below divisional level.

the S-2s of the four divisions in the Ardennes, were not discerning enough. They fell for Giskes' deliberately planted information about the low standard of morale and offensive spirit on the part of the German troops stationed across the border from them.

Admittedly, "Monk" Dickson, a strapping, mustachioed man in his early forties, did consider the captured Keitel order on Skorzeny's formation in his Intelligence Estimate 37 of December 10, 1944. In it he wrote that "a captured order for a comb-out of selected personnel speaking the American dialect to report to HQ Skorzeny at Friedenthal near Oranienburg, by November 1 obviously presages special operations for sabotage, attacks on CPs and other vital installations by infiltrated or parachuted specialists." Dickson, who was regarded as somewhat of a pessimist at higher headquarters in Luxembourg City, felt that (contrary to Giskes's aim) "morale among POWs freshly captured both in the Army cage and at Communications Zone cage, recently achieved a new high. This has been expressed by attempts to escape and avowed eagerness on the part of the prisoners to return and join the battle for Germany." Still he did not draw the requisite conclusion. He believed there might be a limited German attack, but he misplaced its location; and to illustrate how seriously he took the threat, he went off on leave.

He was not alone. With Christmas — "the last one of the war," they were writing in the New York papers — only a few days off, many senior commanders asked for a few days' leave, from Montgomery downwards. In his Intelligence HQ in the shabby, old fashioned Hotel Alpha, General Sibert (who ironically enough would be using some of the men gathering to attack him in his own clandestine operations one day soon)[84]

---

[84] In the summer of 1945, General Sibert was instrumental in sending

discounted any German plan. And as for the Supreme Commander himself, broad-faced, balding General Dwight D. Eisenhower, he intended to give a "little party" for his favorite orderly, Mickey, who was going to marry one of the WAC's at the great Versailles HQ, on the day the great offensive started. From general to private — everyone knew "the Krauts were kaput." Now everyone concentrated on preparing for Christmas: turkeys and chickens were "organized" on the black market; hard "booze" of doubtful quality, but fearsome potency, was brewed from potatoes and raisins; and a solitary, scratchy record of Bing Crosby's was played over and over again as Yule-tide, 1944, came ever closer. "I'm dreaming of a White Christmas," the old groaner crooned with that lazy ease of his. *A White Christmas!*

For many of them in the lonely, snowy Ardennes it would be the blackest Christmas of their whole life. For eighty thousand of them, it would be their last ...

General Gehlen to the USA. There he offered his whole intelligence apparat, which included some of Skorzeny's men, to the U.S. government. The offer was accepted, and Gehlen started to work in the East for the United States one year later. See the author's *Gehlen: Germany's Master Spy* for further details.

17 — GRAB!

At precisely 0600 hours on the morning of December 16, the assault battalions of 250,000 Germans massed in the Eifel came out of the mist and hit the thin American line in the Ardennes. Near the border village of Losheim, they struck the positions of the Fourteenth Cavalry Group linking the two infantry divisions of the V/VIII Corps, the inexperienced Ninety-ninth and 106th.

The Fourteenth Cavalry started to pull back almost at once. The 106th — the "Golden Lion" division, the youngest Allied formation on any front — soon began to break. The Germans exploited the gap between the Ninety-ninth and 106th. But the German attack division in that area — Third Parachute — was about as inexperienced as the formations it was attacking. By midnight it had still failed to clear a path for the armor of the First SS — *die Leibstandarte* — piling up behind, and Skorzeny's undercover men who were to accompany the premier SS division of the German army.

At exactly 12 o'clock that night a wounded and captured Bouck, lying on the dirty blood-stained floor of the little Café Palm in Lanzerath, was trying to comfort "Sak" whose cheek had been shot away in the fighting of that afternoon. His eye lay limply in the bloody wound like some grotesque pearl in a fleshy shell, when the door to the place was thrown open and a hawk-faced SS Colonel entered. He looked around in disgust at the confused mess of sleeping, dirty paratroops and wounded. For a moment he just stared at the scene, his thin nose wrinkled at the composite smell of tobacco, rifle oil and male sweat, then he started rapping out orders.

The café came to life. The paratroop colonel, who had been hauled out of a safe job in Goering's Air Ministry to take command of this regiment was summoned from his bed. The 29-year-old SS Colonel Jochen Peiper[85], a much decorated veteran of the Russian fighting, was not troubled by the fact that the para was very senior to him in rank and age. He wanted to know why the *Leibstandarte*'s armor was being held up. Had he, the para, reconnoitered the American positions personally? The alarmed Luftwaffe officer admitted he hadn't. Without waiting for permission, Peiper lifted the phone and called the commander of the paratroop battalion closest to the American positions to ask him whether he had reconnoitered them. He, too, said he hadn't. But one of his captains had. His disgust and anger growing by the minute, Col. Peiper called the captain. He, naturally, hadn't carried out the task assigned to him.

Peiper gave up on the inexperienced paratroops. Simply commandeering a battalion for use as infantry from the now thoroughly scared, middle-aged, Luftwaffe full colonel, Peiper snapped that he personally would lead the attack that would break through the American lines at four o'clock that morning.

Back at the end of Peiper's long column of tanks and half tracks, which was manned by 5,000 men, Skorzeny fumed also. He knew the success of his own daring operation depended upon a clean breakthrough, with the Meuse being reached by the SS armor on Day Three of the offensive. But already the U.S. defense of the area to the west of Lanzerath had put him back twelve hours. In the end he decided he could do nothing else but wait with the rest of his 150th Panzer Brigade. However, the Stielau Unit would start operating at once. Thus

---

[85] Col. Peiper to author.

the eighty-man group was given the green light, disappearing into the mist to commence an operation which was the only really successful one of the whole costly offensive.

Today it is hard to piece together the exact details of that operation; after the war many of the men concerned were scared to speak lest the Allies take reprisals against them. In addition, the issue was complicated by the sheer number of men arrested as being members of the Stielau group — two hundred fifty altogether — and the confused mess of rumor and frightened speculation which surrounded the operation in 1944.[86]

But, in essence, this was what happened with the seven teams which penetrated the lines that first day.

Up at Sourbrodt, north of Malmedy, the first day of the offensive began normally enough. Third Platoon, C Company of the U.S. 291st Engineers went about their duties in the sawmill, preparing timber for the winterized squad huts of the front. That December the Engineers were on a good thing and they knew it. They had permanent billets, heated with their own timber, fresh rations instead of the cans handed out to the fellows in the line, regular passes to Brussels and Paris, and a nice little thing going with the girls in the border village — "knees under the table," as the Limeys called it. "You never had it so good," the Platoon Sergeant Ed Keoghan told them regularly and they believed him.

But on that Saturday things began to go wrong. Suddenly the village started to flood with rumors. The pictures of Leopold,

---

[86] It is usually assumed that some thirteen members of the teams survived. Skorzeny believes that several are still alive (letter to author, 1972). In 1951, four wrote to a German magazine, detailing their part in the operation.

King of the Belgians, and Churchill and Roosevelt, which had decorated each window disappeared abruptly. A few hours later, the Allied flags followed. Instead of their usual cheerful faces, the villagers looked away when a "Yank" went by and the Americans' greetings were not returned. The platoon officer, Lieutenant Perkins, decided to investigate, leaving Keoghan in charge. Hardly had Perkins gone out when a strange young infantry officer appeared in a jeep, his young face pale and taut. Introducing himself quickly, he asked Keoghan if he could spare some men. "The Krauts dropped a big bunch of paratroops in the woods last night," he blurted out quickly, "and we've got to try to round them up."

Keoghan volunteered to go himself with three or four of his best men. So they spread out into the deep cold woods looking for the paratroopers. They were unlucky. There were none (in fact the Germans had dropped dummy troops there to confuse them, but Keoghan did not know that). Yet if they did not see German paras, they did see that every one of the forest roads was filled with a confused mess of Army traffic heading westwards. Everything was on the road — antiaircraft guns, jeeps, tank destroyers, bridging units, bulldozers, dump trucks — all filled with frightened, white-eyed soldiers, their sole concern to get away from what lay behind them somewhere to the east. As Keoghan told himself cynically this was "the big bugout."

In the end he and his men gave up the fruitless search for the paratroopers, returning the way they had come until they arrived at the crossroads at Mon Rigi. The foot-deep-in-mud intersection was the scene of a massive traffic snarl with over a dozen, mud-spattered, red-faced, and angry MPs trying to sort it out, shouting and threatening above the noise of roaring engines, impatient GIs, and honking horns. "What's going on?" Keoghan asked, giving up and relaxing in the driver's cab.

One of the MPs, hoarse with rage and shouting, said: "We had some boys going down where that breakthrough's at and some damned jokers changed the road signs. They sent the whole outfit on west, *down the wrong road*.... When we got on the trail of it, there was two of 'em still standing out here in the road turning 'em wrong. Hell, those boys have got to go all the way around by Malmedy now to get to Waimes where they were supposed to go."

"But who changed the road signs?" Keoghan asked puzzled.

"Krauts," the MP snorted angrily. "Some of them paratroopers likely. In American uniforms, too. They had a jeep and when we got here they jumped in and made off so fast one of 'em was still standing on the front bumper hanging on to the wire clipper. They hauled out of here going fifty miles an hour!"

The MP was wrong. The men were not paratroopers. The inexperienced paratroopers dropped that night had been badly scattered and were now concerned with sheer survival, not offensive operations. The men in the jeep who had hopelessly snarled up one of Eisenhower's best divisions hurrying to the scene of the German breakthrough[87] *belonged to Captain Stielau's special unit!*

But the misleading of the First Division's Sixteenth Infantry Regiment was only the start.

Lines were cut everywhere behind the front, including probably the main link between General Bradley and General Hodges commanding the U.S. First Army. Sign posts were turned at many important road crossings. The white ribbons indicating that an area was free from mines were removed,

---

[87] The veteran U.S. First infantry.

268

whereas signs were put up in other places to indicate that mines were present where there were none. Lone columns of American troops were panicked by the sudden appearance of apparently scared-stiff GIs "bugging out" from the front, urging them to run for their lives: "The Krauts are coming!"

Nevertheless the teams started to suffer casualties. Retiring from their positions near Poteau, members of the Eighteenth Cavalry coming under the command of Colonel Mark Devine of the Fourteenth Cavalry were approached by a strange-looking group of GIs. A sergeant of the Eighteenth felt the GIs' boots "looked funny." Before he could even challenge, one of the strange GIs called out: "Okay, fellows, we're from E company!"

It was the last words the German spoke.

The suspicious sergeant let them have a burst with his tommy-gun. In the cavalry you don't talk about "companies;" only "squadrons."

Three days later the situation at the little Meuse town of Dinant was tense. Now the Allies knew the direction of the German attack; the defense of the river was all important. But where were the troops to do so? Allied resources were stretched to the utter limit.

Thus it was that a scratch force of British tankmen, U.S. engineers, and Negro service corpsmen had been pressed into a last ditch force to defend the vital Dinant bridge across the Meuse.

That evening, with the air icy cold and presaging snow, British Colonel Brown's scratch force nervously awaited the arrival of the first German panzers and the start of the desperate fight for the bridge. Reasoning, however, that the Germans would approach the little Belgian river town from the south, the British tank colonel had thrown a thin cordon of troops over the river where the approach road had to pass through an opening cut through solid rock.

There his U.S. engineers had strung a necklace of Hawkins mines across the road and erected a strongpoint some yards in front of the deadly mines. If any enemy armour penetrated the roadblock, which was highly likely, the survivors would be able to blow them up on the mines.

Thus the tense, nervous little garrison of exhausted British and second-line American troops awaited the assault which was sure to come. It did. But in a completely different way than expected. The grey day gave way to the evening. The hours passed. It was night. It was silent save for the ever-present background music of war — the rumble of heavy artillery. Then suddenly there was the noise of a vehicle. At their checkpoint the engineers tensed. In spite of the biting cold, they started to sweat. Was this the Germans?

Abruptly, before anyone could react, a U.S. jeep, containing four men came barreling out of the night. "Halt!" someone yelled. Too late. The jeep was through, scattering them on all sides. It roared on. Dinant was a matter of minutes away. The next moment there was the dull crump of high explosive. A sheet of ugly red and yellow flame erupted. The startled engineers saw the jeep rise on the wave of flame. It stopped suddenly and lurched to one side, tires burst, greedy, red oil, flames licking at the chassis. The spell was broken. The men burst from behind their roadblock and ran towards the jeep's bloody mess.

Hurriedly someone began to peel the uniform away from the first of the dead as he lay in the wreckage of the jeep, sprawled out in the violent posture of the suddenly dead. Behind him a broken-voiced GI said in awe at the terrible sight: "God, they're our guys!"

They weren't.

As the dead man's olive-drab uniform was drawn back, it revealed beneath the gleaming runic silver SS of one of Skorzeny's men. The first of the jeep teams had arrived at the Meuse.

But by now the Allied Intelligence Service knew about the Skorzeny operation; on the afternoon of December 18th a military policeman had asked three men in a jeep at Aywaille, south of Liège and some 12 miles from the Meuse bridge at Engis, for the password.

They did not know it and were arrested immediately. On them they had German military paybooks, $900, two Sten machine pistols, two .45s, one German revolver, and six U.S. grenades. The mixed bag sufficed. Immediately they were rushed to Liège to be grilled by U.S. counterintelligence.

They did not hold out long. They revealed that their real names were Officer-Cadet Gunther Billing, Corporal Wilhelm Schmidt and Lance Corporal Manfred Pernass. Pleading for mercy, they revealed their mission and passed on the rumors they had picked up during their training at Grafenwoehr. Corporal Schmidt told his interrogators that "Our unit included a group of engineers, whose job it was to destroy headquarters and kill the headquarters personnel."

The prisoner's statement was flashed immediately from Liège to Eisenhower's HQ at Versailles. Coupled with the name of Skorzeny, the man who had rescued Mussolini eighteen months before, it sufficed to start an unprecedented scare.

Now saboteurs and Skorzeny commandos were seen everywhere. Big, bluff Brigadier Bruce Clarke,[88] the defender of hard-pressed St. Vith was "captured" on the morning of December 20, two days later. His captors were American military policemen!

Over and over again he kept repeating: "But I'm General Bruce Clarke of CCB (Combat Command B)."

"Like hell!" they commented. "You're one of Skorzeny's men. We were told to watch out for a Kraut posing as a one-star general."

While Clarke raged, knowing that the vital rail and roadhead of St. Vith might be lost while he was in jail, the MPs kept him in custody for five long hours. In the end they released him and one of the MPs had the audacity to ask for his autograph. A nonplused Clarke gave him it too.

But Clarke was not the only general to be questioned. His Army Group Commander Bradley was stopped three times on the same day during the course of one of his trips.

Behind the front, from the River Meuse to England itself, a great wave of panic and suspicion seemed to threaten the course of the battle. Colonel Gordon Sheen, Eisenhower's counterintelligence chief, felt that one could not ignore Corporal Schmidt's story. He ordered that the "old man" — Eisenhower — should be given the fullest protection. While Lieutenant Colonel Baldwin B. Smith, a perfect double for Eisenhower, appeared in various sectors of the combat zone in Ike's five-star uniform, Eisenhower himself was confined to his HQ for three vital days. As Kay Summersby, his secretary in those days, wrote later: "Security officers immediately turned headquarters compound into a virtual fortress. Barbed wire appeared. Several tanks moved in. The normal guard was doubled, trebled, quadrupled. The pass system became a matter of life and death instead of the old formality. The sound of a

---

[88] Letter to author, 1970.

car exhaust was enough to halt work in every office, to start a flurry of telephone calls to our office, to inquire whether the boss was all right. The atmosphere was worse than that of a combat headquarters up at the front, where everyone knew how to take such a situation in their stride."

Then Allied counterintelligence men quizzing other Skorzeny men captured in the third week of December picked up the rumor of the Café de la Paix which the eager young Lieutenant had first related to Skorzeny in November. An MP battalion surrounded Eisenhower's quarters. In spite of General Strong's protests that counterintelligence was going too far, Sheen insisted that Eisenhower would have "to obey orders."

It was too much for a very worried Ike, concerned not with his personal safety, but with the outcome of the great battle in the Ardennes. He simply walked out of his office, mumbling angrily to Kay Summersby: "Hell's fire, I'm going for a walk. If anyone wants to shoot me, he can go right ahead. I've got to get out!"

Thus at the most critical phase of the offensive — "the European Pearl Harbor" — Eisenhower was kept virtual prisoner at his own headquarters. In Paris itself, "there was said to be something like near panic" (according to Eisenhower's chief-of-intelligence, General Strong). Described as the "most dangerous Nazi," Skorzeny was given the gangster name of "Scarface." His posters were pasted up everywhere. The French police reported his paras landing near Supreme HQ. Another two hundred were spotted at Bohain. A third hysterical report came from Valenciennes, that some of them were dressed as nuns and priests. As a cynical Strong commented: "All paratroopers *always* seem to be disguised as nuns and priests!"[89]

---

[89] According to Strong, Ike always wanted a full investigation of the

The eighty-man operation paid terrific dividends. The British-run "German" radio — *Soldatensender Calais*[90] — reported that 250 of Skorzeny's men had been captured. Radio Nice stated that a local bank had been looted by Skorzeny's paratroopers — some four hundred miles away from the scene of the fighting! The conservative British paper, *The Daily Telegraph*, informed its readers in all seriousness that specially trained women agents under Skorzeny's control had been dropped in the Paris area where they were to seduce U.S. soldiers. Once the latter had been duly "seduced" and "revealed all," they were to be killed by the handy little dagger which every female agent was confidently reported to carry in her purse.

And so the wild rumors flourished, with General Bradley commenting sourly: "Half a million GIs [were playing] cat-and-mouse with each other every time they met." "Operation Grab" (as the American Intelligence had translated the German designation, though it could also have been translated as "gryphon") was an unqualified success. The twenty-eight-odd survivors of the Stielau jeep teams could be proud of their work — perhaps the most effective operation of the whole offensive.

But what of Skorzeny and the bulk of his clandestine outfit — *Panzerbrigade 150*?

Having finally crossed the border with most of his motorised units, Skorzeny asked General Sepp Dietrich, the tough former sergeant major from World War I who now commanded the Sixth SS Panzer Army, for a mission. Dietrich told him he

---

Skorzeny "threat." But he never got it.

[90] A fake "German" transmitter, run by British journalist Sefton Delmer, aimed at the Wehrmacht.

should take the little Belgian town of Malmedy, and thus open the way to Peiper who was by now trapped somewhere ahead in the hills at the little village of La Gleize.[91] Skorzeny started planning the operation at once, eager to reach Peiper, to whose formations some of his teams were attached.

Lieutenant Peter Mandt, who had been demoted to the rank of GI corporal for the course of the operation, remembers: "As we rolled forward [he was in charge of a Panzer tank camouflaged with an American star and metal sheeting to look roughly like a Sherman], we were listening to the American radio when the program was interrupted by the sound of a volley of shots. For a moment we could not understand what they meant, then the speaker explained: 'This salvo brought to an end another one of Skorzeny's commando teams!'"

Mandt and the rest of his crew looked glum. Now they knew the *Amis* were on to them. But they pushed on down the little side road leading to the shattered town of Malmedy in the valley below. It was already dark when they finally reached their start position. There a mysterious German Lieutenant Commander in the Navy reported that Malmedy was very weakly held. He had gone right through the town disguised in U.S. uniform and had seen little sign of American resistance. As Mandt reported bitterly afterwards: "Thereafter we never saw or heard of him again."[92]

---

[91] For further details see the author's *Massacre at Malmedy*.

[92] Mundt obviously took the mysterious Lieutenant Commander to be an Allied spy (my own inquiries in the area indicate that once the first shock of the offensive had been overcome, the Allies sent agents into the area, who were either native Germans who had been "turned" or their own men.) My guess is that the Lieutenant Commander was the mysterious, elusive von Beer, who always turns up in the stories of this action; or possibly it was another Lieutenant Commander named Schmitt.

Soon Mundt had good reason for his bitterness. His unit attacked that same night, after they had covered their American stars with tarpaulins and dressed themselves in German paratroop coveralls to hid their U. S. uniforms. It was a failure from the start. Mundt's tank was put out of action almost immediately and he was forced to run for his life, blood streaming from a head wound, leaving his dead comrades behind.

The GIs of the Thirtieth Infantry Division, which had gained the nickname of "Roosevelt's Butchers" in the German radio, stopped the attackers in their tracks. Both Skorzeny's group commanders were wounded. Baron von Foelkersam, Skorzeny's Chief of Operations and the man who had accompanied Schellenberg to arrest Canaris six months before, was wounded in the backside, much to his discomfiture and Skorzeny's amusement. But Skorzeny's amusement did not last long.

Later that same evening as he was walking back to his own HQ in the Rupp chalet near the internationally famous Hotel du Moulin, which Eisenhower had used when he visited the front that autumn, heavy enemy artillery shells started to fall on the little village of Ligneuville. Balbina Rupp, the Swiss wife of the owner of the famous hotel saw the big man stagger and almost fall, as he was hit by a fist-sized piece of shrapnel.[93] He had been hit in the cheek, and the blood poured thickly down the side of his already scarred face. A soldier ran from the hotel to help him. The big colonel waved him away. But he staggered inside and grabbed a glass of cognac. Downing it in one gulp, he asked for a mirror; he thought he had lost an eye.

As he recorded in his postwar memoirs: "I felt how the blood ran warmly down my cheek. Carefully I felt my face with

---

[93] To the author, 1970.

276

my hand. Above my eye a lump of flesh was missing from my forehead and was hanging down over the eye. I was shocked. Was my eye gone?"

Fortunately for Skorzeny it wasn't, but Skorzeny's part in the great plan of confuse-and-deceive-the-Americans was over. Three days later he was recalled, but in spite of another meeting with Hitler at which the Führer still talked confidently about another "great offensive in the southeast," Skorzeny knew the great days were over. As he himself wrote: "It was clear to me and my staff officers... that the last phase of the war had begun." Personally he volunteered for a routine front line assignment, where he would fight as a conventional soldier. Von Foelkersam did too, and Skorzeny never saw him abandon the rapidly sinking ship, the task of fighting the "war in the shadows" would be left to that hastily organized unit — the Werewolf. Eager for some last desperate glory, the fanatical young men and women recruited to it in the last months of the war would sacrifice their all in small, bitter, treacherous actions far behind the Allied lines; throwing their lives away almost joyously for a cause which was long since dead.

The great days of German clandestine operations were over. While those in the know in German Intelligence prepared to go again.

18 — OPERATION CARNIVAL

The drone of the captured four-engine Fortress which had brought them to this war-torn, remote frontier area died away in the distance. Now there was no sound save for the icy night wind in the frozen pines.

Thanks be, no one had spotted them. No sudden red flare had shot up into the dark sky to be followed by surprised angry voices shouting in a strange language. Their parachutes had coming floating down into the wooded hills without any enemy reaction whatsoever. *Operation Carnival* had got off to a good start.

But Lieutenant Wenzel, the mysterious young leader of the group, gave them little chance to congratulate themselves on their good fortune. He switched on the small blue light on his paratroop coveralls and ordered them to start unpacking the "food bomb," as the 16-year-old ex-Hitler Youth Morgenschweiss called the two-meter-long container. Hastily they began to divide its contents: hard dark bread, bottles of water, cans of meat, pills, a bottle of cognac — and pistols.

That job done, they set off with Hennemann in the lead, marching single file and heading for the border where they were to carry out their first assignment.

There were six of them: Wenzel, the supposed SS lieutenant in his late twenties, a mysterious figure who had told each of them a different story about his past; Hennemann and Heidorn, two former border guards in their middle thirties, who had been recruited in 1944 to carry out special clandestine duties along the frontier; Leitgeb, the big, broad, balding Austrian SS man who was to be their radioman although he had proved to be the world's worst *Funker*[94]; skinny undersized Erich Morgenschweiss, distinguished by delicate female features under a mop of curly blond hair which contrasted strangely with long, gorilla-like arms; and the woman, 24-year-old Ilse Hirsch, ex-Hitler Maiden Leader and fanatical Nazi. Thus the strange little group made their way through the thick lonely woods, filled still with the rusting evidence of the severe fighting there in the previous September. They were linked only by two things — they all knew the border areas like the back of their hands — *and they had come to kill!*

After about an hour they arrived at the border itself: a line of dark grey, weathered stones running through the woods. Now the two guides, Heidorn and Hennemann, knew exactly where they were on that confusing frontier which separated three countries: Belgium, Holland, and Germany. Wenzel flicked on his little flashlight. In its blue rays they could see the stone where Hennemann was to bury the money. On one side it bore the faint letter "N" — indicating the Netherlands; on the other, there was an equally faint "B" for Belgium. "Will that do?" Wenzel asked.

"Yes," the tall ugly guide, with the heavy chin, whispered as if the woods were full of enemy soldiers.

Swiftly he went to work with his knife, digging under the stone. Finally satisfied with the hole, he placed the yellow waterproof packet containing $5,000 in blood money. Once they had completed their mission, the position of the money would be radioed to a British captain who would collect it as payment for his work for German Intelligence.

They went on.

And then it happened! They bumped into a border guard.

---

[94] Radio operator.

Twenty-year-old Dutch Josef Saive had been combining pleasure with duty that night on the lonely frontier. He had been walking his beat, rifle slung carelessly over his shoulder, his arm curved around the waist of his Belgian girlfriend from just over the other side of the border Mile Straat Now all thoughts of his girlfriend fled from his head as he saw the first of the grey shapes slip through the trees in front of him. He unslung his rifle. Hastily he whispered to his girlfriend. *"Enemy saboteurs! Go back to Sergeant Finders and get help!"*

She started to protest, but "Jost," as she called him, silenced her. "Run!" he urged. "Get help!"

She started to run along the dark tree-lined trail, down the hill, to the frontier post where Sergeant Finders would be preparing their midnight coffee.

Now Josef Saive did not hesitate. "Jost was a keen boy. He had visions of glory," Finders said later.[95] "He wanted action." Licking his lips, Saive leveled his rifle and cried "Hands up!"

"Patrol!" Wenzel hissed frantically, fumbling with his pistol. Panic broke out among the strange little group. Surprisingly, it was diminutive Morgenschweiss who acted first. Drawing his pistol, he fired and at the same time, flung himself down the bank to his right.[96]

Morgenschweiss's shot broke the spell. Josef pressed his trigger almost automatically. Then bullets started to cut the air all around. He was wounded a second time — and a third. Shot in the groin, he sank doubled up to the ground.

---

[95] In an interview with the author, 1970.

[96] It was a quarter of a century later that he learned from this author that the man he had shot — J. Saive — was like himself a miner's son, whose native language was German, and had been born only twenty miles from his own birthplace: one of the mindless tragedies of total war.

As Saive fell, Ilse Hirsch rolled down the embankment to her left and began to run. She was unable later to say how long she ran. But as the first cold white light of dawn began to filter through the pines, she realized that her panic-stricken flight had carried her to the edge of the forest, near their objective.

Before her lay the fields, still covered to knee-level with cold white cotton-wool mist from which loomed the damaged spires of the city's ancient cathedral. It was Aachen, the first major city captured by the Americans in Germany, who were now running it with their German puppets, one of whom she and the rest had come to kill. Who he was, she still did not know,[97] but she was determined to find out.

Stripping off her flying coverall and shivering a little in the cold dawn breeze, she slung her rucksack over her shoulder and set off across the damp fields towards the city from which she had fled under an artillery bombardment six months before.

It was now six o'clock on the morning of March 22, 1945. On the Rhine, the Allies were preparing for their great crossing which would take place within 36 hours. But deep to their rear in territory they had been occupying since the previous October, the first — and last — great *Werewolf* operation was under way.

The fall of the great imperial city of Aachen, which housed the tomb of the great German folk hero, Charlemagne — or as the Germans called him Karl der Grosse — had angered Himmler. When he learned that the six or seven thousand citizens left in the besieged city had received the Americans as if they were

---

[97] Erich Morgenschweiss assured me that the group had not known the name of the U.S. appointed burgomaster when they had set off on their adventurous mission.

liberators, he had been consumed with rage. In a letter to the SS Police Chief for the West, Karl Gutenberger, he said angrily: "From the enemy press it is clear that in some areas occupied by the Anglo-Americans the local population is behaving in a manner without honor. I order that immediately in these areas which have been captured the guilty parties should be brought to justice. Now we should attempt to 'educate' the population in question by the execution of the death penalty *behind the front*."

Gutenberger, who already knew he was classed as a war criminal by the Allies because of his work in Poland and Russia, did not want to get any deeper into the mess. He let sleeping dogs lie. But a couple of weeks later Himmler's head of the *Werewolf* Organization, SS General Pruetzmann, came to visit him personally. Just before the Werewolf chief, who had seven months yet to live, left, he turned to Gutenberger and said: "Incidentally, Gutenberger, what have you done about Aachen?"

Gutenberger looked at him puzzled. "Aachen?" he echoed.

"Yes, that swine the *Amis* have made chief burgomaster."

"What about him?"

"You've got to liquidate him, haven't you?"

"Yes," Gutenberger replied, "I know." But he said the words without conviction.[98]

Thus Operation Carnival, the plan to murder the still unknown Burgomaster of Aachen by the Werewolves, was born.

Lieutenant Colonel Neinhaus, an old party friend of Gutenberger, took over the training of the whole Werewolf organization for the Rhineland in the remote, walled medieval

---

[98] Frau Gutenberger, the General's widow, insisted to the author that her husband did not want to carry out the murder mission.

castle of Hulchrath, some fifty miles from Aachen. He gave the Aachen assignment to the mysterious Lt. Wenzel, who maintained that he had been brought up in South Africa (though he spoke only broken English) and that he had taken part in the Skorzeny operation to rescue Mussolini.[99]

Training progressed rapidly within the sheltered confines of the fourteenth-century castle, whence the six volunteers for the operation would sneak out at night like grey ghosts to carry out their exercises.

Wenzel was pleased with them in spite of Heidorn and Hennemann's lack of enthusiasm for what they regarded as a *Himmelfahrtskommando* — a one-way ticket to heaven. He reported his team ready to go to ex-World War I officer Neinhaus, whose brother would soon be threatened with death by the self-same Werewolves he was training. By an amazing coincidence Dr. Neinhaus, mayor of Heidelberg, would offer to surrender his beautiful city to the advancing Americans. His answer was a mysterious Werewolf death threat.

But if Wenzel and Neinhaus were ready with their volunteers for the murder attempt, Gutenberger still hesitated. He was a family man and determined to survive the war, come what may. He was not prepared to risk his neck for some whim of Himmler's. In the first week of December, however, the SS General received a shock. One of his aides brought him a top secret telex from Himmler himself. After ordering that "every burgomaster in the territory occupied by the Americans is to be shot," Himmler asked the question which Gutenberger had dreaded: *"What has been done in the matter of the chief burgomaster of Aachen?"*

---

[99] Skorzeny could not recollect any "Wenzel" or any one fitting his description when I asked him about the mysterious SS Lieutenant.

The outbreak of the Ardennes Offensive one week later helped to postpone the evil day; but in February, 1945, the Battle of the Bulge won by the Americans, with the latter advancing into the Rhineland itself, Himmler gave Gutenberger a direct order to carry out his original directive. The words were simple and brutal. "The Chief Burgomaster of Aachen has been sentenced to death. The sentence is to be carried out by W" (i.e., Werewolf).

Gutenberger knew that he could only refuse at the cost of his own life. He passed on the order to Neinhaus who gave it to Wenzel. The operation was on. Two weeks later the strangely assorted group set off from the airfield at Hildesheim, flying deep into Belgium in a captured Flying Fortress. They dropped a Belgian parachutist (who was captured straight away) over Brussels, then swung back over the three-country border area called the *Dreilaendereck* just northwest of Aachen, where they themselves bailed out.

We know the rest. But in that third week of March, with the woman lost, the remaining five men prepared to give up. Hennemann and Heidorn were vocal in their criticism of any further attempt to continue the operation, Leitgeb was for having a look at the situation in Aachen at least, whereas Wenzel and the youngest member of the group, Morgenschweiss, dressed absurdly in oversized boots and coveralls, kept their own counsels.

In the end they agreed to send a group from their camp, deep in the Aachen Forest north of the city, into Aachen to have a look at the situation. While this was being decided, Heidorn took to his bed of branches and leaves, protesting he was sick with a fever. However, when it was decided that Leitgeb (the tough Austrian adventurer who had been forced to flee his homeland in the thirties because of his Nazi affiliations) and young Morgenschweiss should go, he raised himself on his elbow and said to Leitgeb: "Sepp, if you get a chance to have a look at my old apartment in the Bismarckstrasse, perhaps you —"

"— Shut up!" Wenzel cut in angrily. "Sepp has more important things to do than look out for your flat, you fool!"

Sulkily Heidorn dropped his head and watched the two leave the camp in silence.

It was Erich Morgenschweiss who first spotted Ilse. He and Leitgeb were standing in the center of the wrecked city in the Auguststrasse, idly watching the Ami trucks go by to the front and the shabby, worn civilians going about their errands from cellar to cellar. Then he saw her plump, unnaturally pale face appear between two trucks. Hurriedly he crossed the littered, shell-holed street. "Ilse," he whispered urgently. She spun round in fright. Then she recognized him — Morgenschweiss in his oversized American rubber boots. She relaxed. The curly-haired youth jerked his head backward and her eyes followed the direction of his movement. Twenty yards away Leitgeb was lounging against a bullet-pocked wall, one big hand dug deeply in his pocket. She knew why. He was holding his pistol. If she betrayed them, she wouldn't live long.

But Ilse, the fanatical Nazi, had not betrayed them. Indeed she had shown more initiative than any of them. Not only had she found that the mysterious Burgomaster[100] was former lawyer Franz Oppenhoff and that he lived at 252

---

[100] Frau Oppenhoff, the murdered man's widow, told the author that her husband had insisted that the Americans should neither announce his name or allow photographs to be taken of him. Unfortunately, an enterprising newsreel camera man did get a shot of him. However, the Germans never saw this shot. Indeed Frau Oppenhoff did not know of its existence until I told her.

Eupenerstrasse — she had actually been into the man's house and knew exactly the layout of the place.

On the pretext of asking for a glass of water she had managed to enter the lonely house, set well back from the suburban street. To her surprise she found that the housemaid had an old acquaintance visiting her: pretty, dark-haired 16-year-old Christel Schütz. For one moment Ilse almost panicked. She knew Christel Schütz too; the girl had once been a member of her own group of Hitler's Maidens! But the pretty girl had not remarked upon the past until later when she caught up with Ilse after she had left the house and invited her to spend the night in her own house. So the woman who had come to kill, occupied herself that afternoon with the typical *hausfrau* chore of helping Christel to clean her living room!

Now she was able to give the others back at the camp a full briefing. Oppenhoff was married with three small children. The house had to be entered by the cellar door because the front one had been damaged. His closest neighbors were well out of earshot. Some Americans were located in the area, but they never ventured out after dark. There were woods on both sides of the Eupenerstrasse, ideally suited for them to disappear in after they had done what they had trained for so long to do.

Wenzel listened to her intently and in silence, hushing any one of the others who attempted to interrupt Ilse's excited monologue. Then he made his decision. "We're going to do it." He pointed to Leitgeb, "You, Sepp, me," and turning to lanky, ugly Hennemann (the former customs official who maintained he had been awarded Germany's highest decoration the "Knight's Cross of the Iron Cross" for his operations behind the enemy lines), "and you..."

It was Palm Sunday 1945, and the last day of Franz Oppenhoff's life. The Burgomaster of the ruined city of Aachen was tired — very tired. For six months he had been the Americans' chief civilian official, he was sick of them and the citizens he had ruled over through these last terrible months. In addition, he was constantly afraid that he would be assassinated by his own people. As he told his pretty, dark-haired wife on her return to Aachen with their three small children in February: "Somewhere or other there is a paratrooper already assigned to the job of murdering me."[101]

Now the full ruddiness of his face had vanished to be replaced by pale concern. There were deep bags under his eyes and the once lively, jolly man, who had enjoyed animated conversation and good wine, had become silent and detached. But on this particular Sunday, energetic Frau Oppenhoff had determined that this day would be one of peace and enjoyment. As she told her husband: "Why next year at this time we'll be celebrating Carnival again. You wait and see."

Thus she planned to make the Palm Sunday weekend a special one for him. With the coal that her husband had "organized," she bought sugar on the black market — Franz had a sweet tooth — and made him "real bean coffee" with sugar. Then after that particular treat, they worked in their vegetable garden for a while before putting the children to bed. The children safely ensconced in their beds and under the protection of their 25-year-old maid, Elizabeth, they crossed to a neighbor's house — that of Dr. Faust — for a couple of glasses of home-brewed "potato schnapps" which Oppenhoff's fellow alderman had managed to "organize."

But even on this holy day of rest, Oppenhoff was not allowed to relax from official duties. About nine o'clock the

---

[101] Statement of Frau Oppenhoff to the author.

little party was interrupted by the excited voice of the dark-haired maid. "Herr Oppenhoff... Herr Oppenhoff, there are American soldiers. They want to talk to you. *Now!*"

The Burgomaster rose hurriedly. American soldiers! What did they want from him at this time of night? But he did not hesitate. "All right, Elizabeth," he called through the blacked-out window. "I'm coming." Pulling on his gloves and adjusting his official armband which identified him as the mayor, he said to Faust: "You speak English. You'd better come with me."

Wenzel was waiting for him, his face concealed in the dark.

Faust said in English: "What do you want?"

Wenzel replied in German. Oppenhoff started back. The paratroopers? But the SS Lieutenant spoke softly and calmly: "We're German airmen," he lied. "We were shot down near Brussels three days ago. Now we're trying to make our way back to the German lines. What about getting us passes, *Herr Bürgermeister?*"

Oppenhoff shook his head. "I can't do that. You should report to the Americans and give yourselves up. The war's nearly over, anyway. It's only a matter of days."

Abruptly Leitgeb appeared out of the trees. His greeting was hard and to the point. "*Heil Hitler!*" he snapped.

Faust started. It was a long time since he had heard that greeting. His eyes fell on the pistol sticking out of the man's pocket. Faust had been an engineer in a German munitions plant. He recognized it immediately. It was a Walther. He noted too that neither man wore badges of rank and both were bareheaded. Fear overcame him. Oppenhoff, who had not apparently noticed what was going on, was just saying: "Let me get you something to eat," when Faust cut in. "I'll go back to the house and see what I can find there for you."

Before the two strangers had time to protest he was gone, walking as slowly as he dared in case they realized what he was up to.

But Faust was not the only one to be afraid. Elizabeth was too. She had discovered the men prowling around the house five minutes before. Oppenhoff tried to calm her. "They're German fliers, Elizabeth. Make them a couple of sandwiches, if you can find something." Then turning to Wenzel, he said. "Just a minute, I'll help her." He followed her through the one door that opened into the darkness of the cellar.

Leitgeb hissed urgently. "When he comes up again!"

In the light of the moon which now came shining coldly through the clouds, he saw that Wenzel's face was a sickly green hue. "Be quick," he urged. "The other one's gone off to alarm the *Amis*. Believe me, Wenzel!"

There were sounds from below. It was Oppenhoff, returning with the thick black bread sandwiches. The footsteps were getting closer. Leitgeb could hear Wenzel's harsh shallow rapid breathing quite clearly. Suddenly the traitor was there, bearing his sandwiches. *But Wenzel did not fire.*

"Do it!" the Austrian hissed.

Wenzel still hesitated.

"You cowardly sow!" Leitgeb cried and snatched the silenced pistol from him.

"Er-what?" Oppenhoff protested when he saw the long strangely shaped pistol.

Too late! In a fury, Leitgeb fired at close range, directly at the Burgomaster's left temple. Up in the kitchen, still cutting the hard wartime bread, Elizabeth heard a sound which she described later "like an unoiled door squeaking." She paused momentarily at her work, then thinking nothing more of it, continued.

Back at his own house, Faust told the little circle about the strangers. Irmgard Oppenhoff's eyes went wide with fear. As she stated later: "the news went through me like an electrical shock."[102] "We can't leave my husband alone with them," she cried, jumping to her feet. "For heaven's sake, if they are Germans and my husband gives them anything to eat, it might cost him his life!"

Later she could never decide whether she was afraid that the Americans or the Germans might execute him. Turning to Dr. Op de Hit, another old friend of her husbands, she cried; "Will you come with me?"

Hastily he rose to his feet "Yes, come on," he answered.

Wenzel, still mesmerized by the sight of the dead man slumped across the cellar steps at their feet, heard them coming. "There's someone coming," he whispered. "Let's go."

Leitgeb grabbed him. "Wait a minute, you pig," he called angrily. "We've got to have proof." Swiftly he bent down and tugged the American armband from the dead man and pulled off his grey gloves.

Suddenly there was a ragged volley of shots from close by.

"*Amis,*" Leitgeb yelled to warn Hennemann somewhere close by. But the guide had spotted them himself.

They had been called out to detect the break in the signal line caused by the latter's cutting of the telephone wires to Oppenhoff's house. Now they had spotted Hennemann and were firing at him in the dark. He began to pelt across the fields. Behind him a machine gun opened up. White and red tracers zigzagged through the night air. Desperately he sprinted

---

[102] Related to the author, 1971.

up the Eupenerstrasse and into the fields on the right-hand side of the cobbled country road.

Suddenly and to his horror, he became aware of someone running after him. He drew his pistol and halted in the shadows. He could feel the sweat trickling down the small of his back. Slowly he began to squeeze the trigger of his pistol. He pulled his hand away just in time. It was Wenzel.

He was gasping for breath and long streams of sweat ran down his pale, frightened face.

"Where's Sepp?" he cried.

Breathlessly Wenzel gasped. "On the other side of the road... he's all right... Come on, let's get out of here... come on!"

Hennemann needed no urging. Together they ran up the side of the road, doubled low, heading for the safety of the woods beyond.

At the house, Irmgard Oppenhoff's hand flew to her mouth. Just in time she stifled the cry of unbearable pain as she saw her 42-year-old husband lying crumpled on the steps. Then she stumbled back against a wide-eyed Doctor Op de Hit. *"Der Franz... der Franz ist tot,"* she moaned.

Operation Carnival was over.

1945: THE AFTERMATH

April is the cruellest month, breeding
Lilacs out of the dead land.

T. S. Eliot

19 — THE BIG BUGOUT

The last dispatch of the last German spy at large in Britain after nearly six years of war reached Berlin on April 20, 1945. It was typical of the depths to which the once famed German Intelligence service had sunk. The agent in London had been queried about the future of the RAF's Balloon Command — this at a time when nearly all of Germany had been overrun and the Russians were at the gates of Berlin itself; and when there had not been a German bomber over London for months! He replied: "Ambler [a somewhat talkative British Air Vice Marshal who was the agent's source] stated that it was no longer needed. Units still left in Great Britain will be absorbed by Fighter Command."

The message had been sent on March 14th, but it had taken so long to reach Berlin. By then the man for whom it was intended had been dead for nearly two weeks, murdered in a most bestial way by his own fellow countrymen, his eyes bulging wildly with pain and fear, his naked body twisting back and forth frantically as the piano wire strangled the life out of him.

They had come for the little ex-Admiral before dawn on the morning of April 9th. The Gestapo officials in their heavy boots clumped down the stone floor of the passage calling out the names of the men who were to be "executed immediately," as Kaltenbrunner had ordered two days before. Dr. Joseph Mueller, once an agent of Canaris himself, relates: "At four o'clock I heard a noise and the voice of a child. It was the daughter of the former Austrian Chancellor, von Schuschnigg.[103]

At six o'clock two numbers were called. Then I heard Canaris' voice. It was the last time I was to do so."

Canaris was fetched out of his cell. He had become a broken old man since that August when Schellenberg had arrested him. His teeth were gone and his cheeks were deathly pale and sunken. He walked slowly, measuring each step as if every movement was important. They were; his whole body was a mass of bruises and bloody wounds where the Gestapo officials had beaten him to make him talk. His pride was gone. The once mighty chief of the Abwehr, who had helped to start the war, had planned to dispose of some kings and elect new ones; who had directed a tremendous, unique intelligence network stretching from the teeming cities of the Far East across the world to the snowy wastes of Canada was now at the beck and call of the humblest guard. Once Mueller overheard a guard say to him, as he handed the one-time commander of a German training cruiser a broom to clean the corridor: "Well, little sailor, you never thought you'd have to swab the deck, did you?"

But on this cold April morning, with the sky outside still the foreboding grey-white of the false dawn, they had not come for Canaris to do the normal routine chores. Today they were going to kill him in the most painful, bestial manner possible — at the express orders of Adolf Hitler himself.

As the prison block which held the doomed prisoners came to life, the harsh naked lights snapping on everywhere, Wilhelm Canaris came hesitantly down the corridor, his hands and feet in chains. Colonel Lunding, a former Danish

---

[103] The Chancellor survived to become an American professor. Mueller, who had been one of the first of Canaris's men to make contact with the "enemy" and had thus entered Schellenberg's dossier which had led to Canaris's arrest, also survived Flossenbuerg Concentration Camp.

Intelligence officer and one-time opponent of the beaten little man in the corridor, peered through a slit in the door of his cell at the spectacle. An official halted the prisoner and bending down stiffly freed him from his chains. He snapped out an order. Slowly Canaris commenced to take off his clothes. Lunding caught his breath.

The ex-Admiral's body was an appalling sight: wounds and great black bruises everywhere. He told himself the German must have been worked over by Stawitzsky, who was notorious in the camp for the brutality of his "cross-examinations." The guard snapped "*Los*," and the one-time chief of German Intelligence shuffled forward and out of the sight of the Danish Colonel. And thus Wilhelm Canaris disappears from our sight too, a victim of his own deviousness, vanity, and yet, at the same time, a victim of his own good qualities and old-fashioned upper-class concept of what was "done" and "not done."

Two hours later Dr. Mueller, who had expected to be executed that same day, was freed of his chains by an SS guard. A little time later there was a gentle tap at his cell door. The "Judas hole" was opened and an unknown male voice said in English: "Do you understand me?"

"Yes," Mueller whispered, scared and intrigued at the same time. "I speak English."

Swiftly the unknown person outside whispered that he was an English officer imprisoned like the rest of them. Then he asked: "Do you belong to the high officers who are going to be executed?"

Mueller answered: "I appear to belong to them."

The unknown Englishman replied: "Well, it's not going to happen. It's all over. They're burning your friends now behind that hut."

With that the strange conversation was over. But a little while later, Mueller had proof that the Englishman had been right. The smell of burning human flesh — sickly sweet — started to penetrate his cell. Soon tiny bits of unburned flesh were blown by the cold wind through the barred window high in the wall. Mueller, known to his intimates as "Ox-Joe" because of his size and bull-like stature, stared at the fragments in horror. Then he broke down. He thought of his friend and former boss slowly burning down below in the anonymity of a concentration camp yard and knew this was the end. "I was shaken by pain and sorrow," he recalled long afterwards, "and I began to sob."

Thus perished the little Admiral, who six years before had said to one of his men[104] in a dimly lit corridor of German Army Headquarters, "This means the end of Germany." And the manner of his death, with its twenty minutes of unbelievable sadistic torture at the end of a meat hook, his bowels involuntarily evacuating, his face turning a violent crimson and the eyes threatening to burst out of the poor strangled face, seemed to symbolize the death agonies of the country which he had served so long...

But in Berlin when the last dispatch of the dead Admiral's agent arrived, it was the Führer's fifty-sixth birthday, and in the ruins of the grandiose Chancellery they celebrated. Eva Braun, who had presented her lover with a portrait of herself in a jeweled silver frame — as if the couple would live for many more years to treasure it — decorated a table in her apartment

---

[104] Now also gone over to the Allies, in this case the OSS.

in honor of the great day. Soon the guests began to arrive. Even the "brown eminence," the man who had really been running Germany for the last three years, Martin Bormann — and Schellenberg's prime suspect as the Russians' number one source of information in Berlin — came. He brought flowers.

Someone else had discovered a battered old gramophone on which the happy little birthday group played the one and only record they could find: a popular movie tune of that year "*Blutrote Rosen erzaehlen Dir vom Glueck.*" "Blood-red roses tell you of happiness." As Eva Braun danced to the tune over and over again, its words seemed to match the days' predominant color; for the sky over Berlin on the Führer's birthday was blood-red, the result of the Red Army's heavy artillery bombardment.

Earlier that same day, Reichsführer Himmler, Hitler's "most loyal paladin," and his now most trusted aide, General Schellenberg, had toasted their master's birthday with a bottle of champagne. Then they had gotten down to betraying him, for they had realized, in spite of the line of office seekers and toadies who were at that moment queuing up to congratulate the Führer, that the game was up. Germany had finally lost the war.

Himmler's face was lined with worry and there were deep circles under his eyes. As he spoke, he twisted his snake ring round and round nervously. For over a month Schellenberg had been urging him to make the momentous decision which would end it all. But he was still scared that Kaltenbrunner, who, with Bormann's assistance, now went over his head and approached Hitler directly, would find out about his treachery.

"You're the only one, besides Brandt (his aide) whom I can trust completely," he told the smooth, attentive Schellenberg, who knew that it was only through this shaken, undecided wreck of a man opposite him that he could save his own skin. Admittedly, he knew that peace with the West could be achieved only if Hitler were removed. But could he, Himmler, shoot or poison the leader he had served so long.

It did not matter, Schellenberg argued, working feverishly on the man who held his own future in his delicate well-manicured hands. There were only two remedies left: remove Hitler or shoot him.

Himmler turned pale. "But if I said that to the Führer," he protested, "he would fall into a violent rage and shoot me out of hand!"

"That is just what you must protect yourself against," Schellenberg said urgently, trying to reassure him. "You still have enough higher SS leaders, and you are still in a strong enough position to arrest him. If there is no other way, then the doctors will have to intervene." Schellenberg meant that the doctors would have to convince the German people — by means of a report — that Hitler was no longer capable of governing them.

On the morning of April 20, while Schellenberg was shaving and American planes above him were making yet another of their daylight raids on the undefended rump of the once proud Reich, he received a call from the Swedish Embassy in Berlin. It was the Swedish Count Bernadotte, who was trying to arrange peace between the Germans and the Allies. He told Schellenberg that he would like to talk with Himmler before he, Bernadotte, left for Sweden at six o'clock the next morning.

Schellenberg got on to Himmler at once. He knew it was his last chance. The Reichsführer who had just returned from Hitler's bunker, where he had congratulated the leader in spite of the cold reception he had received there, met Schellenberg at Wustrow, the site of the Werewolf Radio Station. Himmler gave in and agreed to see the Swedish peace negotiator. Schellenberg breathed out a sigh of relief. He had done it!

Later Bernadotte told him privately: "The Reichsführer no longer understands the realities of his own situation. I cannot help him any more. He should have taken Germany's affairs into his own hands after my first visit. I can hold out little chance for him now." He paused and looked at the smooth, clever young head of what was left of Germany's Secret Service. Then he said: "And you, my dear Schellenberg, would be wiser to think of yourself."

Schellenberg did not reply. Comment was unnecessary; he had been thinking of himself for a long time now.

Thus the last chief of the Abwehr and the Sicherheitsdienst disappeared from the scene, leaving that fantastic world in which nothing could ever be taken at its face value and the abnormal was normal. It had "hooked" him as a drug does an addict, with its heady exciting mixture of blondes,[105] blackmail, bribes, and bloodshed.

Now it was all over. He would have to leave that strange office of which he wrote in unconcealed pride: "Microphones were everywhere, hidden in the walls, under the desk, even in one of the lamps, so that every conversation and every sound was automatically recorded... My desk was like a small fortress. Two automatic guns were built into it which could spray the whole room with bullets." He would no longer need to wear

---

[105] From early 1940 onward, Schellenberg was in charge of a special intelligence brothel run by his organization for prominent Germans and foreigners. Most of the girls were trained SD agents, who passed over the information they gained to Schellenberg or "Bubi" as he was known to them. All the rooms were wired and every conversation was recorded. Today these records are supposed to be in the possession of the East German Secret Service. One can guess why.

that "artificial tooth... which contained enough poison to kill me within thirty seconds."

The days when he could listen to the records of the lovemaking and intimate secrets revealed at *Salon Kitty* were passed. Soon he would fly to safety over the Swedish frontier and live to end his own account of his tremendous activities in the great battle of the spymasters with the words: "For the time being my services were not required." But Walter Schellenberg's services were never — to his mortification — required again.

On that day when what was left of unoccupied Germany celebrated the leader's last birthday, those who were really in the know about Germany's ultimate fate — men like Schellenberg and his old enemies of the last two years, Mueller and Kaltenbrunner — were making plans to save their own skins before it was too late.

Shaven-headed Mueller, of whom Schellenberg had been so afraid ever since they had started working closely together during the great days of the Venlo kidnapping, had just issued new identification papers and "cover stories" to his senior assistants that April 20th, when one of them, an SS *Obersturmbannführer* whose "cover" was that he had been working in a civilian firm these last few years, strode boldly into the Gestapo chief's office.

Mueller looked up from the files of which he had always been so proud (his dream had been to have a dossier on every man, woman, and child in Germany). "Well, what's the matter with you?" he snapped in that thick Bavarian accent of his.

The long-nosed, sallow-looking SS officer was not put out. "*Herr Gruppenführer*," he said proudly, "I don't need these papers." He patted the Steyr army pistol at his hip. "This is my certificate. When I see no other way out, it will be my last remedy. I have no need for anything else."

Mueller sniffed but did not make the obvious comment. He rose and shook the man's hand. He had other plans, and they did not include suicide or anything like that.

"Good luck, Eichmann," he wished the man as he left.

A little later Eichmann would meet Kaltenbrunner, who had left Berlin on that same day, in Austria and tell the scar-faced giant that he was going into the mountains to fight with the *Werewolf.* "That's good," Kaltenbrunner would comment cynically. "Good for Reichsführer Himmler too. Now he can talk to Eisenhower differently in his negotiations for he will know that an Eichmann in the mountains will never surrender — because he can't." Then the last head of the Main Security Office's nerve would break, for he knew what his own fate was to be, and he would snap: *"It's all a lot of crap ... the game's up."*

But on that 20th of April, Mueller did not think so. His underground shelter in the Kurfurstenstrasse — the original building in the Prinz Albrecht Strasse had been severely damaged in a British air raid — was as safe as Hitler's, perhaps even better. There was electricity and plenty of water (a scarce commodity in the *Führerbunker*) and secret little rooms accessible only through cleverly disguised doors. In addition there were several tunnels — one a mile long — leading to emergency exits. In other words, Mueller and his faithful lieutenant, Scholtz, a radio specialist, were in a position to go "underground" in relative safety and reappear in one of several different places at will.

For Heinrich Mueller intended to survive. He was immune to the general hysteria. The man who had joined the Party in 1939, and whose Party "dossier" commented bitterly, "He gave forty pfennigs to the Party Fund this year," believed that this Twilight of the Gods which was taking place all around him was no concern of his. He was a trained policeman — the only survivor of the two who had made up the original command of the Main Security Office (the other was Nebe, whom Mueller himself had arrested with great relish, feeling that he had gotten rid of yet another rival). The Third Reich was about over, but there would be new masters for people like himself who "knew the ropes" and had information to sell. But where to sell it?

To the British and Americans? Mueller knew that the Americans, moral and naive as they appeared to be, would never accept a "war criminal." As for the English, they could hardly work with the head of the Gestapo, the man who had made Best and Stevens, their Secret Service stars at the beginning of the war, talk — although Best would later characterize him as a "nice little man." *All that remained was the Russians!*

We do not know what went on in Mueller's mind that day, as Schellenberg and Kaltenbrunner abandoned the organization which the head of the Gestapo had done so much to build up since that day in August 1939, when he and Heydrich had planned the attack on that lonely border radio station at Gleiwitz, which had started World War II. On April 20, 1945, Mueller went underground in his "foxhole" (as Eichmann called it later) in the Kurfurstenstrasse to reappear briefly on April 29th when he arrested Hitler's brother-in-law, SS General Fegelein. After that he disappeared for good.

A few months afterwards a body was found in newly conquered Berlin. It was dressed in Mueller's uniform and wore Mueller's medals and decorations. But the handful of

302

civilians who reported their "find" to the victorious Russians in the hope that they would be rewarded were a little puzzled by the fact that Mueller's identity card found on the body did not possess a photo, almost as if someone wished to prevent a comparison between the stiff, bloody corpse and the man whose name it bore. The Russians were not interested. The body was buried without ceremony and on December 15, 1945, a freezing, undernourished official at Berlin's Central Registry Office recorded the fact that "Mueller, Wilhelm" (*not* Heinrich), had been buried in "grave number one, first row, section six" at the Garrison Cemetery. The legend read that "dear Father" had "died in combat in May, 1945."

But had he?

Nearly twenty years later, the grave was dug up once more (during the exhumation, it became clear that someone else had tampered with the place some years before) on orders of the West German police. Carefully the bones of one of the most feared men in Europe were sorted out and sent to the Berlin police labs. They were not those of "Gestapo" Mueller. Indeed they were those of *three* men, and the skull was that of a much younger man than Mueller. Thereupon the Berlin authorities ordered Mueller's arrest, but how do you arrest a dead man? *And if Heinrich Mueller was not dead, where was he?*

That warrant for Heinrich Mueller's arrest is still open ten years later, for the war in the shadows still continues, being waged with new "stars" but with some of the old cast.[106] One month after the old war ended the two main protagonists in

---

[106] On the American side, we find such old "professionals" as Gehlen, Giskes, and two or three dozen more who had worked for the Abwehr and Sicherheitdienst; on the Russian side we have Willy Berg, the man who let Trepper go, Naujocks (if we are to believe some reports), *and Heinrich Mueller* (?).

the new one exchanged presents. In Moscow the U.S. Ambassador, Averell Harriman was presented with a hand-carved "screaming eagle," the symbol of the United States. Happy with this token of Soviet good will and portent of future cooperation between the two new super powers which had emerged from World War II, tall, distinguished-looking Harriman ordered the wooden plaque to be hung in the U.S. Embassy's conference room.

Seven years later CIA Agents, carrying out a routine check of the Embassy's security arrangements, discovered a tiny electronic "bug" hidden behind the dusty-wooden eagle which had once inspired such great hopes in those heady days of victory in 1945. Year in and year out, they checked the "bug" on their routine inspections. Nothing happened. It was as dormant as it had been in 1945.

Then abruptly in the first years of the sixties it came to life. It commenced emitting strange microwaves which seemed to have their source in a Russian-occupied building close to the Embassy. But although the CIA agents had discovered both the source and outlet of the microwaves, they still had not ascertained the purpose of the suddenly active apparatus.

Operation Pandora went into action. Back in CIA headquarters a similar device was set up and tested on monkeys and rabbits. Under the hard-eyed scrutiny of CIA agents and scientists a gang of monkeys were set to work to build up a series of wooden bricks while being subjected at the same time to the strange microwaves.

The results were interpreted differently by a select committee of high-level scientists and agents. Some thought the monkeys exhibited "symptoms of schizophrenia," whereas others maintained the test animals remained quite normal. However, CIA Boss Allen Dulles, one-time World War II chief of the

OSS in Switzerland, who so long ago had sent his chief agent to question Aachen Burgomaster Oppenhoff about the German will to resist, moved swiftly and decisively when he heard that the rabbits had exhibited a "much higher pulse and heart-beat rate" under the influence of the mysterious radio waves.

He approached the president of the United States, Lyndon B. Johnson. In a few laconic sentences he explained the Soviets' intentions: they wanted to disturb and perhaps even destroy the ability of U.S. diplomats in Moscow to act and react realistically in Russia. Under the influence of the waves, the confused members of the U.S. State Department would naturally make the wrong decisions and play into the hands of the cunning Russians.

Johnson went into action at once. At a conference with Soviet Chief of State Kosygin in Glassboro, New Jersey, in 1967, a worried President told the sour-faced Soviet boss: "Mr. Premier, I don't know what you intend to do with the rays, but I'd like to request you to stop the business at once."

While the big, broad-faced former schoolteacher from Texas stared at his Soviet opposite number, a wooden-faced Kosygin listened in silence to the embarrassed interpreter's translation.

Then he nodded briefly. He agreed to stop the strange waves. Operation Pandora, one of the Russians' most curious postwar espionage missions, died a sudden death.

Four thousand miles away on the other side of the Atlantic Ocean, the man who had first thought of that particularly ingenious idea — to use advanced radio technology for espionage purposes — must have turned in his lonely, weed-overgrown grave in which he had lain these long fifteen years.

The idea which had been stolen from his files in May 1945, when the victorious Russians had stormed Berlin, had died stillborn. Twenty-two years after the conclusion of the great conflict, Walter Schellenberg's part in the battle behind the scenes had finally come to a belated end. The War in the Shadows was over...

APPENDIX: WHAT HAPPENED TO THEM

Today little can be seen of the tremendous effort in gold and blood that went into fighting the six-year war in the shadows. The area in which Wilhelm Canaris's Abwehr HQ in Berlin was located is called now Stauffenbergstrasse, after the one-armed, one-eyed Colonel who attempted to assassinate Hitler in July, 1944, thus sealing the Admiral's fate. The man who ordered his death, Kaltenbrunner, has had — by an act of supreme irony — his old apartment in the Giesebrechtstrasse taken over by a former inmate of one of his concentration camps. And the gentleman is a Jew to boot! Next door, *Salon Kitty*, Heydrich's spy brothel, where "Bubi" Schellenberg was such a welcome guest and where Naujocks's curiosity about his boss Heydrich's love life caused his demotion and exile to the front as a simple SS private, is also still there. But nothing about the eighty-year-old stucco facade of the rebuilt structure (it was bombed during the war) reveals what purpose it served in the "great game of espionage."

In Hamburg, the center of the Abwehr's espionage battle against Britain and America, the discreet little *pension* where Dasch and SNOW lived while they were trained is still there, as is the Hotel Vier Jahreszeiten to which Major Ritter ordered the drugged CELERY to be taken so that his agents could try to break the code enclosed in CELERY's strange signet ring. But the affluent American tourists who pass back and forth through the swinging doors of the distinguished hotel on the Alster know nothing of the strange undercover battle that went on behind its gleaming white portal so long ago.

It is the same with the busy city "gentlemen" with their bowler hats and neatly furled umbrellas who hurry through Baker Street on their way to the "City" to even bigger and better "deals," their heads full of "stock options" and "gold prices." What do they know of the SOE and their foreign associates who planned the death of Heydrich in this London street? How could they know? Spies rarely leave evidence behind them. They pass silently and stealthily, going to their own particular appointment with destiny, leaving little trace of their passing. A mark can still be seen on the wall of a café at Falize in the Ardennes where one of Skorzeny's camouflaged panzers went through (and stayed there with the cannon hanging over the kitchen stove for two years); a fading "V" sign cut into a tree at *Gut Hombusch*, Germany, to which the survivors of Operation Carnival fled marks a Werewolf arms dump. "Lucy" is buried in a lonely, weed-overgrown grave in Switzerland where he tried to start up the "Red Orchestra" once again after World War II and died a premature death after his second release from a Swiss jail.

In truth, not much really for all that effort, but as Shakespeare puts it — and the Bard can always be relied upon for an apt quote, the history of spying in World War II is "*a tale... full of sound and fury, signifying nothing.*" After all they don't erect monuments to spies, but for those who are interested, this is what happened to the main figures of The War in the Shadows...

1. *A. Naujocks* was sent to the front by Heydrich in 1942. He survived and deserted to the Americans in Belgium in 1944. After the war he made a dramatic escape from them and turned up again in Hamburg in the fifties, where he died.

2. *A. Nebe*, an opportunist always eager to be on the winning side, joined the plot against Hitler in 1944. He was executed just before the end of the war.

3. *Frau L. Heydrich* survived the war. Today she runs a snack bar on her native island. Her many visitors buying her good goulash at DM 3.50 a portion do not realize that the big grey-haired woman who serves them once was married to the man who held sway over 250 million Europeans.

4. *Best* and *Payne* survived the war. They were fired by the secret service after their release, and Payne earned his keep for a while by translating German books into English.

5. *SNOW*, released from imprisonment at the end of the war, went to Southern Ireland, where he is supposed to be alive still.

6. *Colonel Ritter* was released from the Abwehr in 1942 and took over more conventional duties. He is still alive in Hamburg.

7. *Professor Haushofer* committed suicide towards the end of the war while his son was executed at the very last by Mueller's express order.

8. *Schulte-Strathaus* is dead.

9. *Kubis* and *Gabcik* were trapped in a Prague church together with a number of parachutists and resistance workers after being betrayed by one of their number who had landed with them from England. They fought off intensive German attacks on their hiding place, including flooding and poison gas. When they realized there was no way out of the crypt in which they were bottled up, they committed suicide.

10. *Trepper* is still alive in Warsaw to this day, after surviving ten years of imprisonment in Moscow (he flew there with Rado on January 6, 1945, in an American plane). At present he is trying to go to Israel, aided by his son and wife who went on a hunger strike in Copenhagen. So far the Polish authorities have

refused to let him go. Probably they are afraid that Trepper, who is still mentally very alert in spite of his poor physical condition, will publish the real story of the "Red Orchestra."

11. *Captain Piepe* died in 1967, after confiding to cronies that *Willy Berg* who let Trepper go was a Russian agent. Today Berg lives in East Germany after working there at his old job as a policeman.

12. *Kent* is supposed to be alive in Leningrad.

13. *G. Dasch* survived the war and was returned to Germany later. He is still alive.

14. *Captain Ahlrichs*, who planned the operation, went back to his old business after the war, working for the *Organization Gehlen* while it was under U.S. jurisdiction. He was arrested by the Poles on the charge of spying in the mid-fifties.

15. *La Chatte* is still alive, though seriously ill. Pardoned by the French, she changed her name and went to live in the French provinces.

16. *Hugo Bleicher* is alive and well. Today he runs a small tobacco store in Tettnang.

17. *Armand alias BRUTUS* has settled in Britain, being unable to return to his native Poland. In 1967 he met Bleicher again for the first time since that dramatic "escape" in 1942. They got on well together.

18. *P. Dourlein* is still alive. Today he is an officer in the Royal Dutch Navy.

19. *Colonel Giskes*, who after the war worked for the USA within the Gehlen Organization, lives today in Munich.

20. *SS General Wolff* is a healthy eighty-year-old who lives off $150-a-month pension. When asked recently why he had not told the full story of the plot to kidnap the Pope up to now, he replied he didn't think "anybody would be interested in those old stories."

21. *The Honorable Ewen Montagu* is still alive in London.

22. *Lieutenant Commander Jewell* is an admiral in the Royal Navy today. He still does not know who "Major Martin" really was.

23. *TREASURE*, or *Lily Sergueiev*, did not die immediately at the end of World War II. The British got rid of her by putting her in the French Army's Woman Auxilliary. Thereafter she went to the United States where she died about 1952.

24. *Colonel Lane* is still alive.

25. *Major General Donovan* died in 1959.

26. *Otto Skorzeny* escaped from an Allied prison at the end of the war and, after periods in several countries including Ireland, he settled in Madrid where he lives today, running a prosperous engineering business. His enemies have maintained since the war that he has been involved in several pieces of skulduggery in Europe and elsewhere. In 1970, he was struck down by a disease which left him paralyzed. But in his last letter to the author he wrote he was "fit" again.

27. *J. Peiper*, accused of the Malmedy Massacre, was sentenced to death after the war. His sentence was reduced to life imprisonment after irregularities were discovered in his trial. Finally after thirteen years in jail, he was released, an embittered man who confessed to the author that he was still "sitting on a powder keg which threatens to go up at any moment," i.e., expects to be arrested again.

28. *Wenzel* disappeared after the war although the German police searched for him in several countries. *Leitgeb* was killed when he stepped on a mine during the escape from Aachen. Both *Morgenschweiss* and *Ilse Hirsch* were also injured dur-this escape. *Hennemann* and *Heidorn* were still alive in the mid-sixties after being released from jail (the survivors were tried in Aachen in 1949). Today Hirsch and Morgenschweiss live

within twenty miles of Aachen, but Morgenschweiss tells the author that the only thing he would volunteer for today "is to go fishing," his favorite hobby.

29. *Schellenberg* survived the war, as was to be expected. And as was to be expected, he died in his bed in Italy in 1952.

30. *Masterman* went back to teaching after the war. He emerged from the obscurity of his Oxford college in 1971, when he was finally allowed by the British Government to publish his sensational *Double-Cross System* which was held up by the British Official Secrets Act for over a quarter of a century.

31. *Kaltenbrunner* was unwittingly betrayed by his countess-mistress. He was executed at Nuremberg in 1946.

32. *Mueller?*

BIBLIOGRAPHY

Abshagen, Karl Heinz. *Canaris, Patriot and Weltburger*. Stuttgart: Union deutsche Verlagsgesellschaft, 1949. Trans, by Alan Houghton Brodrick, as *Canaris*. London: Hutchinson, 1956.

Buchheit, Gert. *Der deutsche Geheimdienst*. München: List, 1966.

Cookridge, E. H. *Inside SOE*. London: Barker, 1966.

Delarue, Jacques. *The Gestapo*. New York: Morrow, 1964.

Dulles, Allen W., ed. *Great True Spy Stories*. New York: Harper & Row, 1968.

Farago, Ladislas. *Game of Foxes*. London, 1972.

Flicke, *Spionagegruppe Rote Kapelle*. Kreuzlingen, 1953.

Foot, A. *Handbook for Spies*. New York: Doubleday, 1950.

Ford, Corey. *Donovan of OSS*. Boston: Little, Brown, 1970.

Hohne, Heinz. *Kennwort: Direktor, die Geschichte der Roten Kapelle*. Frankfurt am Main: Fischer, 1970.

Ingersoll, Ralph. *Top Secret*. New York: Harcourt Brace, 1950.

Kahn, David. *The Codebreakers*. New York; Macmillan, 1967.

Leasor, James. *Rudolf Hess: the Uninvited Envoy*. London: Allen & Unwin, 1962.

Masterman, J. C. *The Double-Cross System*. New York: Avon, 1972.

Montagu, Ewen. *The Man Who Never Was*. Philadelphia: Lippincott, 1967.

Perrault, Gilles. *The Secret of D-Day*. Boston: Little, Brown, 1965.

Perrault, Gilles. *L'Orchestre Rouge*. Paris: Fayard, 1968.

Piekalkiewicz, Janusz. *Spione, Agenten, Soldaten*. München: Südwest Verlag, 1969.

Reile, Oscar. *Geheime Westfront: die Abwehr, 1935-1945.* München: Verlag Welsermühl, 1962.

Schellenberg, Walter. *Memoirs.* London: Deutsch, 1956.

Shirer, William L. *The Rise and Fall of the Third Reich.* New York: Simon and Schuster, 1960.

Singer, Kurt Deutch, ed. *Three Thousand Years of Espionage.* New York: Prentice-Hall, 1948.

Skorzeny, Otto. *Wir kampften, wir verloren.* Siegburg; 1962.

Strong, Kenneth. *Intelligence at the Top.* New York: Doubleday, 1969.

Strong, Kenneth. *Men of Intelligence,* London: Cassell, 1970.

Whiting, Charles. *Werewolves,* New York: Stein & Day, 1972.

Young, Gordon. *The Cat with Two Faces,* New York: Coward-McCann, 1958.

ACKNOWLEDGMENTS

I owe this book to many people who had nothing to gain by helping me and perhaps something to lose. In particular, I should like to thank the following for their cooperation and information: Frau L. Heydrich, Herr Heinrich Heim (senior associate of both Hess and Bormann from 1931 onwards), Otto Skorzeny, Jochen von Long (Stern), Heinz Hoehne (Spiegel), Dr. Simon (*Aachener Volkszeitung*), Herr Saive, Frau Oppenhoff, Herr Morgenschweiss, ex-Gauleiter K. Wahl, Herr Hermann Buch, Admiral Dönitz, Madame B. Rupp, Dr. L. Bouck, John Eisenhower, and Sir Kenneth Strong.

C.W.

A NOTE TO THE READER

If you have enjoyed this book enough to leave a review on **Amazon** and **Goodreads**, then we would be truly grateful.

Sapere Books

Sapere Books is an exciting new publisher of brilliant fiction and popular history.

To find out more about our latest releases and our monthly bargain books visit our website: **saperebooks.com**